Geese!

To my brother Charles
for guiding me to The Solway.

To Harry Graham (in memoriam) for allowing me
to shoot my first goose

and to Richard Walters (in memoriam)
for handing me his Utopia. Geese!

Geese!

Memoirs of a Wildfowler

EDWARD MILLER

MERLIN UNWIN BOOKS

First published in Great Britain by Merlin Unwin Books Ltd, 2007

ISBN 978 1 873674 13 0

Published by:
Merlin Unwin Books Ltd
Palmers House
7 Corve Street, Ludlow
Shropshire SY8 1DB, U.K.

British Library Cataloguing-in-Publication Data:
A catalogue record for this book is available from the British Library.

Designed and typeset in Sabon by Merlin Unwin Books Ltd.
Printed by TJ International, UK.

Contents

Illustrations

Photographs and illustrations scanned by IE Photography – www.businessphotographs.co.uk

Foreword

This is the second wildfowling book by Edward Miller. His first, *Golden Dawn* (published in 2004), received wide acclaim and sold quickly.

Geese! is written in anecdotal form but is also an in-depth work to help the beginner on his journey through the wild goose trail. The instructional index is a new approach to a work of this kind and helps the novice to find an instant reference to the vast range of subjects.

A lifetime of fowling through north-west England and much of Scotland has produced a wealth of adventures with the gun. The author has never lost his passion for fowling and reckons that any man infected by goose fever all his life is a lucky soul indeed. He tells us he has never been able to shake off the condition and, although now in his seventies and disabled, says he has enough young fit friends around him to make sure he can still reach the flight lines.

Taking care not to make his book read like a manual, the author passes on his considerable knowledge. For instance, when the essentials of camouflage are explored, the reader finds himself concealed in a sandstorm, or behind an innocent lump of driftwood. The technique of goose calling is explained and how to recognise flight lines.

His theories about the type of weapons for large fowl, shot sizes and gun fit come not only from personal experience but also from his years in the gun trade. He was much sought-after as a clay bird instructor and, in his thirties, was the youngest member of the Gun Trade Association Council.

Cooking wildfowl is dealt with and includes a mouth-watering stuffing of wild mushrooms and seashore blackberries. Beware, too, the dinner host who does not heed his cautionary advice about old tough ganders which are turned into a gourmet feast.

There is guidance over the choosing of your shooting companions, what to wear, where to stay, and how to behave in these days of controversial reaction to gun ownership.

Perhaps his most telling words, however, come in the plea to avoid over-shooting – the sort of pressure that has seen the migratory majestic greylag largely driven from its historical wintering grounds in Perthshire (the writer's favourite field sports region). He explains how the greys have been clever enough to move both north and west to Scotland's more tranquil seaboard, there to winter on both coast and islands.

He points an accusing finger at greedy goose guides for contributing towards this harassment. And yet the writer is not anti goose guide. They are, he explains, often the solution for the tyro who wants to fall under the spell of a dawn ambush. There are wise words about how to assess advertisements placed by these professionals and by hotels bent on filling winter beds.

Much of the author's goose shooting has been undertaken, for the past 40 years, on one particular patch in Scotland. There he has seen the flocks burgeon from a few hundred to, at times, around 10,000 at one time. Careful regulation of shooting pressure has, he claims, been the main factor behind the increase – plus the natural growth in world numbers resulting from improved habitat.

His advice on shooting safety is simple. Visit a competent clay bird coach and join a fowling club. Both factions preach safe gun handling from the outset. Clubs will expel a member if he does not conform. And while on the theme of fowling clubs, the author makes an impassioned plea to those Guns who were once avid longshoremen themselves to spare a thought for our youngsters:

'Without young blood, shooting will cease. Every encouragement must be given otherwise they will lose heart. Research has shown that most fowling clubs in the U.K. have an open door policy for juniors (under 18's) but a few don't.

'A lad in his early teens can get very badly bitten by the fowling bug but sadly, in the few clubs without this open door policy, he cannot find access to his local marsh merely because older members, who will never set foot on a salting again, do not drop out.

'I implore these souls to cast their minds back to when they lived for their exciting dawn forays as lads and step aside.'

He urges the reader to join at least one of the two main field shooting organisations, either the Countryside Alliance or BASC (see index for addresses). Over a million shotgun certificates are issued annually in this country and yet only a quarter of the tally are members. So far, over the past two frenetic decades, the rights of the sporting Gun have been largely preserved, and he stresses that the stronger these organisations are, the better we will be prepared for the on-going battle.

In the chapter Scottish Safaris, the author recalls a few of the many expeditions he conducted for selected parties. Perhaps it is worth emphasising how much the lure of Scotland has clearly influenced his sporting career. It shines through his prose and is a sentiment with which so many of us can identify. There is a magic about shooting and angling north of the Border. That the British Isles contains such splendid semi-wilderness areas; the haunt of the red deer, grouse, ptarmigan, salmon and wild geese, is a miracle, or, at least, a blessed accident of history.

Scottish rivers, now recovering so well with their salmon runs, the quite unique sport of open-hill stalking, and grouse, the wildest and most fascinating of game birds, all combine to attract sportsmen from overseas. They flood in from the USA & Europe to enjoy a sporting ambience without parallel: no glut of Alaskan Sockeye or static mid-European forest hunting here.

The hills, the air, the colours and heather moors work their magic to the tune of £200 million per year for the local rural economy. Not to be sneezed at and especially useful ammunition for politicians to digest as they dig away at field sports – and too many of them do just that, to their shame.

Our overseas visiting sportsmen are made welcome. They enjoy real sport in a wild environment and return imbued with the traditions of etiquette of Scottish shooting and fishing.

It does not take long to realise that the author is a traditionalist, but there is one piece of technology – the two-way radio – which he treasures. These days every shoot has them but not for the reason the author uses his.

Though incapable of ever facing the rigours of a marsh again, this old stager is happy to rise in the early hours and drive along unlit byways to far-off Morecambe Bay. There his young son and school pal meet Paul, their guide.

Before the trio drop down the sea wall, to be swallowed by the pre-dawn blackness, the two-ways are checked. On these mornings such aids are alien things to the boys. No contact with the real world for them.

Fifteen minutes later, with the eastern sky stealing ever lighter, his set bleeps. Muted words from their guide, 'The geese are straight ahead, 300 yards off.'

Soon, a mile from the scene, our scribe begins to hear the wake-up calls of 20,000 pinkfoot, breathes the tang of saltings and turns up his collar against the vicious nor'-easter. The Bay is full of geese. Low greylag mutterings are the basses among pipings of knots, dunlins, redshank and curlews. Wigeon, teal and mallard wing high up, making for the sands and backwaters where they will sit out the day.

Another 15 minutes and, suddenly, the first skein lifts. Binoculars pick out a dark line climbing slowly but making towards where the three figures hide. Their magical calling is clear now on the morning air. One end of the clamouring wave could be in range. Abruptly a black shape tumbles out as if it were a giant falling leaf. The crump of a shot follows and a tiny figure springs from nowhere. He stoops, then speeds back, his first goose held tight under an arm.

The old-hand knows the wings will be rearranged and the feathers smoothed just as he had caressed his first goose well over half a century earlier. The boy's pulse will still be racing as he crouches low for the next chance. It is a scene that will never leave him for the rest of his long life.

The radio bleeps again. Paul has negotiated the creek to reach his ebullient charge. 'A pinkfoot. Head shot. We could have a good morning.'

Keith McDougall
Stiffkey
Norfolk

Preface

Much has happened to wildfowling in Britain during the 60 years spanned by this book. When first I rode on Father's back to ford the Big Run on Lytham marsh, at the age of 11, the shooting man saw no restrictions.

The beginning of widespread affluence, and the consequent motor car two decades from then, marked a huge upsurge in the numbers invading our marshes. It called for regulations and sanctuaries, recognised by both the shooter and the conservationist. In fact the shooter became the conservationist. He introduced his own sanctuaries on club lands and was the first to recommend bans in times of hard weather.

No one will ever dispute that those early bureaucracy-free days were good times, but since then the numbers of our migrant fowl have increased dramatically. Indisputably this profundity is the result of the refreshing new approach to wildlife care, which a small minority of short-sighted fowlers at first opposed.

Now, with little effort, the coastal gunner can enjoy his shooting over the length and breadth of the British Isles. Many fowling clubs have vacancies and almost all offer modestly priced day tickets – a useful money earner.

This books helps to guide Guns along fowling's absorbing road whether it be on marsh or stubble. Much of what you want to know about availability is waiting for you at HQ of BASC – the British Association for Shooting and Conservation. How much easier the task would have been for we old stagers when we were planning our forays, had that organisation been as efficient as it is today. What an extraordinary job the folk at Marford Mill (BASC's HQ) do for us. Contact any of its multiple departments and they make you feel as though you were investing the family jewels!

The exploits unfolded in these 14 chapters tell of those distant freedom days among the hard men of our coastal marshes. They step also into the privileged world of the rich. When I was young and energetic I spent time in the gun trade and flew parties by helicopter into stormbound Scottish isles. There we chased geese and stalked the noble red stag.

Affluent clients could have what they wanted, including driven grouse – the most expensive of all our shooting. There was, however, always a strict proviso; geese had to be in the potage. None objected. They wanted to see why I was so impassioned by the grey battalions and all were privileged, for a while, to fall under that spell.

Thus we go, from the humble coastal gunner, to that remarkable breed, the elite Highland stalker/gillie and to the Laird. One common bond does, of course, embrace us all – shooting. It is probably the greatest social leveller of all, apart from the hospital bed, and at its heart should throb that cost-free commodity – good manners.

My active days in the gun trade were some of the best in this intriguing occupation and I was out with the gun just about every week of the hectic 21 years. I was then able to retire from its embrace to reside in the beautiful English Lake District, there to concentrate even more on shooting, fishing and village cricket. I also act as a consultant to a local firearms dealer which keeps me up to date. Before that I had travelled much of the world to seek a better place to live. Nowhere had to offer what these isles could give to a committed and addicted goose hunter.

But how tenuous is man's life in such a Shangri-la? Returning home by bicycle from an inn one night, I was flung from my machine by the sudden appearance of a badger. Left paralysed, the intense rehabilitation lasted 18 months. At first I was unable to hold even a pen, least of all a shotgun.

Shooting was out. Instead I spent as many hours, as I was physically able, sea and trout angling. Kind charter boat skippers baited my rod, cast for me and unhooked the catch when I had reeled in. Weakened arms were incapable of hauling the fish but an adapted chest harness took care of that. Charter boat skippers are near the top of my list of rehabilitation therapists.

On Esthwaite Water, near my home, a wheelie boat for the disabled had, by chance, just been installed. Another piece of serendipity. The rules were bent and I was the only angler allowed to troll for my fish.

Companionship among anglers is close and I thankfully settled for the switch. Previously the pursuit had been only an adjunct to goose chasing.

Then whoever charts our lives devised yet another plot. My wife Annie and I were blessed with the unexpected arrival of a son. I knew I would have to take him goose shooting. What better way to teach a young fellow a love of the countryside?

I reapplied for my shotgun certificate but, before it was finally granted, after four long months, I was to experience what shooting's new bureaucracy was about. Little wonder people of advancing years abandon the battle. Today's shooter must learn not to give in too easily. If those who try to rule our lives had their way, none of us would shoot. Remember that BASC and the Countryside Alliance will look after you.

I also discovered that a standard shotgun was impossible to mount and the stock had to be adapted. Nor was standing shooting possible, but a solid swivel chair gave me wonderful stability and the sitting technique was easily mastered.

All these encumbrances would suggest that the real joys of shooting had been snatched away in that country-lane spill, yet the reverse was so.

In the past the sights, sounds and smells of wood, moor and marsh were always taken for granted. When I lay in a darkened recovery room I felt that they had gone for ever. It was no help, either, to discover I had lost my senses of smell and of taste. Never, I lamented, would I savour the juices from a prune-stuffed pinkfoot goose, but both powers were, eventually, to return.

Now everything is hugely more real. They say there is always an upside to travesty if you look hard enough. Mine was easily found.

Jago was four when we had our first outing, in a pigeon hide. The spring rape was just showing and we had a happy two hours. The first day of September saw us on my Scottish goose grounds on Top Pond for the duck flight and he became a hunter. He shot his first goose at the age of nine.

I wrote this book 10 years after the season of the new beginning and I would like to think that the tyro will learn a lot from its pages. I hope, too, that the experienced Gunner will be absorbed by the stories from dawn and dusk. It has been an intriguing journey.

Ed Miller
Hawkshead
Cumbria
2007

CHAPTER 1

The Solway Years

No world voyager, no African explorer, nobody or anything could have been more full of hope, excitement and overwhelming anticipation than that which filled the raw 17-year-old as he sped northwards to the Solway Firth. That young fellow was me astride the pillion of a gleaming new Triumph Speed Twin motorcycle in the late September of 1950.

At 100 miles per hour villages flashed by and stately sedan motors were left in our wake adding to the intoxication. These were pre-crash helmet days and I suppose we were lucky to have survived when we stepped from our red-hot machine in Carlisle. Here there was real drama not born of the imagination.

'Meet us on the bridge at the bottom of Castletown Hill,' my brother had instructed on the phone. 'We will be in a Land Rover and caravan.'

The Land Rover and caravan were there all right but both were empty. Immediately behind there was a gaping hole in the bridge parapet towards which clusters of people were running. Below lay a giant twisted articulated lorry and brother Charles and his two companions were helping the driver out of its mangled cab.

We were to hear that, as Charles and his pals neared the bridge in the Land Rover, the lorry had careered downhill with brake failure, missing them by inches, and had crashed through the parapet. The driver escaped with no more than a cut hand.

From the age of 12, when I was allowed to roam alone with a shotgun, I had been relaying to my elder brother, via endless letters, just about every step of my excursions over the Ribble saltings near where we were both born in Lytham. Now, a gun owner cannot go it alone until he is 15 and holds a Shotgun Certificate. Days with the gun were not confined to the winter fowling season and a 10 minute bike ride took me to the first of six farms over which I had permission to shoot.

Charles had done his two years National Service in the Royal Navy and for the past year had been a newshound with the Kemsley Newspaper Group based in Newcastle upon Tyne. This north-east base gave him a chance to hunt the Holy Island wigeon. But there were few geese on Holy Island and he was as keen as I was to get under the grey battalions.

It will be difficult for today's fowler, who carries a mobile phone as routine, to appreciate the communication difficulties 60 years ago. By this time I had just left school and started a job with a north-west freelance press agency. We had no telephones in our homes but my brother and I now had direct contact courtesy of our work.

'We go to the Solway by caravan in September and there is room for you,' was the brief message. Today the equivalent would be to hear I had won the lottery!

A caravan was good news. I had little money. My first month in employ had been wageless, 'To see if you are going to make it.' I did but the £2–7s–6d went on board, lodgings, cartridges and Brylcreem.

A convoluted train journey from Lytham to Preston to Carlisle (the rendezvous) was going to be expensive. One of my pals was the new proud possessor of the aforementioned motorcycle – a world leader in its day and one of the first off the production line after the dust of war had settled. He would take me on its pillion. Goose gun was roped naked over my back and fowling gear lashed to the panniers.

To this day you can still detect the repairs to the stonework where the lorry had crashed. The driver was the sole occupant and he was patched up by Ken, one of my companions on our maiden goose hunt. Ken was a photographer in the operating theatre of Newcastle's General Hospital. A first aid kit was, to him, mandatory and he also turned out to be brilliant at eviscerating and jointing game!

The fourth member of the team was Geoff, an affluent estate agent and the provider of the new 18 foot caravan and Land Rover – the first 4WD transport ever available on the open market. It was a team that would remain together for many years.

We left the driver in the capable hands of ambulance men and soon the Solway Firth glinted to our left. A narrow farm track in Old Gretna ended only yards from the Border Esk river. Beyond lay Rockcliffe Marsh which we knew to be private. To the west sand flats, as sweet and clean as my native Ribble, was mud-covered and noxious.

Nowhere to park a caravan. By now it was late afternoon and, to our excitement, the first geese were sighted – a mile to the west and high. Behind were three more skeins travelling from due north. We watched, transfixed, as they crossed the Esk at its junction with the Kirtle then dramatically tumbled from the sky to rest far out on the sands. Geoff's Zeiss binoculars showed their dark line by the edge of a backwater. Most slept but a few splashed and washed.

Redkirk Point lies close to the confluence of these two rivers. As its name implies it is a promontory and huddled among a few wind-blasted trees was an old farmstead. A single track road, gateless and marked as a public route on the ordnance survey map, took us to its meagre shelter.

Redkirk was to be our home for a week. We saw no one on the shore and no land owner troubled to enquire about our presence. You can see

CARAVAN BREAKFAST – *When four novice goose chasers arrived with their caravan on the Scottish side of the Solway Firth in the late September of 1950 it coincided, by chance, with skeins of pinkfoot ending their flight from the north. They parked at Redkirk Point, opposite the roosting grounds, but, unable to ford the Border Esk, they could not get on terms with the geese all week. On their last night they met the local fowlers. They were advised to come later the following season with a boat.*
Left to right: the author, his brother Charles, Ken Watson and Geoff Holmes.

the Point from the main Carlisle to Gretna road, just after the Metal Bridge Inn, and not one journey along this route passes when I do not cast a long gaze and recapture the moments of that week when I was little more than a boy. My wife's standard comment immediately it hoves into sight is, 'All right, all right, please don't tell me again!' But I do.

That evening produced a rewarding golden plover flight in the whin bushes only yards from the caravan. This toothsome plump bird became my favourite dish during our stay.

There were other rewards from the endless shoreline. In those days no fowling clubs existed and the Caerlaverock reserve, further to the west, had not been established. A partridge, a hare and two rabbits found their way into the larder. There were a few snipe to be cooked inside jacket potatoes and always the ubiquitous redshank.

There were even two mallard, ambushed from the salmon stake nets – perfect hides – off Browell, and we sometimes heard distant wigeon when a southerly wind blew. What sport we were to have among them in later years! I found a bunch of teal on the banks of a stream near the Nith and a lengthy stalk produced six with two barrels.

All week we ate like kings. Ration books were still in use and it was a welcome bonus but not the object of the adventure. The geese still eluded us. There was always a restless wind but it was not sufficient to lower the flocks that passed every day at dawn and dusk over our itinerant home two gun shots high.

At dawn we observed several parties lifting from their roost a mile out across the river and making off low over the sands onto Rockcliffe Marsh. Could there be a legal way of intercepting this flight line? Not, we reckoned, without a boat.

We had been unable to make contact with any local fowlers all week. The few shops in Gretna were used to strangers but our enquiries were greeted with a shake of the head. The village was, in those days, a mecca for hundreds of runaway marriages in a year. The moonstruck couples were easy to spot and a source of great amusement to this teenager who was yet to have his first date. Most of them looked about my age, the lads needing a razor but once a week on acned chins. Was love, I pondered, as powerful as goose fever? Then I thought not. Now, as a septuagenarian and three wives later, I know which lasts longer!

THE LOCALS

But our week was not in vain. An inner sanctum was about to open. Friday found us in the Metal Bridge Inn – a favourite watering hole for the famous BB* and his companions on their Scottish goose journeys.

We should have known this was where the fowlers would gather. The first contact I made was with a friendly looking fellow propping himself against the old oak dresser at the back of the smoke filled tap room. A worn Peterson tobacco pipe was clamped in jaws adding a pungent reek to the fetid atmosphere.

'Do you go after the geese?' was my not-so-smooth opener.

'Aye, when the weathers richt.'

'We have been at Redkirk Point all week and can't get near them.'

'Aye, I know.' Harry Graham, it later turned out, only took his gun from its peg when it either blew a gale or the Esk was low enough to cross at dawn when he could tuck himself in at the edge of Rockcliffe Marsh. You had to know the exact spot to cross. Would he be for telling us I wondered to myself?

'Isn't Rockcliffe private?'

'Aye. But if you stay under the bank and leave your gun behind when you go to pick a bird they'll no touch you.'

We invited Harry and his pals for a beer at lunchtime the next day. Crates of Newcastle Brown had come across in the stores from the Tyne and the three who turned up proceeded to reduce the supplies to zero over the next few hours. It would have been a shame, too, to take home the two bottles of Bells that had remained unopened all week.

We had prepared a giant game casserole and Harry, his cousin Nelt Graham and Jim Ritchie saw no reason to move. They didn't even notice the odd curlew breast – the bird ambushed from behind the Lochmaben Stone (see page 6).

It was the beginning of a life-long friendship and we were to shoot many geese together. All three are now buried within sight and sound of Redkirk Point. None made old bones and all were goose hunters until the last.

On that day, so long ago, the three had come armed. A walk over some bordering fields had been planned but no cartridges went into the breeches.

They were intrigued by our armoury, particularly Charles's Thos.

* BB (Denys Watkins-Pitchford) generally accepted as the most lauded modern writer of books on goose shooting. See Chapter 11.

Horsley 10/12 hammer side-by-side. Even then this was a relatively rare piece; weighing eight pounds plus and throwing two-ounce black powder loads out of brass cases. The gun was also chamberless – there were no chamber cones, merely straight tubes from the breech – and would take a 12-bore paper case also. This, however, was when the ballistics went awry and the patterns tended to be erratic and open. The weapon was not proofed for nitro but Charles happily threw his 1 1/16 ounce Grand Prix game sixes out of it. Its open spread also made it the ideal tool for wigeon flighting and walked-up quarry. And, to a fit 21-year-old, its extreme weight was of little problem.

THE LOCHMABEN STONE – *In a neighbouring field to where the four fowlers parked their caravan stands the ancient Lochmaben Stone. It is of Neolithic granite and how it came to be sited in this spot in an upright position in unknown. Centuries ago it was used as a demarcation point for the exchange of prisoners north and south of the Border and as a neutral zone for the settlement of disputes.*
For the visiting raider of 1950 it made an excellent hide for curlew flighting. The wader is now protected. Early in the season, after six months of inland feeding, it made excellent eating.

My T E Lewis magnum they handled almost with reverence. 'One of Bill Powell's men had one of these,' we were told.

'Who was Bill Powell?'

'A bloke,' they said, 'who has a small holding at Glencaple. He arrived soon after the War and has taken out parties of visiting shooters.'

This was the Bill Powell who was to become a legend on the Scottish shores of the Solway. His two books, *The Wild Goose Chase* and *The Grey Geese Call*, were then unwritten. They are epics and sit proudly on my shelves and I know not how many times I have read them.

The Lewis name was, by then, a legend itself in the wildfowling world.

CURLEW IN FLIGHT *by Rodger McPhail – Curlew breast went into the casserole prepared for our new-found friends, the locals.*

Father had travelled down to Lower Loveday Street, in Birmingham, with Grandpa William by rail, in 1920, to order one for his 21st birthday. At eight pounds the gun was also no lightweight. It had 32-inch full and full choke barrels and was capable of prodigious long-range kills. The following year would prove its worth.

Ken had an ancient English hammer double 12.

But it was Geoff's weaponry that commanded most intrigue. His Browning two-shot semi auto also sported a variable choke, which gave the user the option of a super-full constriction through to wide open at true cylinder. Truly a most versatile tool and sweet to handle. The Solway boys had seen nothing like it.

His armoury was completed by a Winchester pump action 3-inch 12 which would take five of the long cases or six 2½-inch loads. Later in life, as a gun dealer, I was to learn of the ruggedness of this particular weapon. Its construction was of the highest standard and I cannot remember one coming in for repair during all my years in the trade and our service became countrywide. Even sand does not jam it and it has to be the most rugged of all fowling tools. This is the gun that many of America's trick-shot clay busters used for their demonstrations. With a magazine extension the gun would take eight cartridges and, throwing all eight clays at once by hand, a demonstrator could break them all, one by one, as they separated – the last just at it reached the ground.

Both of Geoff's guns were new and, by the end of the day, Harry was the fresh owner of a Winchester. He said that it would solve the problem he had with the breech on his nondescript Spanish double which refused to close in a sandstorm – a common occurrence on the Solway and one which, over the years, can remove both blueing and chequering from any gun.

A GOOSE LOST

We were advised to come in November the next year – close to Halloween. They would arrange a handier spot for the caravan and a boat would be a good idea. I was already establishing a rapport with Harry and, just before they weaved their way home along the sea wall, he took me aside.

'Get down to the river tonight at dusk.' He pointed to a scar 500 yards away. 'Lie up there and you'll get a chance at the geese. There is always an odd bunch sneaks in low at last light.' It was my first lesson in goose flight paths and a bag filler in the years to come.

CARAVAN AND LAND ROVER ON REDKIRK POINT – *Big tides lapped the grass only a few feet away and there was an excellent wader flight over the Point. The farm house and buildings are now demolished. The 4WD vehicle had only just been produced for the general public and caused a lot of attention in Gretna Green – the local village. Close examination of the photograph will reveal the author's corduroys drying on the back of the vehicle. He had waded waist deep the previous night in a vain attempt to reach the only goose shot. It had also ruined his week's supply of sweet rations! (Britain still had war time food restrictions.)*

As it happened I was the only one amongst us sober enough to use a gun. In those days not even Newcastle's finest could tempt me to like the stuff. How different it was 12 months later.

I snuck off as lights began to twinkle across the estuary and tucked myself in, just as Harry had instructed. When it was almost completely black I was about to rise from my snug lair when there came a faint cackle from upriver.

Into a kneeling mode and safety pushed forward. There were about half a dozen pinks skimming the water and seeming to make great speed. One quick shot brought the leader out and I was up and plunging into the black water way over my knee wellies. So black I couldn't see my bird.

Quickly I made it back to the bank and sprinted downstream to the first bend hoping to intercept my goose. It was hopeless. The way in front was as dark as the proverbial raven's wing. Old fowlers never carried torches. I must cease this folly. My first precious goose was left to drift into eternity, or to become a grateful Reynard's supper. (In later years we were to find many fox footprints a long way out over the sands.)

Almost as distressing was what was lost in the pockets of my saturated clothing – my sweets allocation for a week while rationing still prevailed!

The next day, Sunday, saw us heading our separate ways home. There is no shooting on the Sabbath in Scotland – another reason for going waterborne. The middle of the Esk marked the Border and the Rockcliffe side would allow us to avoid this restriction.

There would be no pillion transport the following year. The offer was still there but we realised that two guns were essential and no way was this possible on two wheels. The Land Rover and the caravan would be waiting for me at Carlisle railway station. The journey home after our gooseless week was uneventful enough but it was as well that I knew not the horrors awaiting my return trip.

But what had we learned from our virgin trip to goose country?

1. Sort out your flight lines.
2. Work out how to get under them.
3. Make local contacts.

Here lay the storage box of generations of longshore knowledge. We may have been gooseless but, from what was to ensue from the following decades, every minute had been worth it.

I didn't realise it at the time but that meeting with Harry Graham was to be the most significant in my foreshore shooting career. Harry and I became great friends and, over the succeeding 10 years, it was he who taught me so much about estuary shooting.

Harry explained where to expect the geese to flight according to differing tide heights, how wind could alter their course and what effect a moon had on their feeding pattern. I have always been a great believer in seeking the advice of the locals on new coasts but do not expect an instant rapport. It is up to you to make the right approach and form genuine contacts. No fowler will volunteer knowledge to a stranger but you will know when you have cracked that tough outer shell. A few nights in the local bar are totally essential so you need to be of iron constitution, for no Sassenach can out-drink a Scot when you get on to whisky chasers – beer and the amber stuff in tandem!

I was very sorry to read Hugh Meynell's words (see later) describing some of the Solway fowlers as louts but he was unfortunate to have arrived on the estuary as a guest of Bill Powell (the professional 'off comer' guide on the Scottish side). Hugh's arrival as a visiting fowler coincided with my early days in the territory and he stood no chance of integration, for just about all the local longshore gunners to a man objected to the guide's presence.

All the Gretna men remained my friends for life and I am still in touch with some of them well over 50 years later.

SUCCESS

That following year, our second, the instructions were to call at Nelt's house – his full forename was, incidentally, Nelson – from whence we would be directed. It was no more than 200 yards to Tommy Gass's stackyard at the junction of the road down to the Esk where we had first ventured on our initial trip.

The cosy yard, with its neat straw stacks almost enclosing the caravan, became our fowling quarters for many years. We paid rent that first year but from then on Tommy would not hear of it. He had taken over the farm at a young age, on the early death of his father, and eventually his four sisters would wash-up, dust, clean and prepare the vegetables when we were out at flight. (What now BB when you cry that petticoats have no place in goose shooting?)

On this the first day, in these most ideal of quarters, there was soon a gathering of locals – all clad for flight and guns propped alongside bicycles. Our arrival had coincided with their return from Saturday morning flight.

Nelt, Harry and Jim, from last year, were already there and we were introduced to their three pals, Roy, Will and Johnny. We shot as a team for many years when they were off work at weekends and they were grateful for the lifts over in the boat which we had been able to acquire in the close season.

Ruby was a former boating-lake sailing pram-dinghy from my home territory. She was 12 feet long, clinker built and a pig to row with her flat front. It took four strong men to carry her from merse to river but, at £20, she was a snip.

We were to find she could take six on a calm day and, due to the cramped conditions, we then paddled her across. In wild weather, when rain water flood met an incoming tide, the middle was dicey and two trips with four aboard were made.

Our week-long holidays were carefully chosen to coincide with low dawn tides and, at the point where the boat was left, the crossing was roughly 200 yards – a long way in a force eight in the pre-dawn blackness. There were to be some close calls.

On the occasions when the tide stretched the crossing by several hundred yards, and the wind raged, we found we were forced to row upriver in the relatively slack water under the near bank and cross where the river narrowed. The manoeuvre called for considerable seamanship, otherwise we were swept well downstream when we hit the main flow.

THE BORDER ESK – *Gretna local Nelt Graham jr. in Ruby, an ex sailing dinghy capable of facing the roughest Border Esk crossing. Nelt was one of the few able to scull – using a single oar over the stern.*

But all that would come later. Geoff, the caravan's owner, was the oldest by quite a few years in our stalwart team of 10. On the day of our arrival he was happy to christen the event and handed out the Newcastle Brown, but it ended there. There was evening flight to be undertaken and afterwards plenty of Saturday night left to celebrate.

Charles and Geoff had towed Ruby from Lytham to Gretna the previous weekend. The locals – ostensibly her owners – had taken her on sea trials and found her satisfactory.

That afternoon we crossed in two lots. Ahead lay a three-mile walk to the new grass at the extreme seaward side of the private marsh. We were assured by our new friends that the landowners, who lived at Castletown House, Rockcliffe, were happy to allow shooting on this territory.

The grass was creeping slowly westward and the wigeon loved to feed on the new shoots. Droppings were everywhere and we dispersed over a wide area with plenty of time before flight. With me was Harry.

As night gathered we could faintly detect the parties of pinks, far off, dropping in over Redkirk from a great height. To our right the geese that had been feeding at the back of the private marsh, lifted and headed to roost in a dark line on to the sands.

'That is good news,' said Harry. 'They will go back in the morning and we'll have a chance.'

After my abstinency of that first year I had gone into training in the drinking stakes and found the Newcastle Brown most palatable. That evening I had secreted, foolishly as it turned out, a half bottle of dark rum in my copious ex-army smock.

Harry may have drunk half of the bottle but my share – on a thoroughly inexperienced gastronomic processing system – was enough to reduce my marksmanship to rank.

The extra gun I had taken, on this second trip, was Grandpa's beautiful William Powell best boxlock ejector side-by-side hammerless 12-bore. Light and perfectly balanced it was definitely a sin to subject such a weapon to the rigours of marsh life. It was known in the family as 'Grandpa's pigeon gun' and he would have been very unhappy had he known where it was to be used that night. With improved cylinder and half choke 28-inch barrels the Powell was the ideal weapon for wigeon flighting but Harry and his full-choke Winchester out-shot me by quite a few.

Between the team we had a goodly bag and after flight we descended into the local pub in our fowling gear – waders included. We were accepted without much more than a glance. In those unrestricted times our guns were merely locked in the caravan; far from today's paranoia.

I needed no rocking at lights-out and two of the locals opted to sleep on the caravan floor, fully clothed.

Geoff always insisted on a full bacon, egg and sausage start to his fowling day and the next morning Harry and Nelt were well impressed.

Outside there was a stiff westerly and, by the time we had dragged Ruby afloat, the rest of the previous evening's team had mustered and we crossed in two parties.

Harry told me to hang back and we had only a half-mile to make into the edge of the marsh. The whole of Rockcliffe merse is surrounded by a two-foot sheer edge. Big tides break off chunks of the thickly grassed earth and it makes for perfect goose flighting concealment.

As first light was breaking Harry left me 100 yards to his left with the instruction, 'When you hear them coming stick your head into the bank until they are right overhead. Don't move until you think they are past and take them going away.'

There was plenty of shooting that morning but, when full light came, neither Harry nor I had dirtied our barrels.

Harry's theory was that we would get a chance at the greylag which he knew would come off low at this bottom end. Five lots did slip past, to my left and nearer the river, with hardly a croak, unseen by Harry. I should, he told me later, have moved when I saw the leading bunch. My second lesson in goose chasing.

No one had shown themselves a good hour after the first shot had been fired and I was wondering what the next move would be when there was a distinctive 'wink-wink' from Harry's direction. A single goose headed out from the merse and swung along the bank just above my companion. It was no more than 20 feet up and seemed to go directly over where he had tucked in. There was neither shot nor movement from Harry's spot. Had he slipped away up the creek and missed this easiest of chances?

On the bird came, calling constantly. With shaking hand I slipped the safety forward. I wanted to open the breech to make sure I had definitely loaded the gun. The bird veered. It would pass behind. 'Wait until you think they are past', Harry had said. I swivelled from knees to backside. The pink was, indeed, just past and was totally unaware as I swung through its beak with 1½ ounces of BBs.

My bird was still rolling down the sandy bank, towards the backwater, when I hurled myself on top of it. How was I to know the shot had gone through neck and head?

Grandpa had always laid his birds out with the reverence they deserved. It was a family trait followed by son and grandsons. By the time a beaming Harry arrived my first goose lay immaculate on the bank top.

'Didn't you see it?' I asked. 'I saw it drop and that was all I wanted,' said Harry. These Border fowlers really were turning into something rather special.

The bag that morning was six pinks and two wigeon among the 10 of us. Would there be such a crowd on every dawn flight?

Our concern was unfounded. For the remainder of the week our new pals went about their various jobs. Wages were poor in those days and allowed for an indulgence in shooting and ale only at weekends.

THE ONION MAN

However, this was Sunday and there were two geese to be plucked, dressed and stuffed for the oven. We were shown how to identify a young bird, which the locals assured us, would need only 20 minutes a pound, plus an extra 20. Do not, they warned us, try to apply this to an old bird. Steam-roast these and keep testing until they are tender. A peeled onion, they said, was the ideal stuffing but we had no onions and the shops were closed. The Scottish Sabbath was still closely observed in 1951.

That was when an event of biblical proportions occurred. Around the corner came a 'French onion seller,' complete with a festoon of roped specimens dangling from handle bars. This had to be a local joke.

But no, we were told that the same character had been appearing every year about this time since the war. No one minded him plying his trade on a Sunday but whether he originated from over the channel was questionable.

'Combien pour les oigneons?' Charles demanded in best schoolboy French. Our dark blue denim suited, beret-topped, cycle rider was totally nonplussed. He had been rumbled.

A full rope turned out to be cheap but Geoff wanted some fun.

'Pick your smallest onion,' he offered. 'Walk to the gateway and throw it as high as you can. If we hit it you give us one full rope. If we miss we buy the lot.'

Mutely, the 'Frenchman' retreated to the gate having detached a golf ball sized bulb. The gate was a good 50 yards but he kept walking – to the middle of the road. Ten men lined up opposite him and cartridges were slipped into breeches. Harry managed to stuff six into his Winchester. It must have been just like OK Coral, except that the odds were a bit imbalanced.

'Everyone ready?' cried Geoff.

'Aye,' we chorused.

He nodded to the quaking onion seller.

The tiny object sailed high and performed a perfect parabola as guns belched and roared. The stackyard had never seen anything like it. Charles had let go with his black powder 10 and the smoke hung thick and pungent in the still air. When it cleared there was no sign of our 'Frenchman'. A Gun on the fringe had seen him snatch up his bicycle and flee round a nearby building never to return.

The onion was retrieved from the next field. There was just one large nick in the skin of BB proportions.

'You could have done with one four times the size,' advised our local cookery expert. 'But it's better than none at all,' as it was cut in half.

COOKING YOUR GOOSE

The resultant feast was a delight – perhaps the start of the learning curve on how to treat wildfowl for the table. I am a huge fan of steam roasting. We were taught, too, to experiment on various stuffings.

In autumn Rockcliffe Marsh can produce vast swathes of mushrooms (local lore has it that spores were spread there purposely during the First World War years). In the moonlight they shine like a million precious stones. The Gretna men told us to try a few inside a goose cavity along with a handful of blackberries from the hedgerow leading down to the foreshore. The gravy was exotic.

One hard lesson we learnt was that mallard can be as tough as the proverbial tractor tyre while teal are never tough and can be traditionally roasted for as little as 20 minutes in a hot oven. I have consumed hundreds and never had a tough one.

I have experienced this inexplicable phenomena also in roe deer. Why are they, too, always tender, irrespective of age? Red deer can definitely prove exceedingly challenging to the molars and, when this state is experienced, casserole is the only solution.

How gratifying to learn that Clarissa Dickson-Wright's (she of The Two Fat Ladies) favourite Christmas dish is the pinkfoot. She gives us her recipe at the end of the book.

PREPARING DINNER – On our first excursion to the Solway no geese went into the roasting tin but it was very different the following year. Here Charles and Jim Ritchie, one of the first locals we met, pluck a pinkfoot on the edge of Rockcliffe. The bird would be gutted and washed on the way back over the Border Esk before being stuffed and steam roasted in an ultra slow oven for the evening meal. The team feasted on what they had shot every day during their week's stay.

THERAPY

That week was to be a form of therapy for me. I had just been rejected from National Military Service and was mortified at the rebuff. All my pals had made it and some were fighting the communists in Korea. I had wanted to be part of it.

'Your eyesight makes you C3 and ineligible,' they had said.

'But I was in my school rifle squad. I played for the rugby XV without my specs and I can also do the 100 yards in evens.'

'Sorry. You are no good to us with that eyesight. In fact, you could be a liability!'

I felt like seeking the name of the chairman of the conscription board and sending him my goose oven-ready as proof he had it wrong.

For the remainder of the week we had the marsh to ourselves and it was to bring firsts for all of us. Geoff had also secured his bird on day one. He had dropped off half-way along the marsh, where most of the action was expected, and it was his young bird that had also gone into the Sunday oven. It was like savouring tender beef and a culinary first for us all.

Would that he were still here to relive the event in these pages, but Geoff lost a lengthy battle against ill-health at the age of 78. I last met up with him at my brother's Scottish hotel not long before his end. After recovering from a triple heart by-pass he was on a shooting/fishing holiday and looked little different from our Solway days.

We tried the new grass again for the wigeon towards the end of the week but they had not recovered from Saturday's severe attention. Plenty of packs passed over on their way to feed further inland on the private marsh. Their beautiful and evocative whistles announced their approach but there was a strong prevailing westerly up their tails and only the odd bird went into the larder.

Rockcliffe had long been recognised as one of Britain's leading wigeon grounds, if not the most populated. It was closely keepered and, thankfully, little shot. How was I to know that, around 25 years later, I would be shooting the offsprings of these same birds alongside the head keeper?

HORROR

Sunday morning, of that second Solway expedition, saw me transported to Carlisle railway station with extra baggage. This was to be the horror part of my otherwise most successful holiday. The goose gun was broken in two and packed in my suitcase. There was Grandpa's game gun in its immaculate oak and leather case, waders and a sack of birds in the feather. The four of us had two wigeon and four geese each to take home.

We had not, by then, learned that the easiest way to transport our bag was in the oven-ready state. Occasionally one was plucked while on the marsh or walking back over the sands – then cleaned and washed on the way across the river. Most were, however, hung in an airy farm building.

'Put your gear on the rack in front of you,' Geoff had advised. That way I could keep an eye on it.

The early 1950s railway steam travel was at its elegant height. Dr Beeching had not wielded his axe, the carriages were immaculately clean and were adorned with colourful scenic pictures. There were just two rows of seats facing each other in each compartment and there was never any reason to complain about the lack of heating.

Therein lay the problem. The birds had been in a cold airy barn at a temperature not much above freezing for days. Subjected to something nearer to 80 degrees, hitherto congealed blood began to liquefy. Opposite me was a portly grey haired lady intent, I decided, on her Agatha Christie mystery story.

We had not been long into our journey when this innocent lady let out an unearthly piercing howl. Onto her open page had dripped a large deep-cerise pool of blood. It got worse. As she looked up another blob hit her on the forehead, like a villain's neat bullet hole.

It is difficult to describe the mayhem that followed. Someone wanted to pull the communication cord. I had sprung to my feet and snatched the offending sack from the rack, all the while telling the other seven occupants there was nothing to be alarmed about.

Unfortunately, after a weeks fowling, my linen handkerchief, that I used to wipe the sticky mess from the near hysterical lady's forehead, was decidedly grubby and not too sweet smelling.

Thank God there was a Times reader amongst us. Not only did he take charge but he also used the copious advertising pages to swathe my birds. It turned out he had been a high ranker in the Army during the war and had seen a lot more blood and guts than our Pullman sported that unfortunate morning.

Whether it was by good luck or management I know not, but the deeply offended party detrained at the next stop, which was Penrith. The colonel (if he wasn't one, he should have been) had rearranged the seating plan. Me by one window and madam against the other on the same side so that we need not have eye contact.

My new friend wanted to hear all about my expedition and listened fascinated. He told me he had shot geese in the Dardanelles during the First World War. He hadn't found them very palatable. At least that is what he said when we parted at Preston and I offered him one.

Perhaps he wasn't a colonel after all; perhaps he was in the Diplomatic Corps.

(There is a lesson here for the unwary. Should you wish to post game, do so in a purpose-made polystyrene box, leak-proof and insulated to take ice blocks in a polythene bag. When shot game, previously hung in cool conditions, becomes warmer, congealed blood will run. No such advanced technological aids were, of course, available when the above event took place but recently I heard of an incident where a cardboard box containing a shot goose had been opened by the Post Office. Official tape announced the Post Office's action and enquiries revealed a sniffer dog, employed as a drugs detector, had shown keen interest!)

A NEW HQ

The pattern established on our second Solway venture was to continue for five years. The idyllic caravan occupation of Jackie Gass's stack-yard saw many adventures, successes and failures. Each year provided its own adventures under the geese. Sometimes the grey army would be there in legions, at others they would vanish for a reason known only to themselves.

Sometimes we followed the flocks inland during the day but our hearts were not in such tame ventures. We found that we had enough success on the wild foreshore to fill the bag and satisfy the enthusiasm of even an obsessed teenager.

But we did eventually rent, with two locals, a 500-acre farm which produced a wide variety of game including roe deer. In fact, Jim Ritchie's son David still rents the same shoot nearly half a century later and there is an open invite.

By the fifth year, however, Geoff's desire to rise at dawn for seven consecutive days, plus evening flight and wet backsides, had waned and he sold his caravan. Ken, too, had married and dropped out but Charles and myself were just as keen. We found a small local hotel for our HQ for one season before the ultimate solution arrived.

Charles and Jim Ritchie had become close pals. Both were newly married and their wives, too, were kindred spirits. Charles was still living in the north east and when it was suggested that Mrs Ritchie may like a week on the Tyne with Mrs Miller the accord was instantaneous.

Jim could see the marsh from his bedroom window and we now had an HQ as handy as the old stackyard. Besides the annual statutory week, there was also a bed for my lone sorties over Shap.

I had acquired a 1937 Royal Enfield 350cc motorcycle. Flat out she could just hit 45mph. The old girl didn't like Shap's one in four A6 gradient (motorways were still on the drawing board) and, when the tired single-cylinder finally broke down shortly after the start of the ascent one dark winter's night, the scrap yard called. That night my journey north was completed at 3am after hitching various lifts from kindly but curious lorry drivers. I doubt if today's 'Knights of the Road' would have been as receptive towards a wader-clad young fellow clutching a gun and a brace of pannier bags. It saved space to wear the waders and pack my shoes.

The Enfield was followed by another Triumph Speed Twin. Unfortunately this was a 1939 model, the year they were first made, and still sported the old girder front forks. Still much preferable to the horrors of rail travel.

Brother Charles's transport may not have been as speedy but his four-seater Austin Seven, circa 1935, was to take us to and from HQ and the marshes in splendid comfort.

We explored the friendly coastline westward and gloried in not only its clean sandy marshes but also the luxury of the head-high creeks which made stalking sometimes almost too easy. On one occasion Jim and I watched a small bunch of pinks pitch in near the River Nith about 500 yards away. We were unfamiliar with the area and, after setting our watches for zero hour, we separated and took a gully each. Halfway through the time we had allotted we came face-to-face again and were still no nearer! These birds must have known exactly what they were doing but they acted as the perfect decoys and eventually gave Jim the chance of a gratefully accepted right and left from another party which came to investigate.

In those days other shooters were a rarity apart from weekends and, at those times, we stuck to the edge of Rockcliffe.

As the northern Solway became more familiar we learned the art of stalking and driving our quarry. The greylag seemed to be the easiest to manage, though they were outnumbered greatly by their pinkfoot cousins.

GOODBYE RUBY

The year that Geoff decided to give up wildfowling coincided with the demise of our water transport, Ruby. We were never sure who holed her but felt pretty certain it followed an incident when Jim and I had crossed for evening flight to find two locals heading off from Rockcliffe.

They had waded over at low water and must have spent most of the day cut off. One was a squaddie on leave, the other a lad of around 14. They were birdless, fed-up and hungry. They asked us for a lift back but, since we were then a mile from the boat and wigeon territory was still half an hour's tramp, we had to decline. We gave them our Mars bars and pointed out that they would be able to wade back again within the hour.

The flight was fast and furious but, because of the blackness of the night only five birds were collected and Jim resolved to acquire a dog for the following season. The five we picked still made the six-mile round trip worthwhile – until we got back to the river to find the boat missing. In the darkness we thought, at first, that we had lost our bearings until we found the anchor mark.

Jim's words were unprintable. By then the tide was making so we couldn't wade. The three-mile walk off to the Metal Bridge would not have been so bad had we not been so hungry. But we had given our rations to someone else.

We had no covers for our guns yet no one turned a hair when we eventually boarded a bus and sat with them, barrels up, between our knees. Jim's wife, however, was in a great state of alarm since we were many hours overdue.

I heard later that some form of severe retribution was meted out to the squaddie. Something like a black eye and a bloody nose. Soon afterwards Ruby received a large cobble through her timbers. Jim was philosophical. Her hull was found to be rotten and the cobble could have saved us from a wetting, or worse.

We still had the rest of the season to get through and, in those days, dinghies were at a premium. Fibreglass hadn't exploded onto the market and we were stuck.

Jim had a solution. He would build a boat. The result was, to put it kindly, unique. His eight-foot punt floated, and was certainly easy to carry but, with a six-inch freeboard and bearing a three-man load, life was interesting when we hit a chop in the middle of the crossing.

Because of her unsteerability she was soon christened The Pig and sank under us as we reached the shallows on several occasions. Geoff watched her maiden voyage but, the next day, said he would stay on the Scottish shore for morning flight! I think that was, in fact, his last visit.

It was time to pool our resources. We elected to purchase, between us, a sound 12-foot clinker-built craft with trailer. She could be stored at Stormont Farm, a few feet from the marsh, and would be padlocked. The trailer meant two men could handle her. Jim and three other locals, plus Charles and myself, owned her. We hoped she would see out the rest of our years on the Solway.

By 1954 both Charles and Jim, as married men, restricted their annual fowling holidays to a week. That 'thing' which makes Kings leave thrones, which is said to be more powerful than gunpowder, had not yet wrapped its tentacles around my heart and, apart from a week's summer fishing in Scotland, all my spare time was spent with the gun.

SOLWAY SPECTRE

That same year saw me staying at Jim's on my own for an extra week. I had been given a lift to Gretna by car and transport to the marsh, each day, was by borrowed bicycle.

The Pig, constructed basically from marine ply, was still in service and was just handleable by one. On my first day, I crossed before dawn. I had the whole of that part of the estuary to myself. There would be a big midday tide, which would cover all but the top of the merse on Rockcliffe Marsh, and I decided to stay on. I was taking a gamble, a gamble on whether or not I would be spotted illegally occupying the tiny shepherd's hut close to the westerly marsh-edge. The previous season a 'spectre' had arrived at Rockcliffe to strike alarm through the ranks of the Border Esk incursors. It came in the form of a magnificent white charger ridden by the estate's new head keeper.

Arthur Mills had just been discharged from The Guards and, from the safety of the marsh edge, I had witnessed a demonstration of his innovative poaching deterrent.

Timmie and Ossie had driven over from the north east to Gretna and had hitched a lift across the river to the edge of the marsh. This was their first – and last – Border raid. They were warned by the locals not to go into the grass but ignored the advice.

Alerted by their dawn shots the keeper had ridden his steed across the marsh, the magnificent beast making light of the creeks. Timmie and Ossie had escaped by wading chest-deep back across the river with the keeper's threats leaving no doubt about what would happen were they to try it again. Fearing he would follow them over they lay in a field of kale until he rode away.

Jim Ritchie had not crossed with us that day but witnessed it all from the far bank. He took the pair home for hot baths, and a change of clothing, and among his rewards was an expensive new cartridge belt with enclosed leather sockets for each round. They had kept the cardboard rounds bone dry. I believe his son David still uses it to this day.

On the day I took the risk I decided that, if I were accosted, I could claim to have been cut-off by the 'unexpectedly high tide' and, with an empty gun, plead for leniency. No-one, however, interrupted my vigil and, apart from one mishap, it turned out to be well worth the gamble.

The day was one of those stolen from summer, though it was late October. Had there been wind forecast I would not have chanced the venture. Gales can easily put several feet on a Solway tide, particularly so far up its reaches.

The shepherd's hut was a meagre shelter. Built of four foot concrete posts, and corrugated zinc, it had been there as long as anyone could remember. It could only be entered in the stooped position and had room for no more than one man, his dog and his sandwiches.

The tide pushed me into it two hours before high-water after a blank dawn flight. There were plenty of geese in the area but all had flighted too high. Several parties had gone into the back of the marsh and there was every chance they would lift to try some different pickings. Fresh droppings showed they had been in the area of the hut during the last 24 hours.

The first chance came out of the sun, well high, like a covert Messerschmit (the war had been over but a few years). The Lewis tumbled the bird 50 yards out. Gott in Himmel! As it descended its white plumage, hitherto dark against the sun, showed it to be a protected shelduck – the first and the last time I have ever shot this species.

'Don't pull the trigger till you know your quarry.' How many times had I heard that maxim? A lesson read, marked and digested.

I had determined not to move, if I dropped anything, lest I gain attention from the back of the marsh. This stillest of days would allow my shot to be clearly heard for miles but I had to get rid of the damning evidence.

A quick dash to the marsh edge had the bird buried firmly under a heavy turf and no figure astride a white horse appeared. I had once gone deep into the marsh, without gun, to pick a hard-hit bird, and knew the exact path the charger would take.

The shelduck incident lay like a heavy cloud over my head on this most beautiful of days, when a faint cackling snapped me out of my gloom. A cautious peep around the corner of my shelter revealed a skein of some 50 pinks heading straight in from the estuary. They were low enough when they first passed over but I left them; spellbound. One more sweep and they pitched in no more than 100 yards in front. Perhaps I should have taken them the first time. Would they feed towards me? No.

That wonderful guzzling buzz, as they cropped the short grass, was the first time I had experienced this extraordinary phenomenon – like a swarm of giant bees. I doubt if farmyard geese do it to the same degree.

Cautiously binoculars, cartridge belt and iron-rations were shed as I went into the belly position. I had only about 10 yards, in full view of the birds, to make to the nearest depression and I would then be just below ground level on the edge of a flooded creek.

Head flat down, I inched slowly along, all the while waiting for a cessation of the buzz. All was well when I reached cover. It stretched to within a few yards of the flock that was now feeding close to its edge.

After 10 minutes of more slow progress I reckoned there would not be far to go when the buzz stopped. Another skein headed directly in towards their companions calling loudly. When they were 30 yards out I rose to my knees and dropped a right and left as they flared. The noise from those already on the ground was deafening as they exploded only a few feet above my head and headed out to sea in scattered lots. Fearing I would be seen I restricted the temptation to take two more shots.

My two birds lay, inert, only a few yards away, and I controlled the instinct to leap up and gather them in. I was still a 'sitting duck' and remained motionless in my hollow.

How I enjoyed my reverie in spite of my delicate situation. I rolled onto my back. It is surprising what one sees in this mode and it is quite the most certain way of spotting a peregrine if there happens to be one in the vicinity.

By now the tide had begun to ebb and the level in my creek was dropping fast. Time to collect my birds and make it to legal territory.

Years later I was to meet the keeper, the aforementioned Arthur Mills. The event caused much hilarity. Through my shop contacts I had got to know the late Jack Hesmondhalgh. He lived not far from Rockcliffe and ran an excellent walk and drive game shoot to which I had been invited. I believe it still operates today with the Armstrong family of farmers its backbone.

In those days the pie and pea lunch was in a local pub and I found myself next to a spruce Scottish gent perhaps a little older than myself.

'Have you met Arthur?' enquired Jack and we shook hands.

'What,' I asked, 'do you do in these parts?'

'I am the head keeper at Rockcliffe.'

'Ah. I used to shoot it – from the estuary – but it would be before your time, just after the war. In those days the head keeper rode a white horse.'

'Aye. That was my white horse! Jack, do you mind if I sit next to someone else?'

It was to be the start of a rewarding friendship. As a result of that day I took many driven-pheasant parties of paying guests to Rockcliffe. When I had a new team under my wing it would cause me huge mirth when Arthur arrived to brief the guests after dinner. He was a charismatic, commanding figure and his appearance in the room always brought the party to its feet to the last man. I never primed my charges and it was amusing to see their expressions when they realised they had genuflected to the keeper!

How easily comes to mind the memory of that first day I stepped onto Arthur's marsh from the legal end. Guided by Arthur, we slipped through the marsh gate by the shepherd's cottage. I knew it well through the lens on my binoculars. With us that morning was Peter, a solicitor, keen to pouch his first goose. Arthur left me in a dry hollow on the banks of a creek.

'I don't suppose I need to tell you from what direction they'll come,' he had said with a wry grin.

There were no bangs, that morning, from the marsh edge. By then Jim Ritchie was buying his pheasant poults from Arthur and few of the new generation of fowler had chosen to carry on our river-crossing approach. Dawn had hardly broken when the first wave of pinks came in, a long line moving at great speed with a fresh westerly under their tails. Even, after all my practise, I had only time for one barrel as they swept directly overhead at around 40 feet.

Taken as soon as I saw the line my bird came straight out and hit the mud in the bottom of the creek only a few feet away. I didn't move. I couldn't. My first legal Rockcliffe goose was an illegal barnacle! Almost certainly the only one in the flock and indistinguishable in the poor light.

When Arthur strode over, after flight, my bird was still where it had dropped. He spoke only two words and they were expletives. He pushed it into the mud where it had landed.

'It once happened to me,' he said to make me feel slightly better.

Peter didn't get his goose that morning and the tale of his first is told in a later chapter.

There is a highly significant footnote to this saga of tide stranding and I have purposely used the incident to emphasise what might befall today's miscreant. Then I was poaching. Today it would be classed as armed trespass.

I was a gauche 19-year-old when I embarked on my reckless venture. Had a keeper approached, my gun would have been empty and my plea would have been that I had been caught out by the unusually high tide. Were I to have been prosecuted, the fine would probably have been 10 shillings (50p).

Today I could lose both my shotgun, ammunition and the boat I had gone over in. My shotgun certificate could be revoked and the fine could be up to £2,500. There is also the possibility of a gaol sentence not exceeding three months.

LOST TROUSERS

The earlier reference to the Armstrongs reminds me of the night I 'lost' my trousers.

We had ended a most splendid and bountiful day when the bag of pheasants grew and grew. All 20 of us were feasting on one of Mrs Armstrong's sumptuous hotpots in the static caravan/gunroom when our banqueting hall began to rock with the arrival of a sudden, westerly gale roaring in from the Solway Firth. This became a full blown storm when a deluge of rain thundered on our roof so loudly that we had difficulty hearing ourselves speak.

'Who's for a wigeon flight tonight?' asked someone. We all knew that none of 10,000 resident flock would want to be on their estuary feeding grounds in such a tempest. 'Haggiston's flood?' said John. 'Aye,' was the unanimous reply.

The fact that I would be two hours later than my ETA at home was of no consequence. Those at home were used to my dalliance on away shoot days.

But where, I pondered, would we all find cover? I knew of this flood and there were a mere four pallet hides. I need not have been concerned. Only three youngsters out of the entire team were fired up enough to turn out in such conditions, plus myself, the oldest by many years. There was no way I was going to pass on this one for I knew the Solway pinks sometimes dropped into this spot on this sort of night when the sandbars in the Firth proved too hostile as a roost.

Our hides were meagre shelters in the saturated violence. I must, thought I, discreetly suggest an L shape to the shoot captain. There were plenty of wigeon that night. We shot steadily for half an hour until the light had faded too much, even for the eagle-like vision of my three young companions. The dogs were constantly at work retrieving birds, sometimes almost a field away, as the gale plucked them down-wind.

My contribution was, however, meagre. No way could I match both the eyesight and the lightning reflexes of the young Guns. I had the added disadvantage of wearing spectacles. Disappointingly the geese did not come. No doubt the fury of the wind had persuaded them to pitch in at less exposed quarters.

Most of the Guns were still imbibing when we returned. We had divested ourselves of our waterproofs and I declared how pleased I was that, underneath, I wore my substantial Derby tweed plus-two suit. That was when Robin Armstrong, the middle of three brothers, chirped up, 'What about the pair of breeks you were supposed to be having made for me two years ago?'

Not like me to miss a sale – but I obviously had. Robin no doubt had placed his order one day between drives in the gun trailer because my golden rule, as a journalist, was to write down everything vital. Time for some fun. The whisky had taken hold and the smoke-fetid room was awash with riotous mirth already.

Robin was taller and appeared much leaner than I – by about three stone I reckoned. 'I'll tell you what. If my breeks fit you (they were of identical cloth to Robin's Norfolk jacket) you can have them. If they're too slack around the waist you pay me full retail for a new pair.' 'Done,' said Robin. Here, at last, was a chance for me to extract the full mark-up from a farmer. The Armstrongs were generous with their pennies but I have never, in all my years in the gun trade, sold anything to an agronomist at the advertised price. I dropped my trousers with full confidence.

I know not if the prolonged cheering came from the sight of my naked limbs or from the fact that the new trousers fitted their new owner like proverbial gloves. I hear they've only just fallen apart 30 years on.

(If you are wondering whether I was forced to travel back trouserless, the answer is negative. A lesson to all shooters straying from home territory: always to carry a spare pair.)

BOAT PROBLEM

Over the years boats became an on-going problem for all the fowlers at Gretna. Not even the locals could sleep easily. One morning Old Nelt discovered his eight-foot dinghy missing. It was the end of the season and he was prepared to wait a while in case it turned up.

It did – in Northern Ireland! On the stern he had affixed a plate with his address. Since it would cost too much to recover the craft he wrote a letter of thanks to the honest finder and asked him to keep it with his compliments.

Ken Watson – he of our maiden venture to the Solway – also arrived pre-dawn to discover a dinghy he had recently acquired missing. Later that day the boat was spotted two miles downstream on a sandbank and a daring plan was hatched to execute her recovery. She was too far out in the firth to be dragged to a channel so Ken and a pal decided to take another craft down-river on the ebb tide beyond where the stranded vessel lay and, with the coming of the tidal bore, row across the current to its position and attach a tow rope.

To anyone who has witnessed a Solway bore the plan certainly sounded fraught. On a big tide the onrush of the sea can outstrip a running man.

Those of us not participating in the jolly affair secured a ringside seat by motoring to a point opposite the promised drama and were not disappointed. As the tide swept in – you could plainly view the two-foot wave – Ken and his pal were swept rapidly up-river, the oarsman working frantically while the other thrashed valiantly with a paddle.

The plan worked like a rehearsed commando raid and soon the two tiny craft sped back up-river. We motored as fast as we could to the mooring but were well beaten by the courageous mariners.

FOGGY DAYS

Foggy days on the Solway often produced a great deal of excitement. My first experience was many years before the appearance of the brilliant American goose calls on the UK market but, in those early days, the fowler who had mastered the art of using his vocal chords to lure his quarry could often swell the bag in these murky conditions.

In my boyhood I had been taught by my Father to bring in various species by calling, in particular curlews and redshank, but the art of luring geese was alien. One young Solway local highly versed in the art, however, was Nelt Graham. He, in turn, had been tutored by his father and possibly his father by *his* father.

The morning I was to first experience Nelt's prowess had dawned clear and still. Six of us had crossed by boat to the edge of Rockcliffe and dispersed along its westerly edge. The system for departure later was always the same at dawn and dusk. The one who had moved the furthest southward collected the others one by one as he made his way back to the boat.

A fair number of birds had dropped in to the back of the marsh at first light after passing over us two gunshots high. Then a fog descended and I had pulled my ex-army gas cape (complete with rucksack space on the back) over my head and, wrapped in my voluminous sheepskin thigh-length waistcoat, had fallen into a most comfortable slumber.

Goose talk woke me with a start. All around was a thick blanket of fog and a distant calling announced a small party of pinkfoot making its way unseen up-river. Close by came a more insistent call which ceased as the far-off pack moved on and I decided to investigate.

After a stealthy five minutes of half-bent movement along the marsh edge I was greeted with a quiet hail – Nelt. I joined him in his cosy lair and, for the rest of the morning, was given my first lesson in goose calling.

Although Nelt's cries did not sound, at close quarters, very realistic they worked on the real thing – often with devastating effect. As the fog thinned that morning he called a singleton so close in to us you could see its head twisting inquisitively as it searched for its source. I was allowed to make the kill – the outcome of an indelible demonstration.

It is certainly a skill worth practising. The note comes from the back of the throat and is delivered in two short sharp bursts at a high pitch. Have a go next time you see a singleton.

The thing that struck me most with Nelt's technique was the great volume he employed – intensified by cupped hands. I use the skill to this day, but only if I have forgotten my call or dropped it out of reach. (I am now too disabled to stoop to ground level. Everything has to have a cord which can be retrieved by my shepherd's crook stick and that can be a lengthy procedure.)

How easy things are for today's tyro. Not only does he have his artificial calls but also the most realistic of lightweight decoys. These can, at times, be almost too deadly. What would the fellow of only a few seasons' experience, who struts like the proverbial turkey cock because he has succeeded in holding a first-year goose over his head while he plays his merry plastic tune, do if he had only his own skills to employ? I really do feel that, with these extra aids, the job can sometimes be too easy. This is when those who have control of inland goose shooting must exercise discretion.

For the uninitiated I must, however, stress that the use of goose calls, be they a manufactured device or the employment of one's own vocal resources, are vital. There are times when the calling of long lines of flighting birds may appear futile. However, on occasions, over long seasons, I have played my seductive melodies to seemingly totally disinterested throngs only to find the odd skein detaching itself when almost out of sight and then homing in to my decoy pattern with complete abandon.

A skein does not, of course, drop down in such an incautionary way every time. Often they will circle with great trepidation, particularly in full daylight. This is when the decision over whether or not to shoot has to be made. Sometimes the timing has to be split-second in order to give the other Gun/Guns a chance if you are not alone.

Ideally, of course, all true fowlers would prefer to shoot alone but this privileged situation is not always the case. If your birds do make the direct approach then wait until they are about to settle before pulling the trigger.

At times, when geese have been using a flight pond – not a roost, for roost shooting must never be undertaken – I have called to distant lines of birds on their way to their night quarters. Occasionally the odd pack will break off for a look-see and my shooting causes no disturbance to the main body.

At other times you may be considering whether to pack up when a faint croak announces a small party unable to overcome their curiosity. A couple of floating decoys can be invaluable under such circumstances, tempting the birds to come straight in. But a word of caution, if more than the spasmodic bunch is tempted in to your water, make a modest bag and depart speedily.

Judging your lead when birds are dropping in to water can be difficult. One much-respected writer – for me he is the most revered – makes an extraordinary statement in one of his works. He advises the tyro not to pull the trigger until he can see the eye of the goose! One cannot forgive the talented scribe by offering the plea that he was having a 'senior moment' for though he wrote about the wonderful chase into his eighties, this particular pontification was issued in early middle age.

Quite simply, the inexperienced fowler will, or should, quickly learn if he is fortunate enough to have a wise mentor. My favoured counsel to the uninitiated is never to squeeze the trigger if you have the slightest doubt about range and then to double your lead. It is very difficult for the tyro to conceive the speed of such a large bird. If an incoming bird has spotted you with a wind up its backside, a goose can be romping along at a cool 50mph and more. For an unsuspecting target my method is to blot and squeeze.

BILL POWELL

But back to the charismatic years on Solway.

On another foggy morning four of us had gone down to board Ruby at Stormont and had to rely on the good nature of the aforementioned professional goose guide Bill Powell. It was the morning when we discovered the hole in Ruby's timbers. Although Bill was not happy at our presence – he had three guests with him and had always looked on Rockcliffe as 'his private marsh' even though he, too, was obliged to stick to its edge – he was man enough to recognise our misfortune and to offer us a lift. He did, however, pull rank and suggest we remain at the northern edge of the merse while he took his paying guests to the normally more productive middle.

I had gone up on a lone sortie and had joined three locals including Harry Graham. When Harry heard the professional's suggestion he couldn't stop chuckling – but then he was always chuckling. This time he could hardly contain himself.

'The silly old sod doesn't know that the geese always follow the river off on a foggy morning,' he had chortled. 'We should fill our boots.'

The geese, mainly greys that day, did, indeed, follow the river until they reached the Rockcliffe grass when they cut in. We put up a fair old barrage – none was too high, only wide to right and left – and we finished with 11 between us.

Bill's face was a picture to behold when he finally led his party off, never having fired a shot. We had ferried our bag across the river by the time he arrived and one of us returned to row our benefactor back. We felt almost embarrassed when he asked us how we had got on.

One of my regrets is that I was never able to do this fine man a good deed in return. It was towards the end of his fascinating guiding career. He could not have made much of a living at the job but, these days, I know something of how he must have taken pleasure at presenting a youngster with a chance to get under the enthralling creatures he hunted.

In his writings Powell is sometimes disparaging towards the local fowlers. He obviously projected these feelings towards his paying guests for, in his book Saga of a Goose Trail (2002) Hugh Meynell also castigates fellow goose chasers for positioning themselves in front of Powell's Guns and for playing transistor radios on the marsh!

Here I must leap in to the defence of these splendid folk. From the very beginning we received nothing but immense warmth from these iron men on The Solway. Many of them earned much of their income from haaf netting, which involves standing in the river on a flood tide to trap the spawning salmon and sea trout. The paraphernalia of net and frame were heavy and cumbersome enough without coping with the catch on the return journey.

The occasional pony was still in use transporting equipment and catch when we made our first venture to the estuary but the number of fishers was declining as more lucrative work became available.

Powell obviously refused to acknowledge that he was a usurper. Some of our Gretna friends supplemented their incomes with the sale of geese. The interloper was, ostensibly, taking bread from their tables.

In the later chapter Kindred Spirits I tell of a dawn flight I spent with the brothers Wilkins who live in the hinterland of Morecambe Bay and who are still avid goose chasers as they near three score years and ten. On that most memorable of mornings on the Bay I learnt that both of these brothers, David & John, were clients of Powell's in 1958. In those days the fee for a week's stay was £14 including full board and a daily guiding service. You could also hire one of two double 8-bores for £2 per week – cartridges extra. David killed his first greylag with one of these muskets.

There was, however, a hidden expense when you lodged in Bill's cosy bunkroom, part of a traditional fisherman's single storey cottage in Glencaple. Visits to the nearby Nith Hotel were part of the everyday routine and the ageing guide's whisky intake was legendary.

'He never bought a round,' said David. 'And I never saw him refuse one!'

Had Powell taken note of what John Guille Millais wrote in his classic work of 1901, The Wildfowler in Scotland, his relationship with the men of The Solway would have been much different. In his opening chapter Millais observes that the resident Scots fowlers could not be expected to look on the visiting Gun with a 'kindly eye'. But he says he shot over much of the land's coastal regions and found all the locals could be won over by kind and considerate treatment.

'I have never had any trouble after going out of my way to make friends with my brothers-in-arms,' wrote Millais.

Following their first visit to the Solway, and for many years afterwards, the Wilkins team made persistent, but unsuccessful, attempts to shoot on Rockcliffe Marsh. Head of the clan was Pa Dick Wilkins, a lifelong goose chaser who shot geese until the last year of his life at 82. He wrote to the Mounsey Heyshams, the owners, whose home adjoins the territory but was always refused permission.

'We were always told that they felt there were already enough Guns shooting there,' David told me.

However, I suspect the owners were merely wanting it left in peace. I know the very occasional friend did shoot it lightly and, as previously outlined, I was one of those to do a lightning dawn flight when I was among a driven pheasant party staying on the estate. But, during my expeditions from Gretna I never heard, or saw, anyone shooting the territory from inland.

On one occasion the three Wilkins called on Arthur Mills, the head keeper, in spring and were given permission to gather gull eggs. 'It was a wonderful day,' recalled David. 'There were great numbers of birds nesting there, mainly herring gulls, and we came off with a small bucket full.' (Gull eggs were considered to be a great delicacy until their collection was banned by the Wild Bird Protection Act of 1981.)

BIG GUNS

The goose-calling Nelt junior was also the first man I had come across who could use a big bore gun to good effect. His mighty single hammer 4-bore (I forget the make) had been in his family for many years. I suspect it was only proofed for black powder but he cheerfully threw three ounces of BBs from its 42-inch full choke barrel using nitro home loads.

His efforts inspired me to lug my grandfather's single Tolley hammer 8-bore to the Solway. It had already proved itself on the tightly packed wigeon flocks on the Ribble but I had never succeeded in bringing down anything I shot at singly – be it mallard or pintail. With the 8-bore on a rope sling over my back and my eight-pound Lewis magnum 12-bore under my arm, I had to be the best armed fowler but I still never downed a goose with the Tolley. Many times I used the eight first, missed, and, snatching up the 12, killed cleanly.

While still in my twenties I did, however, acquire the ultimate in big bore shoulder guns – a muzzle loading 2-bore by Thos Hawkrigg. This was the only inscription on the weapon which was capable of throwing four ounces of BBs from its 45-inch barrel. I used the tool on the Morecambe Bay wildfowlers' territory at Pilling and did succeed in downing geese with it. My enthusiasm was, however, dimmed by the irksome business of muzzle loading and the urgent necessity of diligent and laborious barrel cleaning on my return home.

The supreme efficiency of my Lewis was probably the reason for my relatively short love affair with big guns, though I once possessed the *piece de resistance* – a Holland & Holland single hammerless sidelock 4-bore. How I came to acquire the weapon is worth recounting.

I had then entered the gun trade at the age of 26 and had advertised a list of guns in the Shooting Times. I received a call from a German businessman based in Belfast. He was interested in a Holland & Holland Gold Name 12-bore I had listed and had, he said, a single 4-bore of the same make to trade in.

My excitement was difficult to disguise, even on the telephone, but there was a problem. The Troubles were at their height and the transferring of weapons to and from Northern Ireland carried the strictest security. The carriage costs alone, due to these restrictions, were exorbitant.

I was, however, doing a regular trade in side-arms, supplying civilian executives in Northern Ireland who had been advised by the authorities to arm themselves. I invariably suggested a snub-nosed .38 special Smith & Wesson revolver, which could be worn in a covert shoulder holster.

Eventually, through a piece of sheer good luck, a method of transferring these weapons became not only foolproof but also free of charge without having to trouble the routine postal service. There was an undercover police unit based at Squires Gate airport, Blackpool, solely for Northern Ireland operations and, knowing of this organisation from my newspaper days, I contacted one of its officers. They had light aircraft making regular flights to and from the two territories and were more than happy to make sure my small packages arrived intact.

Large parcels were, however, a different matter they said. I also needed to check the 4-bore with my barrel gauge. Then one of my gunsmiths, on hearing of the problem, came up with the ultimate solution. He had recently qualified as a small plane pilot and could borrow a single engined aircraft from a pal. All it would cost me was the fuel.

Conditions were ideal on the morning of our departure. We were soon off the Stranraer peninsular and dropping into Newtownards airport. The perfect three-point landing put me at ease until the plane began to shake violently. My pilot had forgotten to tell me that the runway went from tarmac into grass!

Within seconds of pulling to a standstill a car drew up alongside our plane. We were met by an RUC sergeant in plain clothes. He introduced himself as Bill. He was very friendly but distinctly edgy. As he drove us at high speed in his unmarked car towards our appointment with the German businessman I enquired hopefully, 'Any chance of a quick pint of Guinness Bill?'

'Neither the Queen, the Pope nor the President of the United States could get a pint of the black stuff today,' replied our new friend, who was a native of the Emerald Isle. 'We had the shelling of one of our police posts last night and the sooner we get this job done and you two back in the sky the better I will be.'

We drove on in silence. RUC and Army presence was everywhere.

When we arrived at my client's sumptuous home Gunter was delighted with the Gold Name Holland and I had great difficulty in keeping my hands from trembling as I hefted the fabulous 4-bore – one of only a few, I was to discover, ever made by that illustrious company. I had taken a set of barrel plug gauges and found the bore clean and well in proof. Overall the weapon was in excellent condition.

Gunter told me what deal he wanted and we shook hands at his price. He seemed surprised that I didn't try to bargain but I cannot reveal what the 4-bore stood me at, lest the dealer who eventually bought it from me reads this. Let me say that had all deals been like that I would have been retired from the gun trade in my thirties instead of in my forties!

Bill was perspiring profusely by the time we climbed back aboard our plane – which had been guarded in our absence. All the same the diligent sergeant carefully checked it for explosive devices. I could not help feeling sad that a country of such natural beauty had been so abused by strife and blood shed.

The 4-bore was nitro proofed and came with a supply of brass cases. I nailed the odd Lancashire goose inland – I was loath to take it on to a marsh – but there was nothing I could not have killed with my Lewis. After using this unique weapon for a season it was sold to the dealer – the first person I had offered it to. Perhaps even then it was under-priced. The only true way of knowing the full worth of such a rare weapon would have been to submit the piece to auction.

The pros and cons of big bore guns will rage for as long as we are allowed to go wildfowling. That these weapons have a charisma all of their own is undeniable. They are a sheer joy just to touch.

With their banning in America in the 1990s came the deadly 3½-inch semi-auto gas-operated 12's with their 2¼ ounce cartridges – sweet shooting, easy handling weapons capable of prodigious killing power. But that there will always be a market for the old fours and eights is as certain as the fact that the pinkfoot arrives in late summer!

My advice to a beginner is to acquire a modern over and under 12-bore with interchangeable chokes and three-inch chambers. A competent dealer, or clay bird coach, will ensure a correct fit and this weapon will cater for all forms of shooting from clays to pigeons, pheasants and geese.

These days gun fitting is made easier by the fact that thick layers of clothes are not now needed to ensure winter warmth. Modern fabrics give both insulation and total rain protection with the minimum of bulk ensuring a stock length suited to all seasons.

NOON GEESE

It has often crossed my mind that, just as Lord Lovat recruited largely Highland stalkers into his ranks of Lovat's Scouts (sniper/commandos) in the Second World War, surely Sir Peter Scott could have had a band to rival that cunning breed had he chosen to enter the Army rather than the Navy and enlist wildfowlers. Both pursuits are equally as adept at covert approach and concealment and fitness plays a large part in both. Of course, I couldn't possibly have qualified for Scott's lot since I had failed my National Service medical on poor eyesight.

The nearest I got to armed conflict was wildfowling. That pursuit could, also, be exceedingly exhausting and, one day in our little Solway caravan Harry decided that, after almost a week of pre-dawn alarm calls, he would stay in his sleeping bag an extra three hours. He would, he said, guarantee us geese if I also wished to stay in the land of nod.

It would not have mattered how much noise the other three made as they departed from the caravan that November morning. It was a delicious feeling to roll over and slumber on. Harry even produced bacon and eggs to send us on our way with the sun well up and little breeze. By then the ice had melted on the caravan ceiling and we left the kettle on a gentle simmer for the return of the early shift.

NOON GEESE *by Rodger McPhail*

Geoff, Charles and Jim had taken the Land Rover but the stackyard, into which the caravan was tucked, was only a mile from the shore and it is all down-hill. There was still a two man punt for us to navigate the Esk to the edge of Rockcliffe and, as we landed on the far bank, our companions hoved into sight gooseless.

'We'll be back after lunch,' shouted Harry as we headed for the nearest edge of the merse.

AUTHOR AND MENTOR – *The author, left, with his mentor, Gretna fowler Harry Graham, on the day they missed dawn flight, went out at noon and had bagged three pinkfoot by 1pm. Harry reckoned the late shift would come off low and he was proved to be correct.*

'There will be some late bunches coming off the sands for another hour and we need to be close to cover,' said my totally confident guide. There had been a waxing three quarter moon during the night and Harry's theory was that some of the geese, a mixture of pinks and greys, would have fed under it and would be sleeping in – just as we had done.

After a short walk along the sand, where a backwater swung in close to the three-foot high merse bank, Harry called a halt. 'We've no need to spread far apart,' he reckoned. 'When they come keep your head into the bank and shoot when I give the word. They haven't been troubled at this spot all season and should be low enough.'

I had total confidence in Harry's reckoning and, in little more than five minutes, a thin black line appeared far out to the west. There were around 100 pinkfoot covering a wide front and it looked as though we would be under the left leg of the vee. When Harry shouted, 'Now!' I thought he had left it too late. We rose on our knees as one. The two shots were simultaneous and my bird dropped like a stone 50 yards in to the grass.

Harry's bird slanted out and he was up and off, his gun left on the thick grass of the merse. 'Empty my gun,' he shouted as he went away at a steady jog, his gaze fixed firmly on the featureless landscape. I did not give him much of a chance but, after 10 minutes, he was on his way back with a bird in his hand. He said he had marked it against the end of a distant wood and had found it belly up half a mile into the marsh. And there had been no sign of keepers.

While Harry was gone another flock of pinks came in and I collected my second.

In all the years I shot Rockcliffe we were confronted only once when we went into the private merse to pick fallen birds without, of course, our guns. The locals contended that we were observed often through scopes or binoculars and Arthur Mills, the keeper, and his team were quite happy with our behaviour.

SOLWAY GUARDIAN

Years later, in fact when I was compiling this book, I learned of another guardian who also kept watch on our safety on Solway's vast open spaces.

I had contacted Ken Watson in case he had any photographs from the early days and it was he who told me of the watch kept by Old Nelt.

SEASHORE AMBUSH – The locals taught us to use the smallest amount of cover to get under the Solway flight lines. Here the author lies behind a clump of sea thrift on the shore-line. It was ideal for intercepting waders – before most of them were put on the prohibited list following the 1981 Wild Bird Protection Act.

His farmhouse lay only a mile from the shore and its views to the edge of Rockcliffe Marsh were uninterrupted. He had a powerful spotting scope, tripod mounted, in a top floor window. His prime concern was for our safety but I did wonder if it was he who had told Harry of the late skeins that went off at the bottom end of the marsh.

Harry Graham gleaned much of his deep knowledge of the Solway flight lines from Old Nelt and, towards the end of his days the old chap did, I hear, have at least one trip a year with his gun on the foreshore, but only when he knew he would have a chance to bag a goose. I was never present when he made one of these rare sorties but did learn about the day one of these special outings saw him fall foul of the law.

My narrator was Whitie, the same Whitie pictured on page 233 and about whom I write later in this chapter also. I let him tell his own story:

'Two of us persuaded Old Nelt to come with us one February for dawn flight. We knew he would put us under the birds and we all three got geese.

'But one had gone down on to Rockcliffe Marsh and we all decided to look for it after flight. We knew we were allowed to pick birds that had been shot on the foreshore and had dropped on private land but didn't know we could not take our guns with us even if they were unloaded.

'We were still searching when two keepers appeared. Old Nelt told us to run for it even though we thought we were all right. The old chap couldn't move beyond a walk and when they caught up with him they told him he would be charged with trespass. It cost him 10 shillings in court and a good telling off. I think it was Old Nelt's last outing.'

SANDSTORM

While fog can often give the fowler the advantage over geese, particularly if he is a proficient caller, a good old sandstorm can also provide deadly cover – at a cost, however, to one's musketry.

There had been a week of low tides on one of our visits to Solway in the early years. Coupled with either an east or west high wind, sand storms rage along the track of the Firth. Wind from either the north or south produce little more than a flurry, where the multitude of waterways, crossing their path, swallow the particles.

The dense grit-laden columns are, conveniently, often only around waist high and prostrate, with feet towards the flight path, the ploy often produced supper once the flight line had been determined.

My Solway mentor was with me approaching evening flight when I first experienced this phenomenon. We were half way to the edge of Rockcliff merse when Harry suddenly ordered the prone mode. With plenty of daylight left, a bunch of around 15 pinks was heading straight for us from up-river. At ground level the damned stuff got everywhere – up the nose, between teeth and in ears. As a specs wearer I did have an advantage but Harry also employed his experience.

He always wore a thin mesh scrim-style scarf and this he drew over the bridge of the nose. American GI khaki peaked woollen headgear was pulled down to protect squinting eyes.

The birds could be faintly observed holding their line and, with a shout of 'Now!' Harry sat up and proceeded to work his five-shot Winchester pump action 12 at an impressive rate. Out of the corner of my eye I could see geese flailing down. This was the easiest of chances as the birds fanned back against the wind and I dropped my two.

Harry reckoned we ought to stay put while the wind held and make a run for the wigeon flight at the last minute. There was comfort enough while we stood in the midriff-high column. When we spotted a party of geese we would sprint one way or the other to intercept our quarry and sink out of sight in our most uncomfortable ambush.

That day the tactic was, however, to work well for me only twice. After the second immersion my father's lovely 1920 Lewis magnum, with its original colour hardening and its trade-mark mallard drake engraving, refused to close. While Harry merrily carried on spewing the rounds from his highly efficient Winchester I was busy stripping my side-by-side into barrels forend and action pieces. A thorough wipe with a handkerchief (obligatory in those days for the specs wearer) had the musket operational for only one more immersion.

After several days of this treatment, or rather abuse, the gun had altered its appearance. All the colour hardening had disappeared, plus a lot of the blueing from barrels and furniture. The stock and forend checkering, crisp at the start of the week, was now worn almost smooth. On my return home I had to keep the revered weapon out of sight from my father until it had been given a facelift at the gunsmiths.

I know of only one other gun to receive more abusive treatment than this at the hands of the Solway. I refer to the new Purdey deliberately trampled into a ditch by the aforementioned Hugh Meynell in his successful ploy to escape the clutches of a gamekeeper.

The story is told in Bill Powell's *My Wild Goose Chase* and later by Hugh himself in his book. I make no apologies for repeating it a third time for it is surely worthy of recounting into eternity. My excuse is that I am able to print a photograph of Hugh and Purdey to prove that both have worn exceedingly well in spite of the horror.

For the uninitiated the facts are that Hugh and a pal were staying with Powell for a week of fowling in his Glencaple cottage bordering the River Nith. The date was around the same time that Harry and I had immersed ourselves in the sandstorm.

Hugh and his pal were walking back along the road after dawn flight towards base, when a bunch of geese pitched in to a nearby field. The birds were on keepered land but the pair were gooseless and crawled off up the said ditch.

Unfortunately for them a keeper had spotted their trespass and headed for their position. Their only hope was to trample their guns into the mud beneath their feet and make out they were bird watchers.

It worked and Hugh tells me he retrieved his Purdey (it was only months old) under cover of darkness in great fear for its condition.

'After a long and careful cleaning it appeared to have suffered very little,' Hugh recounted when I got in touch during my book research.

Today a similar weapon would cost £60,000 plus.

THE ABUSED PURDEY – *In his book 'Saga of a Goose Trail' Hugh Meynell, above, tells how he buried his new Purdey in the mud to escape the clutches of a gamekeeper. The incident happened at the same time the author made his early outings to the Firth and is re-told here. Hugh was, at the time, staying with goose guide Bill Powell nearby at Glencaple. The shotgun suffered no permanent damage and is pictured, 55 years after the incident with Hugh and Skipper the Lab. Today, the same model would cost £60,000.*

CAMMO TAPE

These days, if you know you are to be subjecting your gun to such dire conditions, there is a simple solution – cammo tape found on the shelves of most gun shops. I have used it now these past five years and can vouch for its effectiveness.

The ultimate is, of course, the purpose-made camouflaged gun. What a stride forward in technology. The patterns are photographed onto both metalwork and carbon fibre stock and are consequently nigh on impervious to wear.

Cammo tape is just as effective in aiding protection and also, most importantly, eradicating barrel reflection. I was initially sceptical but, after plastering a Berreta 301 gas-operated 12 in the product for a season I found, upon its removal, that the original finish was unblemished. I must stress I have experience only of the waterproof variety and applied a fresh batch after 12 months. There is one of porous nature and I cannot vouch for its properties when it comes to keeping rust at bay.

GUN CARE

After this horror story of gun abuse it would not go amiss to offer some advice on the care of shotguns subjected to other untimely indiscretions.

While it is routine to clean your weaponry as soon as possible upon returning from an outing, more attention must be given when on a sortie away from home involving, perhaps, a week in a hotel. There it is too easy to leave your gun in its slip, albeit in a safe place, while you repair to the bar.

Make it a rule to check your gun immediately, particularly watching for any splashes of blood on barrels and action. Blood is one of the most corrosive elements there is on metal and will destroy blueing quick-time.

In my gun trade days many were the customers who arrived in despair simply because no-one had warned them of the careless practice of leaving game on top of a gun in the back of a vehicle. 'Wipe off instantly' must be the strict rule. I have known corrosion to occur within six hours.

Splashes of fruit juice can be as pernicious. An orange, carelessly quartered near a gun barrel, will put cash into a gunsmith's till faster than the proverbial ferret up a trouser leg.

Another no-no is the long-time storage of a weapon in a gun slip. Unless the lining is one of those wonderful silicone-treated damp repellent jobs, there is danger of moisture attacking the barrel finish with expensive results. I have seen rusting on the outside of barrels so deep that they were rendered unsafe.

A lesser, but nonetheless unforgivable, offence is to hold the barrels with the naked hand when placing the gun in its safe. Grip them, instead, with a lightly oiled rag. Naturally occurring acids on one's hands can cause rusting, if only slight. Should rusting take place, use a small piece of the finest steel wool and rub with a helping of oil. If the rusting has not been in place long, there will be no lasting damage.

Should you be storing your gun for a lengthy period do give the inside of the barrels a good oiling. But be sure to rod this out with a dry patch before firing. Excessive oil can, and does, cause barrel bulging.

Another most heinous offence is to store your cleaning rod inside a gun barrel. However stupid this may seem it does happen, particularly when on a shooting trip away from home. I was once at a clay shoot when a Gun arrived late. He grabbed his semi-automatic from the car boot, rushed onto the line, loaded, called for his bird, and, on report, out went a cleaning rod! Fortunately for the Gun in question, and for those nearby, the barrel did not, amazingly, burst. In fact, by a miracle, there was no evident damage. In today's regime of strict regulations I am sure the perpetrator would have been sent packing.

Finally, after a session of hard fowling do take your gun to a gunsmith. If it is a standard o/u or side-by-side it will take him only seconds to open the action to check if cleaning is necessary. More often than not it will need no attention.

Semi-autos are a different matter. Once a year, particularly if you are a 12-month shooter, have the action stripped, cleaned and oiled. During a season if you do get some malfunctioning due to a build-up of deposits, there are wonderful de-fouling sprays made exclusively for autos. I use Hoppes No. 9. Apply a good dose of the wonderful stuff, leave overnight, wipe off the excess fouling and re-oil.

When I began my shooting life, the attention one had to give to one's shotgun and rifles involved far more care. Then there were highly corrosive percussion caps employing fulminate of mercury and sometimes even black powder ammunition. You neglected your tools at your peril. Barrel pitting was all-prevalent and unscrupulous lathe operators lapped out barrels thus rendering them dangerous. This is why it is imperative to have all old guns checked by a gunsmith before you buy. An internal barrel micrometer reveals all.

SCUTTER BOOTS

If I were to be asked which of those Solway fowlers of long ago were at the top of my table in the art of concealment, it would have to be a tie between brother Charles and the late Nelt Graham junior.

Charles had such a distinctive gait that we were all amazed when he made it into the Royal Navy. He did not, after all, possess flat feet! As he disappeared over the horizon, on one of his lengthy covert goose chases, up would go the cry, 'Charlie's got his scutter boots on!'

Both Charles and Nelt would vanish within minutes and, on an October afternoon in the early 50s, we saw them walking back over the sands with a dozen geese between them though they had chosen different directions to melt into the merse. It was all the more commendable when one learns that the remaining four of us had empty bags.

On the particular day the dry westerly was around force six with a thick cloud base. Neither would say where they had been in the 12 square miles of creeks but none of us had heard shots so we concluded that they may have been into the back of the marsh – where only the brave ventured.

Charles had found half a dozen old 10/12 brass cases the previous summer for his Thomas Horsley and had loaded them with black powder and two ounces of BBs for the left full-choked barrel and two ounces of fours for the improved cylinder right barrel.

His first shot, he told us, had been at a party of pinks crossing at 25 yards. Five had dropped with the open barrel and he had rightly been too busy marking the fallen in the maze of creeks to use his second.

There was, of course, another very good reason why Charles bagged more than his fair share of geese – he was an outstanding shot. He began his shooting life, as we both did, when he was strong enough to tote a shotgun.

But there was also another talent, developed at an early age, which was to prove tellingly critical by the time he reached 20. Woodland pigeon and rabbit stalking had taught him to shoot from either shoulder as he approached behind the back of a tree and he was able to readily switch to the left-handed mode following right-eye damage while serving in the Royal Navy.

His form did drop slightly for a short time but he proved his remarkable prowess when, in 1967, he won the Lancashire Clay Pigeon Sporting Championship.

On another occasion five of us had motored west to Browell, where we had hoped a noon tide would push birds on to the grass. The day was memorable for me.

Following a lengthy stalk I had spotted a pack of teal pitching in half a mile away and got to within 50 yards. Two barrels had yielded five birds as they jumped.

These, plus two wigeon at dusk, comprised the biggest bag on the day but, for drama, it was inevitably surpassed by Charles. The occasion was not, however, without a scare.

We had gathered at the Land Rover after flight with no sign of older brother. With an hour gone beyond ETOA we were all worried. Jim had seen Charles at last light heading south-west, ie. towards the Solway mouth wearing his scutter boots. A great quantity of geese had gone in to roost high up on the still wind but no-one had heard bangs other than among those of us under the wigeon flight on the grass.

The vehicle headlights had been flashed at regular intervals and we were about to employ the fowler's emergency signal – three shots followed by three more – when the ears detected a faint plic-plac far out in the night. Presently the errant fowler appeared bearing three pinks roped over a shoulder.

We were to hear that Charles had decided to track the stream of geese out to their roost, 'Just to see how far they went.' He reckoned he must have travelled four miles over the hard sand before total blackness descended. The geese seemed close and he had sunk to his knees and then his belly.

'I decided to crawl as near as I could and hadn't really thought about a shot.' Very soon, and soaking wet, he could make out a vast array of dark blobs on the tideline.

'When there was a squabble I eased forward and when they fell silent I stopped,' he told us. Charles reckons he was around 30 yards off when the vast horde exploded. He knew he was out of order but discharged both barrels and dropped three stone dead.

Charles still remembers this remarkable occasion well, after nearly 60 years, and says he was glad of the flashing headlights when he finally turned for home. It was his first, and last, such sortie. About this time Bill Powell and Arthur Cadman were involved in fierce arguments over 'sand crawling' – digging in close to the goose roosts – and we kept well out of it. The practice is now banned.

THE VANISHING WILLIE

They used to say that the Scottish Border fowlers were as hardy as otters. Sometimes they needed to be. They certainly seemed more impervious to cold than those of us who had sedentary jobs.

Their toughness was illustrated, one morning, by Andrew who, because of work could only make rare mid-week trips with us across the river to Rockcliffe. He had taken a day off and was the only local to turn up for a lift over one January morning.

There was a severe pre-dawn frost following a light covering of snow and, as we reached the far side, Andrew slipped on the icy gunwale as he was disembarking. He went full length in two feet of water but, after draining his waders, he said he would soon warm up with the three-mile walk to the tip of the marsh.

There were few geese about at the time but the four of us had a bird apiece as they came in to the new grass where the night tide had cleared the snow. Andrew had continuously moved position in his creek during the flight in an effort to keep circulation going but never asked for an early return. We had half expected him to turn back on the way out. He could have taken the boat, gone home to change, and returned for us later.

He was, however, the first to head off back and when we caught up with him he certainly did not look too well. He was gripped, sporadically, with severe shakes and a hefty swig on Geoff's brandy flask helped somewhat. Once over the river he readily agreed to leave his cycle for a lift home by car. (Hypothermia is dealt with in Chapter 9.)

Fortunately his wife was also not at work and, we were to learn, stripped off his sodden gear and stuck him under the hot shower while she ran a bath. Later we were also to hear that, upon glancing down, Andrew had let out an ear splitting bellow. His 'tackle' had disappeared into his stomach!

He could smile about it when he graphically explained how he directed the hot water hose onto his lower belly all the while vigorously rubbing with shower gel. Eventually the little fellow popped out and he assured us had suffered no long-lasting ill effects.

Dame Nancy Rothwell, a professor and Assistant Dean at Manchester University, where she is a Research Fellow, explained that this was a natural reaction to intense cold – the body's way of protecting a vital part.

While on the subject of severe weather, I have often been asked why we switched our annual weekly visit to January when October would guarantee the presence of geese on the Solway. Meteorological records prove that the winters were considerably colder in the mid-1950s but we still chose to take our longer Solway excursion late in the season merely to avoid blowfly problems in our hanging birds – the laying of eggs on bloodied parts,

My last caravan had an insulated shell, double glazing and a catalytic heater that ensured night time warmth but, in those days, there were no such refinements. Our breath often froze on the caravan roof, to fall in sheets over our breakfast!

THE TRUANT AFTER FLIGHT – *Schoolboy George 'Whitie' White in 1955. He had begged a lift across the Border Esk at dawn and made friends with the team springer Chip. Fifty years later I met the same 'Whitie' exercising a springer where they had crossed that morning. He continues to shoot the edge of Rockcliffe Marsh. Note the team's transport – a 1930s Austin Seven. Left to right: Nelt Graham, Jim Ritchie, Charles Miller and 'Whitie' with Chip.*

Towards the end of our Solway years it was good to see more and more youngsters turning out. Most were there at weekends. However, one mid-week morning 14-year-old 'Whitie' was on the shore awaiting a lift across the Esk.

'Shouldn't you be at school?' enquired Charles.

'I'm ill.'

'What with?'

'I have a fever.'

'What sort of fever?'

'Goose fever!'

A CHANGE OF OCCUPATION

Nine years after my first Solway trip I moved out of journalism into the gun trade. The decision to go into self employment and take on a large debt was massive. I also had the weight of a mortgage, having just married. A family was planned and I felt I needed to create for myself a better income.

When I heard that the old firm of Entwistle, Gunsmith, was for sale in Blackpool I acted fast and never regretted it. Shooting opportunities beyond my most extravagant imagination were to be offered but I moved cautiously. Always I put my business first until I could see that all those invites to prestigious venues would be of benefit.

Eventually I gathered around me a trusted and talented staff and was confident enough to leave them in charge.

Though we were very busy in summer looking after the shooting gallery trade, the winter months were the most interesting.

Blackpool is sandwiched between two of the most heavily populated wildfowling grounds in the British Isles – Morecambe Bay and the Ribble estuary. By the early 1960s I spent most mornings in the fowling season, when the tides and weather were favourable, on one or other of these saltings. And I knew full well that, by mid-morning back in my shop, I would be regaled with the exploits of like young fowlers.

One such zealot was Ted Leen, an ardent member of the Fylde Wildfowlers Association. They then had marshes on Morecambe Bay and the River Wyre. Ted's tales were always full of drama. So much so that my two young smiths, on hearing his voice, would hurry from the workshop, don outdoor jackets, turn up their collars and crouch down behind the counter in case the oncoming line of tightly bunched pinkfoot spotted us.

Sometimes the lights were even doused and, if the wind howled up the street from the Irish Sea, the door was flung open. Even black Labrador Jess knew she had to adopt her keep-your-head-down mode. She honestly appeared to enjoy these bizarre scenes and always greeted Ted with great enthusiasm whenever he entered the shop.

Ted took it all in good part. To shoot a goose at dawn on that club's territory was a rarity and he was re-living the moment.

SOLWAY PILGRIMS

I suppose it was tales like these that inspired two of my staff to make the Solway pilgrimage in the winter of 1962-63. Eric Cooke, gunsmith, and Mike Mogilnicki, Saturday assistant, were both about 20 years old. They took with them the latest in long range weaponry and ammo but, as Mike said, their main armourment was, 'The rashness of youth.'

How could I tell them that the expectancy of bagging your first Solway goose was about one in five years?

There were four in the party, including Ted and his unquestionable appetite for goose chasing. Mike, now the owner of my old Preston gun shop, recounted for me the remarkable events which went into making their trip outstanding by anyone's standards.

They made the journey in an old banger that was as draughty as a colander. It would not have been so bad had it possessed a heater but that accessory was a thing of the future. Besides four men and all their gear there was Jess, my Lab. She had listened for long enough about Ted's exploits and no way was she to be left behind. It was a long haul, pre-motorway days, but the lads knew they would be warm in the Nith Hotel – it had boasted central heating.

'That's when things started to go wrong,' said Mike. 'They were overbooked and we were sent to a cottage down the road. The bedrooms were bloody freezing but the old lady told us we would be roasting in no time.'

Fires were soon roaring in the grates of both cosy bedrooms and never went out for the next five days. Apparently it was the old lady's custom never to use precious and costly fuel until her guests actually appeared. 'We get a lot of city gents and when it is as cold as this they just don't turn up,' they had been told.

Cold it certainly was. From the upstairs windows the lads looked out directly across the river Nith where sheets of ice straddled its banks.

The marsh beyond was white over, a mixture of snow and frost. The hotel game larder had its share of geese and ducks and the landlord, the effervescent Billy Houliston, who had only recently ended his professional footballing career with The Queen of the South Football Club, wasn't exaggerating when he assured them there were plenty of geese in the locality.

There were, however, more surprises awaiting the team.

'We downed plenty of ale that night but, about 3am in the morning, we were all awakened by a deafening crash. We flung open the windows but there was nothing to see.' No street lighting in those times in a little Solwayside village.

Pre-dawn they learned the cause of their violent awakening. During slack water, at high-tide, the river had frozen solid and, when the tide ebbed, it had finally collapsed from the bank top like an imploding drum. The thunderous boom had frightened the locals as well as the visiting Guns. No one could remember such an event.

'We crossed the river next morning in the dark in a dinghy no bigger than a bath tub. I shudder at the memory of three of us paddling across swaddled in Barbours, waders, hats and scarves, with guns, cartridges and a Labrador and the dinghy showing no more than four inches of freeboard,' said Mike.

'Somehow we made it. One of us was sent to return for the fourth member of the party while the others struggled to climb a steep bank of almost sheer ice. The only thing which kept us going was the distant call of geese. None of us fired a shot that morning, or for the next two. Although the temperature was lower than any of us had witnessed before – there was no wind.'

When the team had reached the far bank on that first morning they had been met by a guide. He knew his stuff and told them where to go each morning as the tide altered the roosting grounds. Each time they were under plenty of geese but to no avail. All were too high.

'On our fourth day it clouded over and the temperature rose to minus five. It started to blow and we knew that evening flight would present us with half a chance. Sure enough the wind kept the geese low enough for us to bag one each. It was well celebrated in the bar that night.

'The following morning my three companions went out for morning flight – I opted to stay in bed having developed a heavy cold. Needless to say I missed the best shooting of the trip. They returned with more geese and several ducks.'

STORMONT FORESHORE – *In the 1950s, when our boat was out of commission we sometimes transported up a lightweight sectional job. It didn't like rough water! The shot was taken at the end of the track leading to the Stormont Farm foreshore opposite Rockcliffe. Then it was flintstone and grass. Today it is tarmacked with car parking through the gateway.*

The trip also produced for Ted his first 'driven' pheasant. At the age of 68 Ted is still a part-time keeper on an east Cumbrian grouse moor near Barbon, a post he has held for 36 years. He was almost sheepish when he described how he had come to achieve an event which is indelible in the memories of most shooting men.

'We had moved close to a wood on the edge of the marsh. At dawn there was a chorus of awakening pheasants and, after a while, I sent the dog in. Suddenly an old cock rose from behind some high trees and swung over the marsh above my head.' A full choke and a load of BBs did the job.

Mike concluded his written account. 'In the intervening 40 years I have shot driven pheasants, grouse and all manner of game, deer and wild boar. I have many memories of red letter occasions but none is clearer than my first goose on that bleak and frozen Solway.'

An epic it certainly was when one learns of all the years spent by so many erstwhile goose slayers in seeking the wildfowler's Holy Grail.

Hugh Meynell, author of the afore-mentioned *Saga of a Goose Trail*, tells how he made the long haul to the Solway from his Midlands home for nine years before downing his first goose. For Hugh the magic of that wondrous expanse of sand, mud and merse was such that he did not finally give up the adventure until it had stretched to 11 years.

HARD WEATHER – *Hard weather throughout Britain during the 1958/59 winter drove many geese to feed in the hinterland of Morecambe Bay. I shot several whitefronts (in excellent condition) close to the Bay. They were, and still are, rare in Lancashire. The photograph shows me and Dick Eaves, secretary of Lytham and District Wildfowlers Association, on the northern banks of the Ribble estuary among ice floes. The bird is a whimbrel (now protected). Later that day I shot a pinkfoot (also in good condition) – the only goose ever to fall to my gun on that estuary. In those days all the geese flew off to the south apart from the occasional stray.*

It is also good to learn that Hugh continued his goose hunt for many more years to come. His final haunt was way up in the north-east of Scotland and his book, describing his expeditions, is a must for all wildfowlers.

During my compilation of this book Hugh and I exchanged letters. I was hoping that we might, intriguingly and unknowingly, have encountered each other when Bill Powell took his charges to our territory on Rockcliffe but Hugh was never privy to this part of the Solway.

I was amused, however, when a bulkier than usual communication arrived from Hugh's home. It contained a fired old cardboard Eley 8-bore case. Its pungent burnt powder was not of today's propellant and it still sits on a shelf in my den where my young son stuck in it a pinkfoot's tail feather. No finer ornament graced any man's quarters.

Chapter 2

Lancashire Geese

A fortunate combination of circumstances was to lead to a highly privileged chance to indulge in my number one winter passion in my early twenties. Most game shoots take place on Saturdays and, as a football correspondent with the local newspaper, chances of that day of the week free were almost nil. There were, of course, the bonuses. My days off were mid-week and I was able to roam the marshes invariably alone.

Besides being a founder member of Lytham Wildfowlers, on the Ribble, I was, soon afterwards, able to join both the Fylde and the Morecambe Bay Wildfowlers Associations with their combined huge coverage of the north Lancashire coastline. Pick your days and there were some good flights to be had under the grey geese at dawn. Then, during a particularly hard spell of January weather frozen soccer pitches meant that I had a Saturday off.

One of the many reasons I had found a certain young lady extremely attractive was that her father had acres of prime game shooting in various parts of the county and, when I let it be known that I was free to beat the next day I was, instead, invited to take my gun since they were one short.

On this particular shoot, close to Morecambe Bay, the prime quarry was ducks – mostly mallard, teal, wigeon and pintail with the odd pochard and tufted included in the bag. A few pheasants were also put down and there was a small stock of grey partridges. The reason for the profusion of wildfowl was that the land flooded heavily in wet winters – almost on the lines of the Somerset Levels (water meadows) though on a far smaller scale.

On this particular day I was a walking Gun and had just reached a thick hawthorn hedge – they left them high and deep to combat the violent winds roaring in off the Bay – when I spotted around 100 pinkfoot feeding in a sheltered hollow. 'Stop the line,' I urgently whispered. 'We have a goose drive on here.'

One of my hosts was amused to see me crouching low. 'We never bother with those things. They are no good to eat,' he declared as, almost distraught, I watched them lift and disappear behind a wood half a mile away.

Over lunch the same Gun, who was also the shoot captain, must have observed my despair which I genuinely tried to hide. 'Do you like goose shooting?' he asked.

After explaining my addiction his reaction was instant. 'Come whenever you wish to and bring a pal. Just avoid our shooting days and keep in touch with the farmer. He has been complaining about their numbers and you will be doing me a good turn.'

How clearly I recall his words 50 years later. I did not abuse the privilege and kept my visits down to around once every 10 days, always departing the territory an hour after full light.

Parts of the area were the nearest you could get to being out on a marsh. On stormy days one could hear the roaring of the surf in the Bay and, with the wind in the right quarter, catch the clamour of the flocks of pinks when they lifted from the sandbanks.

My first goose from this privileged terrain was memorable. It came on my initial visit. My companion was a mad-keen fowler, four years my junior and desperate to bag his first. The shipping forecast had promised a south-west gale and this time they got it right. When I had contacted the farmer the previous evening he told me which field the birds had been in that day. 'Get rid of them,' he had said, 'I'll be glad to see the back of them.' He was delighted to learn that I would be paying regular visits.

There was no sound of the geese lifting from the Bay that morning. We arrived pre-dawn and the wind roared through the compact hedge as we tucked in 50 yards apart. I had stood for a moment by one of the stunted wind-bent oaks that dotted the small field edges and, underneath my feet, felt the ground move as the mighty storm strove to tear its roots from the earth.

We had sited the two dozen silhouettes (this was still before the days of shell decoys) in the middle of the field knowing the birds would be low coming off their roost. If the wind changed the thin plywood shapes would move like weather vanes on their round pegs.

The first lot certainly were low – just above a lone, gnarled tree 100 yards away. We moved and were rewarded with two birds from our four shots as they crossed between us only 10 yards up. We joyously shook

Lathwaite Geese *by Rodger McPhail – When I first started shooting the geese on Lathwaite, near Cockerham, Lancashire, many of the fields became water meadows in winter. Pinkfoot and a few greylag flew in at dawn from nearby Morecambe Bay and for many years I was the only one to shoot the geese there – with occasional help from one other Gun.*

hands as we retrieved a bird each. You may think we should have downed more than two but, at the first shot they had scattered like leaves.

During the next hour four more lots came in small bunches but on different tacks each time, the result, we concluded, from probably having been dispersed by the storm during the night. They still homed in on the decoys but out of range and we realised we should have placed the silhouettes much closer to our hedge – another early lesson in the glorious art of goose chasing.

This was the first time I had used this type of decoy, laboriously and lovingly fashioned and painted matt goose-grey with white bums. I was pleased to see the way they pulled the birds but noted that none actually pitched among them. The birds would wheel a fair way out, glide in then flare with alarmed cackling when they disappeared as the outline was lost. They did their job, however, and were in constant use for many years until the advent of today's shell decoys.

Much later, when I joined Richard on his Scottish goose grounds, (eventually christened Ponkey's) the birds did actually land among the silhouettes, obviously encouraged by the two additional stuffed decoys.

This exciting Lancashire shoot was also to produce my first European whitefront, in the winter of 1956. There had been no hard weather in the north-west but there must have been a considerable spell elsewhere for they arrived, unusually, amongst us in fair numbers. The first I knew of their presence was one morning on the farm with Charles. Nothing had moved at first light and, in fact, the sun was just topping the Bowland Forest hills when I heard their distinctive bell-like calling – a new sound but instantly recognisable from the bird book description.

The black bars on their chests were clearly distinguishable as I stood up in my hedge hide and took out a right and left. What magnificent birds. One was a large mature specimen, its bars appearing blacker than black and the stark white of the forehead contrasting with the yellow bill.

Later in the season, when I thought they had gone back to their winter quarters, I was out in January again with Charles. It was one of those mornings of heavy cloud and dawn was late. In those days I had a voluminous waistcoat fashioned from three large sheepskins. I found that if I lay in the dry grasses at the base of a dense hedge I could pull the waistcoat over my head and doze in great comfort. A shout from my companion disturbed my slumbers on this morning and I had just time to swing a snap shot at three birds as they disappeared over the top of the hedge. I saw one crumple but, when I made my way into the field via a

ILLEGAL GOOSE – In my gun trade days I took Ben Lodge, a Yorkshire customer, to one of my goose reserves near Morecambe Bay. Ben inadvertently strayed over the boundary. He escaped being caught and bagged his first-ever pinkfoot. You had to be fit to negotiate steep-sided dykes. This shot was taken on Lathwaite where the water courses were deepened to take the flood-water away quicker.

distant gate, I found two dead birds – a pink and a whitefront!

Those inland Lancashire days were also valuable in furthering the art of stalking and driving geese. All the ditches were assiduously maintained in an effort to drain the land more quickly. In fact they were constantly being deepened and often it was a struggle to ascend their steep sides once one had reached the bottom. In places the dykes were so deep that, while it made stalking a cinch, one had to rely much on guesswork to locate the quarry.

On one occasion, just after I had taken over the Blackpool gun shop in 1959, I had rendezvoused with a Yorkshire customer in the early hours of the morning at an A6 all-night transport café.

As I have already stated, it was never my practice to use any of my personal goose shooting for commercial gain but Ben Lodge had rung up about a rare AYA o/u 3-inch 12-bore I had advertised nationally. Ben had never shot a goose and wanted the gun for a Scottish trip. He sounded as fanatical as myself about goose chasing and would make the journey over to view the gun that week. There were plenty of geese in the Bay so I suggested we meet at The Jungle Café at 6am on the following Friday. Ben was self-employed and could come back to the shop to look at other weaponry if the AYA did not suit.

This particular model was a one-off. There was nothing like it in the importer's price list and I could only assume it had been brought into the country individually. At 7¾lbs and with 30-inch full and full choke barrels it shot sweetly. The trigger was single selective and the boxlock action had deep, relief wildfowl engraving.

Ben fell for the gun even before he had shot his goose. We had met on time and I left him in the best spot with the decoys laid out in a field which the geese had been using all week. Unfortunately it was a field almost bereft of cover and I had to position my guest where two drainage ditches met. I had instructed him on what to wear and his Barbour, deerstalker and waders blended well. Giving strict instructions not to move until I had collected him, I made for the opposite end of the farm.

There was little wind that morning and Ben's chances looked slim as the day lightened. What geese there were did not appear to go near his field and I did not fire a shot myself. Nor were there any bangs from my guest's direction.

In the hope of late birds coming in to the decoys when the farm hands moved in to the surrounding fields – it was muck spreading time – I walked over to Ben. To say I was gob smacked to see two pinkfoot lying next to him was putting it mildly. He had a smile broader than a Blackpool landlady's backside.

'Where the heck did you get those from?' I asked.

'Up there,' he said, pointing beyond the boundary.

'How far up there?'

'Oh a long way. I saw a small lot dropping in by that wood.' He pointed to a no shooting zone where the farmer would only tolerate reps by appointment and kept a rottweiler to deter intruders! 'I just kept walking along the stream until I reached them and got two when they jumped.'

There was little point in telling Ben he had been very close to a prosecution or worse. After breakfast at The Jungle, bought by an ever-grateful new owner of an AYA o/u, Ben sped off over the Yorkshire border singing a very happy song. I wondered if he knew I could have lost my gun and him his car for trespassing in pursuit of game.

In those days the pinkfoot population in the UK was put at around 40,000 and, in the south-eastern area of the Bay they had a set pattern.

Wilf Holden, late father of Raymond who operates Hy-Fly game farm in Preesall, always maintained that they did not visit his territory at the extreme southern end of the Bay until the second half of January. He would, therefore, have only a bare two weeks of goose shooting on his own land. What a different story these days. Raymond, whose game hatchery is now the largest in Europe, has purchased much of the land in the area. What he does not own he largely rents and the geese feed there in great numbers from the end of September throughout the season. Raymond shows them great respect and has a rule to cease shooting by 9am. Perhaps it is lack of disturbance that has drawn them.

My days on the farm of green and thick hedges ended when it was sold and the new owner introduced a drainage scheme which finished the territory as a water meadow shoot. Those were the days of lavish grants for land improvement and it is doubtful if today the powers would have approved the loss of such wetland to the environment.

NATEBY

The loss of the Lathwaite goose shooting was, however, to coincide with yet another piece of fortitude.

Bernard Shaw, not he of literary fame, but someone held in almost as much awe by this avid goose-struck fellow because he had copious access to the great birds, was landlord of the Horns Inn at Churchtown village near Garstang, Lancashire. Bernard was shoot captain of a walk-and-drive syndicate covering around 3,000 acres close to his hostelry.

I was quite aware that the likeliest reason for my first invite to the shoot was my excellent black Labrador. She was from the then-famous Midnight of Mansergh line, created by Mrs Roslyn Williams, in her day a leading field trial judge.

Jess was in her second season and was one of the most intelligent among the many dogs I have possessed. Fearless in cover, she was rock-steady to shot – unless she was on a marsh and that was a trait I had no desire to cure. She had quickly learned that a fowler's dog should move to the drop of a bird. There are many times when your four-legged companion knows when a bird is down, and you do not, particularly at dusk. On formal days it was as though she, like her master, knew she had to be on her best behaviour!

Besides the shoot providing excellent bags of pheasant, partridge, woodcock and duck, Bernard's hospitality was legendary. The Guns would meet for starters at 9am and, if you preferred to begin your day with a lashing of bacon and eggs, so you could. Lunch was invariably a side of beef and the Stilton was enough to die for. These were pre-breathalyser days and most Guns stayed on at the end of the day for duck flight, which was always there for those who wanted it.

Here, too, the geese fed in large numbers, coming in from both Morecambe Bay and the Ribble estuary. Yet again the Guns, all much older than myself, were not interested but Bernard's wife was, I quickly learnt, very fond of them as a table bird. Mary was born in Southern Ireland and, from childhood, had learned to cook a goose to perfection.

Eventually I could never decide whether my regular invites were down to the excellence of my dog, the fact that I found pheasants on low terrain easy, or because I was willing to turn out at dawn on every shoot

MISSION ACCOMPLISHED
In my gun trade years I was a regular guest on a Lancashire driven pheasant shoot when my days would begin at dawn ambushing the teeming flocks of pinkfoot which fed there. No-one in the shoot was interested in turning out at that hour but wild goose was the favourite roast bird of the wife of the shoot captain. The fowling gear (note the sheepskin waistcoat) was exchanged for a formal suit for the remainder of the day.

day to add a goose or two to the bag! I suspect the latter, for Mary always glowed like a honeymoon bride when I was successful. I assured Mary that the feeling was mutual for I, too, felt like the nuptial groom!

How I hope that today, 30 years on, the fields in that secluded land are still as unspoilt and that no hedges have been ripped out nor ponds filled in. Had I been able to persuade any of the other Guns to turn out at dawn, filling the bag would have been much easier. Small fields, thick hedges and a network of shallow ditches made shooting more simple than any territory I have ever chased geese on. I made it a rule, however, to stop at four birds and Bernard seemed happy at my abstinence.

Nateby was where my little bitch learned to belly crawl. When I first detected her following me in this mode I went into paroxysms of laughter. A bunch of pinks had dropped in at first light at the far end of the field from where I had set up my silhouettes (notoriously bad to spot in poor light). I could have left Jess at 'sit' and she would not have moved a muscle but decided to try her on the stalk.

Telling her to 'heel' I set off on the 100-yard manoeuvre behind a hedge with a well-laid, thick bottom. After a couple of minutes I glanced back to find her doing a perfect imitation of a snake – her head flat to the earth and inching forward on her stomach. She also was 'laughing' like some dogs can.

I found, too, that I could use her to drive geese. I sat her down-wind on one side of a field I could circumnavigate (if there was a handy ditch.) I would then call her through the flock with an Acme whistle. It was a truly deadly manoeuvre. On these occasions I do not know who was the prouder – handler or dog!

I have to stress, however, that this method cannot be executed without diligent training. At first, when I whistled, the dog merely followed the route I had taken. Much practice, by showing myself on the opposite side of the field before I called, was undertaken during training before the dog understood what was needed of her. It would be interesting to hear what a professional thought of such an attainment.

Invites to this most hospitable of shoots continued throughout my 21 years in the gun trade but, as shooting pressure on the geese increased in the surrounding area, the syndicate's policy was more and more towards non-disturbance, a move to which I whole-heartedly subscribed.

In all those years I was never accompanied by anyone else on any of these goose forays. This solitude gave me a feeling of great confidence and the huge anticipation before each trip was probably due to the fact that

I knew there would be no-one else to make a balls-up! Or was it just the fact that fowling is, by its very nature, a lone pursuit?

MARTIN MERE

By the time I was 30 I had bagged my fair share of Lancashire geese and liked to think I had not overdone it – though the opportunities for big killings had been there.

There was one territory, however, that I had coveted – the mosses around Martin Mere, near Southport. It had not then become a sanctuary but the whole region was controlled by large estates and the chances of finding goose shooting were hopeless.

There then came yet another gesture from Lady Luck. Jack Shepherd was a Blackpool solicitor who had kept a Gun for many years in the Martin Mere shoot where, today, The Wildfowl & Wetlands Trust has its most excellent and successful sanctuaries. My first invite was for September 1, a mid-week and three weeks too early for the first of the geese. The territory was totally unfamiliar and, when dawn broke, I was struck by the lack of trees on this endless mossland.

A keeper had placed sparse hides over the 1,000 acres that the shoot encompassed with just enough cover for man and dog. The sky was full of birds at dawn and, on the stillest of mornings, I was glad I had taken a fully choked gun. As shooting increased birds got higher and higher and the 1¼oz of five's produced some spectacular results. The dog and I soon had an interesting mixture neatly laid out. My tenth bird was a fine mature drake shoveller – the first in a busy fowling career. Teal predominated, with a fair show of mallard, and the bag also included golden plover and snipe.

The horn called us to breakfast and then we spent the rest of the morning walking the maze of drainage dykes for mallard and teal. The shoot carried a healthy stock of grey partridge and there was plenty of evidence of a good rearing season. They were definitely off the quarry list on that day but there could be no complaints about the size of bag.

Redlegs* had not then arrived on the British shooting scene and it was not, in fact, until around 10 years later that I personally experienced

* Redleg partridge (native of Spain). This is a game bird now reared in huge numbers in the UK.

them on a mixed goose/game and stalking trip to the Highlands.

On that most charismatic of first visits to the Mere I had guided the talk over breakfast to geese. Yes, they did use the territory, in great numbers and Peter Scott was already visiting to net and ring them but not until after the shooting season was over. I was told I would be invited again when geese would be among the bag but, sadly for me, all shooting, apart from September 1, was on Saturdays – my busiest day by far in the shop. Invites came as promised and I had to send my brother Charles in my place. After all was it not he who had first guided me to Solway?

Charles and a friend shot on the Mere regularly until his move to reside in Scotland. Jack Shepherd then asked if I could find two more Guns, 'as compatible as your brother.' Chance to pay back a kindness offered by a farmer friend in the long ago. I was 14 when I had pedalled four miles to George Taylor's farm on the edge of Lytham to ask for permission to fish a carp pit on his land. I had grown up on tales of mighty fish coming from this spring-fed pond on a strictly keepered piece of land which George had just rented. He would see what he could do.

Permission was eventually granted and I spent many hours hunting the elusive double-figure leviathans. Sometimes my vigils lasted all night, so obsessed was I. Often I was broken and I never landed a double figure fish.

Twenty years later I phoned George Taylor, still Mr Taylor in days when protocol ruled, with the invite to shoot on Martin Mere. He was delighted and would be very pleased to take his young son Richard. George and Richard shot the Mere until Peter Scott finally turned it into what it is now.

There was a sequel to this little story that had begun with the kindness of one of nature's gentlemen to a youngster he had never met before. With George long gone to his eternal shooting ground I found myself sitting, at a wedding reception, opposite his son Richard, still as keen on the gun as he was as a young man.

I quickly steered conversation to shooting. 'What were your days like on the old Martin Mere?'

Richard enthused and lamented the day it all came to an end. But did he know how he came to get the invite? He had no idea and it was a nice story to tell on a day when everyone was telling nice stories.

The Wildfowl Trust took over the Mere in 1972 – 10 years after my first visit. At the heart of the sanctuary was a 363-acre farm which they acquired for £52,000 – around a million in today's terms. The transition to sanctuary status was not without its controversy. One of the bordering farms was worked by the late Gerald Sephton, whose son Colin was a rising star in the clay shooting world. Scott had tried to stop Colin from using his private skeet range, alleging it would cause disturbance. Gerald sent him packing and Colin's continuance with his practice was to prove to have no detrimental effect on the geese. And it did lead to Colin representing England at the Olympics.

I practised often on Colin's layout and had a standing invite to flight geese on his land whenever I wished. It was an offer I was not to take up until the end of the century in circumstances that were, to put it mildly, unusual. (See Chapter 9.)

My next visit to the Mere, after that September 1st invite, was soon after the sanctuary had opened its doors. Crowds thronged through the turnstile and headed for the splendid array of hides approached by the 10-foot high banks and blinds. Man and creature side-by-side. Youngsters learning, one hoped, to respect wildlife and their parents perhaps taking something in themselves. An elderly gent manned the gate and, during a lull, I ventured to tell him how I had been privileged to visit the land in its natural state. What the heck if he wished to berate me when he heard that I had a gun in my hand at the time.

'You lucky devil,' was the surprising retort. 'What was it like?'

One has to admit, with total approval, that Scott got it right. How much better that thousands can enjoy the battalions of wildfowl rather than we chosen few?

OYSTER CATCHERS

During my shop years countless invites came over the counter to shoot at a variety of venues as enticing as wild boar in Tunisia and sand grouse in Libya, but none as odd as oyster catcher slaying in Morecambe Bay in March! I checked that the date was not April the first!

The offer had come from a North West Fisheries Protection Officer – officially hatted, badged and authorised. The good chap was desperate. The cockle and mussel gathers of Morecambe Bay were seriously on his back. He had spent a considerable portion of his department's budget, allotted to the depletion of the otherwise protected oyster catcher, to little avail. Rocket netting he had first of all decided was the answer and could we please manufacture the launchers?

The equipment we produced, on lathes in our Blackpool high street

OYSTER CATCHERS *by Rodger McPhail – For a year I was registered by the Ministry of Agriculture, Fisheries and Food as an official oyster catcher destroyer in the 1950s. The birds were plundering thousands of mussels a day. Carrying 200 cartridges I at first killed close on that number per outing, but the birds quickly became wary and the project was abandoned. The species were, and still are, protected and are useless as a table bird.*

workshop, functioned to perfection but, unfortunately, the oyster catchers were unobliging. Apparently they are not good rocket netting candidates – something to do with not staying in the same spot long enough, unlike geese.

So, as a last resort, it was down to the gun. It transpired that the ardent Fisheries Officer had already tried his hand at slaying with his game gun with paltry success. 'Have you anything that will kill at a long range?' It was more of a plea than a query. What a splendid opportunity to air the deadly Lewis magnum. During the close season I did take the trusty musket out of its cupboard from time to time for an outing on the clay bird range but there was nothing like the real thing, even though they were black and white, protected and inedible.

I was asked to report to the officer's steading on the edge of the Bay, near Preesall, one mid-morning on an ebbing tide. Transport was an ancient grey Ferguson tractor kept solely for Bay work. The mollusc beds were teeming with oyster catchers and it was fascinating to observe their ploy. A mussel would be plucked from the bed whereupon the bird took to the wing and, from around 20 feet, hurl it to the ground, preferably a stony one. The rest was easy. I never did count how many mussels any one bird devoured in an hour but Fisheries Officer had done his homework and he reckoned that the estimated 25,000 birds in the Bay accounted for quite a few tons in a year.

At first the unsuspecting sea pies* provided simple targets, reminiscent of tame pheasants, and I soon had half a sackful. When they became wary I concealed myself behind a convenient boulder and was tumbling them with ease at 50 yards, courtesy of 1¼ ounces of number fours out of a full choke. When the birds moved to this extreme range the FO's artillery was totally ineffective.

FO strode over, 'I don't know how you are doing it,' he wailed. 'I'm wasting my time. I'll leave you to it until the tide is making.' But I had some bad news. I was out of cartridges! The 100 I had distributed in belt and pockets had gone.

The following day we were back. This time I carried a 200 capacity cartridge bag (all paid for by HM Fisheries & Food). FO had a few shots and retreated. I proceeded with the execution but for no more than half an hour longer. The sea pies were not foolish and moved to the other side of the Bay.

Footnote: *Sea pies. In some areas a commonly-used name for oyster catcher.

This was to be the format. One good day per fortnight and the birds became as educated as any duck or goose in the open season. The project was abandoned and the oyster catchers allowed to proliferate.

FORESHORE GEESE & DANGERS

It was soon after losing the Lathwaite shooting that I was fortunate to gain entry to the Fylde Wildfowlers Association which had a narrow stretch of marsh towards the southern end of the Bay. It was so narrow that the chances of getting under a flight line were slender. On each side were substantial stretches controlled by the Morecambe Bay Wildfowlers Association to the north and a private syndicate to the south.

I had been on the waiting list of both fowling clubs for some time and at last entry into the Fylde organisation gave me a slim chance of bagging a dawn pink or grey. For two years I persisted, most of the time watching helplessly as gale-lowered skeins battled their way inland on either side.

Then came the day membership of Morecambe Bay fowlers arrived closely followed by a chance to join the private syndicate. I enlisted in both for the fees were modest.

I never exceeded more than one goose on any of my outings on these patches and, without question, the most memorable was the pink killed stone dead at a prodigious height by my then 11-year-old second son William. I had been out at morning flight on the two previous mid-week dawns without firing a shot in the light winds. The third day, a Saturday with Will off school, the forecast was for a strong westerly. The birds would have the wind across their starboard beam and they could be low enough.

Will had been keen to use his Grandpa Fred's goose gun for a while. He was a lanky lad and the stock – built to fit his short forebear – was close enough in length for him to handle comfortably.

I placed him slightly ahead of me in view and to my left. The first skein came directly over my hole but I reckoned they were a touch too high. Did not want to teach the young fellow bad habits and I was pleased when he also resisted giving them a barrel.

The second lot came in at the same altitude but this time over Will. My 'Too high' shout was either unheard or went ignored and a single shot brought the third bird in line slanting out. By the time it slumped to earth it was stone dead. I sped over to check that it was going nowhere but for the time being it was in an inaccessible spot.

The rest of the flight passed wide and Will's shot was the only one between the two of us that morning. Together we hurried over to where his first goose lay on a mud bank on the far side of a gutter. So deep was the mud that there was no reaching the bird by fording the creek and I instructed Will to tuck himself in to the bank opposite his kill while I made the mile-long trek inland and out again to retrieve the bird. It was the perfect opportunity to instruct a beginner into the perils of marsh and mud. In those times redshank were still on the shooting list and Will spent a happy 20 minutes trying vainly to bag a few with game sixes.

The goose lay in a hollow of liquid mud to one side of a hard ridge. I was able to traverse 20 feet along its upper limit and reach down to grab a wing. I pushed my stick into the ooze to demonstrate to my young charge its peril. A step onto this morass would have meant almost instant submersion.

Very soon after this outing there was a grim tragedy on the banks of this very same creek, though further out in the Bay. It outlined, in an horrific manner, the dangers awaiting the unwary on what, from a distance, appeared to be a harmless vast stretch of clean sand.

Two local teenagers were racing their trials motorcycles on the sands. The lads were both around 15 and as they were on private land they could legally ride there without breaking any highway laws. One of them strayed too close to the edge of the gutter and was thrown from his machine when the vehicle's wheels sank into the glutinous sludge.

Unfortunately the lad tried to retrieve his machine and became trapped. The rescue services, including the fire brigade, were called but nothing could be done. Frantic efforts were made to extract him but the relentless tide swept in and he was drowned next to his helpless would-be rescuers.

Since then, and as a direct result of this horrific tragedy, the local rescue services have a revolutionary system whereby the mud can be forced away from a victim by air and water pressure.

QUICKSAND

I was prompted to include this piece about the dangers awaiting the unwary on our marshes by an article in the 29th September 2005, edition of The Times newspaper. The headline read, 'Science sinks the myth of a slow death in quicksand.'

However, the scientists of the Ecole Normal, in Paris, were delving up the wrong creek. There really is something called quicksand which, as its name implies, acts quickly. I suppose the scientists of that illustrious place of learning were looking at the general dictionary definition; 'A deep mass of loose wet sand that sucks anything on top of it inextricably into it.'

The scientists claimed that the object would not keep on going down. It would merely be held in its grip. Any experienced wildfowler will tell you that this is not real quicksand. In quicksand you just keep going. I could, when I was fit enough, take you to an evil patch of the stuff on the channel side of the River Ribble wall far out on the marshes off Warton in Lancashire.

My pater had warned me against setting foot on the seemingly solid surface but, one day while in a daydreaming state, aged about 16, I fell into its clutch. On the north side of this particular marsh the mud is glutinous and deadly in parts but is easily avoided. If you have any doubts while traversing such terrain, merely avoid stepping anywhere unless it bears old footprints.*

As I topped the channel wall on that day and left the thick stuff behind, there appeared to be solid clean sand at its seaward foot. I stepped boldly into the sand and, frighteningly, shot downwards almost as though in pure water.

Pivoting violently, I flung my arms back on to the substantial rocks which comprised the wall. By then I had plunged up to my waist with no

*Footnote: Paternal Grandpa Will (born 1875) one of a long line of Lytham Marsh marauders was often heard to cynically say, 'Believe nothing of what you hear and half of what you see!' Certainly the latter could have been applied to two incidents which happened to me on the Ribble. Both involved footprints in the mud.

I was fooled totally one February morning after dawn flight by the first set. They led to the main run and I stepped boldly into the racing water at low tide only to go in waist deep. The prints had been made by a fowler who was using a punt to cross the run when it was in flood!

The second set were so odd they had me totally mystified. They bore only one footprint at such a long interval that they appeared to have been created by a giant. They also stretched over what was a seemingly treacherous terrain where from time immemorial we were told not to venture.

When I recounted what I had seen to the next monthly meeting of our fowling club it caused great mirth. It transpired that one of our committee members had been caught out by an early tide and had to swim for it. The single bounding print was where he had kept thrusting a foot downwards to spring his way into a short breast stroke till he reached *terra firma*!

sign of bottom beneath wadered legs. The gun barrels were scratched, but mercifully undented, and, having successfully arrested my plummet, I laid the weapon carefully on the sloping wall. A heave had me safely back on to the security of the stones and I went about the task of brushing off the thick gritty sand. Little had entered my waders since my immersion had been but brief.

A close observation of the surface of the sand showed a distinct change in its consistency compared with the adjacent terrain. Where the greedy maw had tried to trick me it stretched for perhaps 20 yards. I hunted the wall until I found a trapped length of driftwood. It was all of 10 feet and disappeared from view as I plunged it down through its seemingly innocent surface. I somehow felt that the covert sinister mouth actually smacked its lips and the slap of an incoming roller against the wall sounded horribly like a belch!

But what to do if you do become trapped in thick mud? I am pleased to report that due, undoubtedly, to my early training, it has never happened to me. I have it on good authority, however, from one unfortunate, that your release is best secured by falling onto your back and, with gun behind elbows, easing yourself to safety.

Another peril, just as deadly to the unsuspecting, are treacherous tides particularly when combined with adverse wind and torrential rain. Many are the stories of inexperienced fowlers perishing on the marshes all round our coast line when caught in such conditions.

The simple facts are that gale force winds can stem the flow of an ebbing tide which then mixes with floodwater from inland. We have two tides in 24 hours and when the next surge occurs, the height of the combination of fresh and seawater can climb many feet above the predicted level.

Often on the Solway we were forced to go in over the tops of our waders to retrieve our anchored boat when the waters were held back. But we always had the safety route inland over the private Rockcliffe Marsh where not even the most zealous of gamekeepers would have had the temerity to effect an arrest.

Similarly we always kept a weather eye on conditions on the Ribble marshes where devastating floods in the 1920s caused such havoc. On that day the tide should have been tiny. At 22 feet it was 10 feet below a spring tide but it actually inundated the town.

Chapter 3

Ross & Cromarty

Jim Ritchie was the one who inspired our expedition to Ross & Cromarty in the far north-east of Scotland – just about the furthest one could go in those days from Solway to guarantee migratory geese. Now shooting pressure has driven many as far as the Orkneys – particularly the greylags. We suspected there were small pockets of greys perhaps higher up but we had gleaned that there was often a build-up of the pinkfoot in the area during January with the promise of mallard, wigeon, teal and sometimes pintail.

By then I was in my first year in the gun trade and had acquired a Morris 1000 shooting brake. Unfortunately my bitch was in season so we relied on Boy, an ageing, portly yellow Lab which had been gifted to Charles. A customer had appeared in the shop with Boy a month earlier and asked if I knew of a shooting man who would like him since he was going to work abroad. It would, he said, be a shame to retire him at eight years old. Charles had moved down from Newcastle to take over the family monumental masonry business and had just lost a young Labrador bitch to Viles disease. Boy stepped into the gap.

My trip to Ross and Cromarty had been arranged before I knew I was to own a gun shop. I had to ask myself the question: Should I be taking time off to go fowling in this most critical year in my new venture? The gut feeling was no, but it was pointed out that January was traditionally one of the quietest months in a gun shop's calendar and it would do me more good than harm to have a break. We compromised. Both Charles and Jim were totally understanding and we agreed to shorten the holiday from two weeks to one.

I was also able to fit in a deal with a new customer on the way north. I had begun to advertise extensively and a client in Penrith had 'a few antiques' to trade in for a bar-in-wood Westley Richards 12-bore. The contact was, in fact, to prove most beneficial over the years. We did the deal and Bill Thomas (fictitious) traded with me for the duration of my time in the gun trade. The added bonus, too, was that I sold one of Bill's antiques at a Highland hotel and covered my expenses for the holiday. I was learning fast.

Snow and ice had gripped the whole of the northern part of Britain for nearly a month when Charles and myself headed for Gretna to collect Jim with Boy in the back of the brake. Oddly the dog did not seem to be his usual laid-back self on the journey but we thought nothing of it. The reason for his restlessness was to be revealed later, much to my extreme embarrassment.

After collecting Jim we suggested that he did the first spell on ice-bound roads, which he knew well, and we would then take turns. I sat in the rear seat with Boy seeming to get more restless behind me. We were only around 20 minutes into the journey when the wretched animal let out a howl and hurled his immense bulk onto my shoulders, his tongue in one ear and the rest of his body striving to stick his giggling tackle into my other ear all the while his howling becoming more anguished and urgent!

Disaster quickly followed. Jim turned his head at the onset of Boy's abuse and lost control on the ice-rink of a road. The car careered into the heather banking and flipped over. Thankfully it was enough to throw Boy from my shoulders and jerk him out of his fit of passion. We slid to a halt with the car lying on its offside.

Charles was the first to react, thrusting his door upwards like a submarine hatch. But, with all thoughts of love-making expunged from him, Boy was the first out followed by Charles, myself and the hapless Jim, who was wedged under the steering wheel.

A passing motorist helped us to right my lovely new vehicle. Fortunately the damage was restricted to a burst front tyre and a rear wing that resembled a used toothpaste tube.

We then discovered the reason for Boy's amour. While we were rearranging the gear in his space we realised that the hessian sack I had used for the goose decoys was from my bitch's bed. Since she was heavily on heat it was saturated with her pheromones! Poor Boy. And poor me and poor motor car.

The offending sack was swapped for something sweeter at the next garage where our tyre was mended. Boy immediately returned to his usual docile self for the remainder of our vacation.

The roads actually improved the further north we went. We were on

TEAL by Rodger McPhail – *When I drove with a couple of friends to the east coast north of Inverness in the January of 1962, we located large quantities of teal, wigeon and mallard. It wasn't until we were introduced to a local fowler that we discovered goose territory.*

territory where they were used to snow and ice and the gritters had been out in force.

But the cold had not abated and we stayed only one night in the bothy we had rented for the week. It was in a lovely spot, on the shores of Nigg Bay, but there was no heating, apart from an Aga stove a long way from the bunk room, and we were forced to sleep fully clothed.

The next day we moved into an hotel (where I sold my antique – a fine brass barrelled blunderbuss with flick bayonet).

An indication of the extreme cold can be gleaned from the fact that when we came to break the breakfast eggs in the bothy they were almost frozen solid and boffins reckon this would have put the temperature at around 17° below freezing!

Though costly, the move to a relatively expensive hotel proved to be a winner. Not only were we cosy and well fed – with breakfast any time from 8am to midday – we were also served by a very pretty waitress who had a boyfriend who was a wildfowler. Sandy Holmes turned out to be a real find. He, too, was in his twenties and came from a long line of coastal gunners. By day he was a postman, or rather from early morning to midday. It gave him plenty of time to show us all the likeliest spots and we soon had the hotel game larder festooned with mallard, wigeon and teal.

But it was geese we had gone for and it would be two days before Sandy's day off when he would be able to take us to a dawn ambush. Sandy had no transport in those far off empty-road days, apart from a cycle, and was delighted to be conveyed along his native coastline in comfort. He resolutely refused to tell us where to find the geese until he could be with us. All our efforts to seek them out had come to nought and we began to wonder if, in fact, there were any in the area. In the end there were fewer geese than we had hoped for, probably due to the weather, but a great weight of ducks. They fed where tides cleared the grass.

We were still scornful, at that age, of hunting the Grey Army inland, although Sandy was keen to have a go. Fifty years ago the resident winter goose population in those parts was but a fraction of today's numbers and Sandy said we could expect either pinks or greys.

When we were first introduced to Sandy he carried an ancient double barrelled 12-bore of Belgian origin. It had 2¾-inch chambers and, though it bore only black powder proof marks, he happily used nitro ammunition and even fed it three inch cartridges with apparent impunity! The gun was so loose in the action that it rattled like an old farm gate. When I suggested that he take it to his local gunsmith to have it tightened he there and then unhooked the barrels, lay the breech across a tussock, and beat the lump with a stone! After reassembling the weapon he handed it to me. 'Try that,' he urged. It was as tight as the proverbial drum.

Sandy would take no cash payment for his services. Cartridges, he said, would do and we saw him well stocked on our departure. He was grateful, too, for the transport and took us to endless farms where he had permission to rough shoot – courtesy, no doubt, of his job as the local postie.

One day Jim shot his first woodcock and, such was our enthusiasm at bagging the species, that Sandy said he knew of a place where he could usually guarantee to find several of this elusive mainly migratory quarry. We were guided to a narrow inlet, north of Nigg Bay, where there were many acres of gorse bushes on the higher part of the marsh. A recent spring tide had washed the area and, within the hour it took to slowly work the gorse, we succeeded in pouching three cocks with a few rabbits to boot. We were puzzled at so many of these enigmatic birds being on the east coast. Usually they had moved by January to the west. Were they fresh arrivals?

In all of my 60-year shooting career I have never been among more of these delightful birds in such a short period, though one morning before dawn on Jura when, on the way to the ferry, after an October stalking trip, there had been a fall of cocks during the night. The road was full of them and, so weary were some that they didn't move and we had to steer carefully on the single track highway.

But, back to geese. On the day prior to our promised goose sortie it had snowed heavily again and we had been greeted, at breakfast, by Jean with the words, 'Ye'll be needing a shuffle this morning boys.' (Jean hailed from Glasgow.)

'A shuffle?'

'Aye. To dig your car oot – it's under a snow drift!'

A feature of the Inverness region is, incidentally, that here the purest English in the British Isles is spoken.

Sandy was worried that the geese would have headed for easier pickings on the west coast, where the snow was reported to be lighter. In our favour, however, were the high tides which would wash the marshes clean. When Sandy arrived at the hotel, an hour before dawn, he asked if he could borrow my game gun – the sweet-shooting lightweight William Powell. When I told him it was totally unsuitable for geese he insisted it was 'for the bunches of wigeon.' I reluctantly consented after he had

Postman Sandy
Sandy Holmes, the Tain fowler who showed me and my pals where to find geese. The picture is of Sandy with my best William Powell boxlock damascus barrelled 12-bore ejector through which he shot 3-inch BBs. The gun was proofed only for 2½-inch loads!

A Morning's Bag
The bag from morning flight on Beauly Firth: greylag geese 3, mallard 8, wigeon 9, teal 2. Total 22. Guns 4. The Morris Traveller shooting brake bears damage only to the rear wing after rolling over on ice on the journey north. The rugged ash frame had protected it – and the passengers – from serious problems.

assured me he would be using his tightly choked Belgian weapon for the geese.

Sandy's directions took us to the Beauly Firth. There is, or was, a stone jetty on its northern shore and we stood on its extremity in the darkness before dawn while he directed us to our stations. Snow clouds hung heavy on the stillest of mornings. Goose talk came from the estuary and there was the occasional call of a cock wigeon. Though the creeks were shallow they offered sufficient cover for an experienced fowler and it was not long before someone was in action towards the head of the firth.

It materialised that this was where the main gathering of pinks had roosted. Charles, Jim and myself were restricted to a duck flight – mainly mallard. With the arrival of daylight we all three waited back on the stone jetty for Sandy to show. A distant figure hoved into sight far up-river, well loaded with birds. It was Sandy with four pinks and a grey. And only one gun – my Powell!

'It kicks a bit with 3-inch,' he grinned rubbing his shoulder.

My reply was unprintable. I fully expected such abuse to have shaken the old girl (circa. 1895) loose but all was well. Suffice to say that our friend never laid a hand on the gun for the rest of the trip.

By now it was snowing again and the fields, that were once walkable, lay under a foot of the stuff. Pheasants were pushed into woods and we soon had more than we needed. Sandy's day off had produced a bonanza.

One of the marshes, which later proved productive for geese, bordered Nigg Bay, and we added both pinkfoot and greylag to the bag on the midday high tides. At no time, during the whole of the six-day stay, did we see another fowler – apart from Sandy. There were then no fowling clubs or sanctuaries on that part of the coast, free shooting on Crown land foreshore ruled and still, of course, does.

Daytime often produced some rewarding stalks and drives between the three of us as we followed the coast roads and scanned the marshes from various vantage points. One such venture did, however, produce its drama.

Parties of geese seemed to be arriving daily and we found a small gathering of greylag on the grass bordering Nigg Bay when it was my turn to do the flushing. The birds were across a tidal creek and the plan was for me to be dropped off on the south bank while Charles and Jim motored round to the north, approaching along the marsh edge between the birds and the bay. The flock of around 20, were some 200 yards from the edge of the marsh and everything looked set for success.

The tide was not due to start making for another two hours so we set zero hour at 45 minutes. There was some low level crawling for myself before I reached the creek. When I made it to the middle of the water I was surprised at its depth and the force of the flow. We had reckoned without the melting snows and, instead of the expected foot depth, it was at least double that. No real problem, I thought, we had time to spare before the tide started to make.

Once in the shelter of the far bank, safe from a vicious north wind, I looked at my watch. Fifteen minutes to go with the geese feeding peacefully in the same spot 300 yards away. It was then that I had a call from nature and downed trousers, hidden under the marsh edge. 'Always remove your wallet when you drop trousers and remember to place a stone on your money,' had been Father's advice from an early age.

Bang on zero hour I stood up and the geese lifted to plan and headed for the bay. They were only 20 yards above the grass and four barrels pulled out four birds.

I turned back to the creek. This time there were only inches to spare, and once on the far bank, there was time to turn round and reflect on another cunning plan brought to fruition. Somehow, however, all did not seem right and that was when I patted my back pocket – like those of us do who are not used to carrying large bundles of notes. Empty. The wallet still lay under the stone under the far bank and the tide was fast approaching the spot where I had tarried.

The icy water was scrotum deep when I reached the middle, and even higher by the time I had retrieved my treasure. Wet waders were not, however, to be a problem. The bag for the week was beyond expectations and, soon after dawn the next day, we lashed two sacks of birds on to the roof rack for the return journey. We followed the snowplough south along the A9 above Inverness and were the first car into the town from the north for four days.

A DIFFERENT MCNAB

Two years later I would return to the same territory with two different companions. This time we were on a mission to secure our own version of a McNab, (a salmon, a grouse and a stag in one day) and we would go earlier to avoid the snows. The affair had been hatched in my shop one day when four of us discussed the wealth of field sport to be had north of

SNOWED IN – *The three visiting fowlers had to follow a snow plough from Tain into Inverness on their return journey. Theirs was the first car into the city from the north for four days. Jim and Charles check one of the drifts. On the roof rack two sacks carrying the week's bag in deep freeze mode.*

the Border now that pernicious taxes were forcing the big estates to open their lands to paying guests.

In those days all roads wound through picturesque glens, small townships and villages thriving with the woollen and whisky industries. Once you were past the horrors of Glasgow, or the laborious affair of crossing Edinburgh's Firth of Forth by car ferry, the rest was a delightful, leisurely, journey.

As the road climbed the northern banks of the Forth, to the west down below were extensive lagoons, their shores and tiny islands dotted with duck hides. Who were the lucky ones who crept into them for evening flight?

Not much further on the road took us past the famous Loch Leven, where the flocks of pinkfoot geese were noted for later attention. The highway sped through the Carse of Gowrie where here, too, were burgeoning flocks of greylag, some feeding only 100 yards from the road. These, too, were eventually to pull me there, though in much more secluded surroundings out of sight and sound of roadway and dwellings.

The four of us who planned that 1964 sortie were Bob – who was desperate to get under the geese for the first time in a shooting career that had begun 20 years earlier on his father's east Lancashire farm when he was 12, John, a pub landlord who wanted to shoot a red stag with his 1897 Winchester under-lever .44 black powder buffalo rifle, Sid, an architect who was coming because he happened to be in the shop when the discussion took place, and myself.

In the first year of my shop tenancy a fit, bronzed young fellow had appeared in a well-worn safari jacket. 'Mick Roberts,' he had declared, thrusting an iron-like hand over the counter. Mick had just ended a career in Africa that had taken him from oil prospector to big game hunter, police officer and part-time mercenary during the Mau Mau troubles in Kenya. He would, he told me, be looking for a post as stalker on a Highland estate in Scotland and wanted to trade his .357 Holland & Holland magnum big game rifle for a .270.

Mick's family lived in Blackpool and he joined the Blackpool and Fylde Fullbore Pistol & Rifle Club, which I had just formed with its headquarters on the nearby Weeton Army range. He was one of the few professionals we had in the club and the members were to learn a lot from his expertise both with rifle and handgun. He was no slouch, either, at clay birds and he and I had a firm friendship until his sad, and untimely, death 12 years ago.

But what had Mick to do with this McNab trip north? He had soon found employment near Fort William and I had received a stream of letters telling me about the 'paradise' in which he had found himself. 'I should have come up here 10 years ago,' he wrote.

His latest communication was a call for help, which he hoped I would be happy to fulfil: A cancellation meant that he had a week of stalking, free, on his estate running up to October 20 – the end of the stag season in Scotland – and he had five beasts to take off his ground. Might I be interested? Does a child like toffee?

He had also told me of a friendship he had developed with a clan who had been tenants on a neighbouring small estate for generations. Their land held a heavily wooded glen and supported a stock of grouse, ptarmigan and blackgame. The ptarmigan would be around 3,000 feet. The family held the sporting rights and, for a modest sum, we could have two days with the shotgun.

So it was that we planned a trip to the Highlands for our version of a McNab: stag, ptarmigan, blackgame and geese – all new to each of us, apart from me and my geese. But then, woe is me, the walls of Jericho came tumbling down north, south, east and west of our careful plans. The week before we were due to depart, the thatched roof of John's pub caught fire and he had to cancel. Then Mick rang to say his boss had decided to shoot the five stags himself. Lesson one in life: never try to do anything on the cheap.

But Bob and Sid were raring to go and Mick was waiting for us when we reached our Highland hotel. With him was Andrew, he of the blackgame and ptarmigan land. Things looked up when he said he thought he would be able to 'find us a staggie' too.

First we had to meet the rest of his clan, something Mick had not alerted us to and which proved to be probably the most memorable event of an intriguing week. Mick said we were to be fed by Andrew and discreetly suggested it might be a good move to take FIVE bottles of malt with us. To say that all three of us were second division drinkers when it came to standing shoulder to shoulder with the Scots and downing fortified Highland burn water was an understatement indeed.

The route to Andrew's HQ fell away to a flint track, heavily grassed down its middle. Stunted birch, willows, alders and hazels crowded us in and rabbits scuttered ahead. There was an aura of calm about the place. A good mile led on to open hillside and the family home, single storey and whitewashed, was reached by stepping stones over what could only be described as a bog. Something of a challenge, one would have thought, at night.

Five sheep dogs greeted us from a sheltered pen. We would meet them again around midnight. Inside a huge mound of peat glowed in a fireplace more suited to a baronial hall. A large, blackened, stock-pot hung from a hinged bar and an equally black kettle steamed gently on a swivelled hob.

Head of the household was Rabbie, a leathery, fit 74-year-old, and Andrew's brothers were Jamie and Georgie. The fifth member of the household was Flora – a lass of around 30 winters (I purposely use winters rather than summers) with an eye that fixed the object of her attention and another that hit a high corner of the room. Her hair was a wild bush but she had, Andrew assured us, a heart as soft as thistledown and was a miracle worker with skillet and peat embers.

Mick explained that, each spring, either Andrew or Jamie went down to Glasgow to find a housekeeper. Flora – her surname really was MacDonald – looked after all their needs that year.

Bob wanted to leave immediately.

'What have you done to us?' he whispered.

Mick thrust a large whisky into his fist and assured him, 'It will all be well worth it. Think of the shooting.' Sid and I found the whole affair stimulating. We were about as far as you could get from a shop on Blackpool's main street.

Flora's mutton stew was scrumptious, especially when one dunked a chunk of her crusty bread, fresh out of the fireside oven. Bob, too, soon relaxed to the sound of Jamie's pipes and was the first to call for an encore when Rabbie demonstrated his team of five dogs' outstanding skills.

They were brought in to the now fetid room, sometime in the early hours, and ordered to sit. Rab invited each one of us to ask his charges to leap onto the sofa by name and then proceeded to make them change places with each other using only verbal commands. Like; 'Gip change places with Fly.' 'Fly change places with Fern.' And so it proceeded, faultlessly. They were, apparently, famous at Highland shows, had appeared on TV and were good money-earners.

By midnight Georgie, who suffered from some form of degenerative condition, had passed out and Andrew asked me to take his feet while we carried him into the only other room in the abode. There was no bed, just piles of blankets, and we lay Georgie gently in a corner. If we were to be up early next morning it was time to leave.

Navigating the bog between the bothy door and our car on a night blacker than a raven's wing was, we felt, a big problem when we came to depart. But not to Andrew. Though of only diminutive stature we were ordered to climb, one at a time, onto his back whereupon he skipped as sure-footedly as a pack mule from stone to stone. Not even Sid's 15-stone proved much of a challenge.

The same iron Andrew was the only clan member astir when we made it back to the bothy at 10am later that morning. His pace was sympathetic to three chaps not used to one-in-four gradients and, by lunchtime, we had three blackgame in the bag plus a woodcock and a couple of bunnies. One of the five sheep dogs worked quietly and efficiently to flush the game. We had to do our own retrieving but the splendid animal marked each kill for us.

We found the quarry in the wooded glen not far from clan HQ. When the woodland gave out I killed a grouse and then Andrew handed me my rifle and took the shotgun. Time for the staggie.

Andrew led me straight to not a staggie but a 10 pointer, black from his recent rolling in a liquid peat bog. At 150 yards it was a cinch for my .270 Steyer Mannlicher carbine and its 4x40 Khales Scope. On the crawl in we had disturbed a covey of eight ptarmigan, still not in their full winter white. A good omen, perhaps, for the hunt on our way down while Andrew dragged the beast.

But it was not to be. No more of these elusive birds showed and the next day we headed for goose territory. Andrew had offered to take us out again the following day for the ptarmigan but Bob would have none of it. The light of day had not lessened his first impression. Offers of cash to the generous clan were very firmly turned down and to push any harder would, we felt, have caused offence. All we had shot, including the venison, was theirs and one more bottle of malt was not rebutted.

BIG PIGEONS

When we arrived at the coast Jean no longer worked at the hotel where we had been snow-bound two years earlier. We did not enquire about Sandy in case he asked to borrow my Powell!

On the first morning's recce we hit the jackpot. Taking the same road where Sandy had led us on my first visit, Sid, scanning to the right, while I drove and Bob concentrated on his side of the road, laconically observed 'What bloody big pigeons!' Sid's big pigeons were 100 greylag feeding on a field immediately adjoining the marsh.

At the nearby farm Sid was elected to do the asking and soon came back with an affirmative. The farmer had also asked if we could attend to real pigeons on his newly-sown winter wheat.

Our first objective was, however the geese.

I would have liked Sid and Bob to make their way by a torturous route to the marsh edge while I drove the flock over them but neither was as familiar with the terrain as I was so Sid elected to do the driving. I would place Bob under what we hoped would be his first goose.

We allowed 30 minutes before the birds would be flushed. Sid had what appeared to be an easy approach behind a dry stone wall leading from the road. I took Bob on a wide circular move to the marsh edge where I had lain in wait for the wigeon on my last visit. It entailed a hands and knees approach, empty guns in the crook of an arm in the classic mode.

Bob was using a 2¾-inch Remington five shot (the three shot restriction had not then come into force). In pole position he stoked up with 1½ ounces of BBs and I left him in a state of high anticipation.

I reckoned I could get within shot of the flock myself with a further 500-yard crawl up a ditch that cut into the marsh, but, with only 100 yards covered, the birds jumped for no apparent reason. There was much satisfaction in seeing them head straight over Bob's position and the two lead birds crumpled instantly. I waited for more shots from the auto but Bob was up, out of his hole, gun on bank and his brace held high aloft, one in each grasp.

When Sid reached us he had a sad tale to tell. The geese had moved to within a few yards of his wall during his careful approach and were,

THREE OLD HANDS – *Two years after my trip, in arctic conditions, to Ross and Cromarty, I went with two more pals (this time, in softer October) to coincide with the end of the red stag season. We found plenty of geese and more drama.*
Forty-five years later, we met on Bob's Lancashire shoot for the February pigeon roost shooting.
Left to right: Sid Wild, Bob Rhodes and me.

he felt, too near for a heavy load. He was swapping his cartridges for 5's when they lifted, his gun empty.

It transpired that both pinks and greys were using our friendly farmer's fields and had arrived only a few days earlier. We all had geese over the next few days, plus a goodly bag of pigeons. This time we were there in October and the weather was so different from our first visit.

Still we saw no other shooters. Surely we must have enjoyed that particular part of Scotland at its best in terms of lack of disturbance.

This time, however, our greatest problem lay in saving the birds from becoming fly-blown. We were lucky to have an excellent hotel cold room and they eventually made the journey back south in one day in a cold boot.

These days the whole of that coastline, which I refer to as Ross & Cromarty after the old shipping forecast area, is controlled by wildfowling clubs but is still open to visiting fowlers and if you are lucky Sandy may still be there, but don't lend him your game gun!

BROTHER CHARLES planning a strategy for a goose stalk in Nigg Bay, Ross & Cromarty. The photo shows the deep sides to the marsh edge.
I remember the stalk well. Charles and Jim secured a right and left each, and I filled my waders after forgetting my wallet on the wrong side of a creek as the tide flooded *(see page 82)**.*

Chapter 4

Greylag Country

How I came to discover BB's secret Perthshire greylag lands was another piece of sheer serendipity. Within a year of becoming a shop owner there appeared, through the doorway, a fellow who was to have a considerable influence on my shooting life.

Peter Waugh was one of those characters determined to bounce back whatever might befall. Recently divorced, he had come to Lytham intent on fulfilling an ambition – to learn the art of wildfowling and the Ribble estuary seemed as good a place as any. But, being a healthy 30-odd-year-old male, he must first find himself another partner. That is how he came to walk into my shop. A cab had delivered him to the dancing academy, 50 yards up the road. Learn to do the two-step and, he reckoned, the fillies would be there for the taking. Fortunately for me – and, I like to think for both of us – he turned left after his lesson and came upon a shop window full of guns.

By chance, too, he had leased an apartment in the next avenue from my Lytham home and that was five minutes from the marsh. After half a dozen day tickets had enabled Peter to learn the ropes under my guidance, he gained membership of the Lytham & District Wildfowlers Association and was well and truly bitten by the bug. Lytham offered some outstanding duck shooting but, after a highly rewarding season among the wigeon and the pintail, Peter wanted geese. Charles agreed to let him join us on our annual Solway week in the October but, on our arrival, the hordes of grey birds had deserted Rockcliffe Marsh. Jim Ritchie and Roy Martin had scoured the whole of the area and declared that they had totally departed.

That was when Peter suggested we all head up to the Highland glen where he had lived for the previous two years in a small, cosy inn. The hostelry had, Peter told us, its own grouse moor and he had gained permission, during his stay in the area, on various farms yielding goodly mixed bags including pheasants, partridge and blackgame. When the two Solway locals, who had taken the week off to chase the geese, heard that the shooting was free they gleefully agreed to the venture. Two car loads transported five fowlers and their dogs northwards.

There was a potential problem when we arrived at the inn. Another Gun had arrived the day before and also wanted to shoot its land. In deference to Peter, who had become one of the family during his two year sojourn, permission had been refused. The visitor had, it transpired, called on Peter's other shooting grounds and received the same response.

As we drove up the track towards the grouse moor we rounded a bend and were greeted by an extraordinary sight – a crowd of large grouse-like birds feeding on silver birch buds in the upper branches of a belt of trees guarding the moor. They were greyhens, new to all of us bar Peter. Charles slammed on the brakes and went into reverse gear until we were out of sight of the birds. He took charge.

'How big is the wood?' he asked Peter. After learning it stretched for no more than 100 yards he deployed all of us to make a wide detour onto the hill beyond the wood. He would give us 10 minutes and would then drive the belt of trees towards us.

As the first bird lifted from its lofty perch I saw it crumple to Charles's shot. A positive barrage followed and we picked five greyhens and one blackcock. Some of the shots were of prodigious distances since most of our guns were heavily choked fowling pieces.

Peter had told us he had found little success on the moor during his two years and, because of its apparent unproductiveness, had left it alone. But he had always been alone and had no dog. We had a brilliant Labrador that missed nothing. Our bag at the end of the day – we shot it clockwise then anticlockwise – numbered nine brace of grouse plus the blackgame. We had walked widely spaced and found heavy charges of BBs devastating on coveys which had become tightly packed at the end of the season. The purest game shot will cringe as I surely did when I became familiar with formal driven days later in life.

The other resident Gun appeared at dinner that night and made no acknowledgment of our presence. Afterwards, in the bar, a tall weather-beaten figure in tweed suit and deerstalker asked how we had fared during the day. He was headkeeper on a prestigious neighbouring grouse moor/ deer forest and looked at us in utter disbelief when we told him our bag had totalled 24 head.

'Would ye mind taking me to see them?' he asked and stood rooted as he gazed upon the fine array in the hotel game larder. He was still shaking his head at closing time and probably went to his maker wondering how we had achieved this extraordinary total so late in the season. We kept quiet about the BBs!

The other hotel guest had breakfasted early the next day. Our host told us he had found some shooting on an estate in the next glen. Dinner saw the same display of aloofness and no attempt was made at contact until he came into the bar later that evening.

TROUBLE

Also staying at the hotel were three Yorkshire lads in their mid-twenties on a drinking spree. The outlaw Gun was drinking with them and, by midnight, one of these lads had taken to his room. But Outlaw was having none of it. 'I'm buying from now on,' he suddenly declared. 'Bring him down!'

Dutifully his two pals 'brought him down' but in a sorry state. Unable to stand they propped him in a chair, his string-like tie undone around his neck. Outlaw plucked it off, dropped it into MY beer, held the glass aloft and declared, 'Landlord. There's a worm in this man's beer. Buy him another.'

The room went quiet.

'I think,' I said gently 'You have made a terrible mistake. Outside. Now.'

'No,' said Outlaw. 'We shall settle this a gentleman's way. We shall arm wrestle. The loser pays.'

Having only ever seen Spencer Tracy arm wrestle in 'Old Man of the Sea', circa 1943, we all thought it a wonderful idea and the bar was cleared. Outlaw instructed the landlord to call 'Go' and I instantly flattened his arm. Outlaw stared hard. 'I wasn't ready.'

I suggested he called 'Go' then promptly did the same thing. 'That's impossible,' he cried. 'My name's Lou and you and me are going to make a lot of money!'

Nonplussed, we all listened. Our new friend was, he told us, a greetings-card wholesaler and was wont to carry his samples around in thick heavy binders one under each arm and one gripped in each hand. The practice had given him, he said, arms of steel and the only other time he had been beaten was in the next glen by a huge Highlander famous for his strength. Lou was sure I would have the beating of him since he, himself, had not proved an easy opponent. Please would we all go over the next night and he would organise an evening of wagering. By now we were warming to Lou. We agreed if payment could be made in whisky!

Come the night, the giant Highlander met the same fate as Lou and we all had a riotous time. The Scots paid up happily for their round but no one was out of pocket. We all kept buying rounds until we could neither sup no more nor hardly stand.

The next day we were homeward bound but, before we left, Lou took me to one side. I had already regaled him with my passion for geese. 'Give me your phone number,' he urged. 'I have some rather choice goose shooting not a million miles from here and I would like you to join me next year.'

What wondrous patterns life can sometimes weave.

MAD MONK PENINSULAR

So it was that, in late October, nearly 12 months on, I met Lou and his younger brother Malcolm at a grey-walled friendly hotel hidden away at the end of a sweeping laurel-fringed driveway. Below, beyond the lawns and the field, lay a small loch where, Lou told me, we hoped to find some action at evening flight.

Donald, the landlord, had confirmed that the greys had been using the roost every night since their arrival about 10 days earlier. Nor had they been shot. The hotel did not advertise its shooting and Lou had only found it by dint of hard searching two years ago.

The weather forecast was encouraging, but the northerly wind was no more than fresh when Lou guided us to a bay each as the evening drew in.

The first lot came early and reacted instantly to my goose call. The party of around 20 greys were well out of gun shot on their approach, with the wind up their tails, but a quick tune on the Olt call had them swinging towards me and dropping quickly.

With paddles down they homed in to the bay like wasps to a honey pot and gave me an easy right and left. The dog had them picked in an instant.

Most of the birds did not come in till close on darkness but I was able to account for two more. Neither Lou nor Malcolm had fired a shot and my success was down entirely to the call. The brothers had no experience of this essential piece of equipment: in fact it was Malcolm's first goose trip.

By morning the wind, bless it, had risen to gale force and Lou asked me if I would take his young brother under my proverbial wing. He had handled the call with great reverence after I had shown him how it worked at the end of the previous night's flight and was probably hoping that the magic flute would work its wonders at dawn.

After dinner, the previous evening, Lou had called on a local landowner for permission to shoot the remainder of the fields surrounding the loch which was largely tree-lined. Malcolm and I headed for the western shore where I hoped some of the birds would flight off low in its relative shelter. I had noted a long peninsular jutting out into the loch during yesterday's visit and fancied it greatly under the violent conditions.

Lou went to the head of the loch where most of the population had flighted in the night before. The fierce head wind should give him a chance.

Malcolm and I found the 50-yard-long promontory thickly wooded and we had to fight our way in blackness over fallen trees densely covered in lush ivy. The same tangle cloaked the wide walls of what was once a considerable structure. There was no way round, for its foundations reached each edge of the peninsular and more climbing was necessary.

Who had inhabited such a place and how long ago? I hoped landlord Donald would be able to give me its history but later he told me that all he had been able to discover was that it had some religious background. We promptly named it Mad Monk Peninsular.

Waves crashed against the boulders at the extremity of the spur and there was plenty of cover for two men and a dog in the shoulder-high king ferns. This bracken species, twice the height of the native strain, was further proof of man's manicure.

The 19-year-old Malcolm may not have done much wildfowling but he certainly had the eyesight for it. As the sky gradually lightened he whispered, 'There is a flock of about 20 coming towards us.'

They were battling slowly into the gale from the far end of the loch at less than tree height. As they reached our position, no more than 30 yards out, I urged Malcolm to shoot and the outside bird folded instantly to crash into the boiling waves. Before I had time to stop him Malcolm had plunged into the surf, eager to retrieve his first goose, and immediately filled both waders. Dog or no dog he was desperate not to lose his valuable prize but quickly gave up when the loch bed shelved steeply. He was then treated to an immaculate display of waterborne retrieving by the experienced Jess. She had seen the bird fall and headed into the breakers without hesitation. I doubt if she had ever faced such a maelstrom but seemed to enjoy the challenge hugely.

Three more were added to the bag, though the main weight of birds had headed off up the middle of the water. Lou had been in action and we hurried off to see if his half dozen shots had produced anything and if a dog was needed.

THE BROTHERS VENABLES – *I was introduced to greylag country by Lou Venables, left, the previous year following a bar room disagreement. It was the start of a lifelong friendship. On the right is Lou's brother, Malcolm, with his first geese. This was Malcolm's first visit. He was so captivated that he found a job as a gamekeeper in the same glen and still lives there!*

He had two geese but, because he felt that anything he shot would be lost in the water if he got too near its edge, he had moved uphill. The first skeins had been low and he had collected a bird. After that they were well up, in spite of the wind, and he reckoned he had been lucky to add one more. All our birds were greys.

Ten geese for the first two flights was, however, an excellent start. In the remaining two days we added another half dozen, plus eight mallard and a brace of pheasants apiece. We could have put many more of the longtails in the bag had we tried but happily Lou, like myself, placed geese at the top of the quarry list.

EPIC FLIGHT

The following year we met again on the same territory but Malcolm was missing. He had gone in to game keeping and remained in the occupation all his working life. Besides Lou and myself there was the ageing Albert plus Urch and Harry.

In spite of his years, Albert's enthusiasm for shooting had by no means diminished and his heavily choked Browning u/o was often more than a match for my trusty Lewis – or was it that he was merely a better shot? He certainly appeared less infected by the all-powerful goose fever.

This was the trip when I made my audio recordings of several dawn flights – tapes I still have today. How they stir the soul upon their playing and leave youngsters in awe at the picture they conjure as the staccato bangs, thumps and expletives assault the eardrums like ten Hallelujah Choruses!

The final morning of that trip was to produce an epic flight that rarely happened in those far off days when geese were much thinner on the ground.

The birds had suddenly changed their feeding grounds and, the evening before, had poured into one of the numerous lochs in our territory from a fresh direction. A strong southerly was forecast for the morning and, if they returned to their new dining quarters, they would be heading directly into the gale over a belt of trees bordering our ground.

The 100-foot larches grew at the edge of the water and we positioned ourselves, before first light, on rising ground 30 yards beyond the loch. We were spread out as if for a driven pheasant shoot and could just glimpse the gradually lightening roost through the leafless timbers. The birds must have spent the night a good mile up the loch for their clamour,

GREYLAG *by Rodger McPhail*
Unknowingly, I stayed at the same inland hotel used by BB (Denys Watkins-Pitchford) as his HQ in greylag country. In those days – the 1950s – fowlers were a rarity in the area. Now, because of shooting pressures, the birds have moved to the west coast on the opposite side of Scotland.

when they lifted, was barely audible.

Would they take the same path? The calling grew louder and louder but it was too dark to see the first lot before they swept over the treetops. A salvo of six shots brought four birds out. We were dogless and there was barely time to retrieve the fallen before the next wave arrived.

This time two more tumbled before there was a lull. We could now hear concentrated muttering on the loch and expected the remainder to head off in a different direction but, with daylight coming rapidly, we were able to see another long line approaching at eye-level through the timbers. Like heavy bombers the long skein had to lift to clear the trees and we had the easiest of targets. Our only reason for missing – only another four fell to 10 shots – must have been due to lack of lead. Such large targets are deceptively fast at close quarters.

There seemed to be no end to the flight on this extraordinary morning and, when the bag reached 20, we stopped as one man. The birds were still pouring from the loch as we departed and, as the aged Albert commented, 'If all goose shooting was like that I think I would not bother.' He was another fowler who liked to work hard for his birds.

These days – 40 years after this event – the numbers of geese (pinks and greys together) have multiplied hugely and such gatherings are commonplace. But with the burgeoning numbers came commercial goose guiding and I hear the birds no longer go to that magical place.

The same team gathered the following year but it was the last time that I was to shoot with Lou. Like so many fishing/shooters approaching middle age he abandoned the gun for the fly rod.

I courteously asked if he minded if I went on to shoot from the hotel and he thanked me for the respect. I visited there many times over the years and only once took another Gun. I was so well aware of how such a place could become over-shot.

NEW GUN

This other Gun was to be Richard. (He features greatly later in the book.) He had a new goose tool – a relatively rare weapon that had arrived over the counter of my Blackpool shop a short time earlier. It was a Greener three-inch magnum 12 with 34-inch fully choked barrels. He was desperate to try out its killing power and soon had the chance.

We decided on a November two-day sortie to greylag country to tie in with a gun deal I had in Perth.

The days were cold, bright and windless and, while the geese flew high over land, they were invariably much lower as they headed up and down the loch particularly off Mad Monk Peninsular. One morning, above the mysterious ruins, we were also treated to some aerobatics from a tiny shrieking merlin hawk. There was certainly a plentiful bounty of small song birds for his picking among the dense ivy.

With us was my new dog a strong, rangy, yellow Lab named Henry. I had acquired him as a pup and he had proved to be the easiest of pupils, eager to learn and eager to please. We had accounted for most of our birds well out over the water and Henry made light of the retrieves, including one that had landed on ice where I feared he would crash through the crust. We had spotted it, belly-up, an hour after a dawn flight half a mile from where we had been shooting and only let him go after testing it ourselves.

There was an odd incident on the second morning. We had decided to split up at dawn, Richard to man the raspberry canes between two lochs, where there was invariably a chance from either roost, myself to head for a small grass field where we had seen around 100 greys feeding the afternoon before.

There was zero cover in the grass pasture so Henry went with Richard into the canes. I took the gamble of lying down in subfusc clothing in the middle of the grass before first light. There was no way of knowing from which direction the birds would come, otherwise I would have tried a hedge. I reckoned that once the flight line had been established I could move.

I got it right. At the first hint of light a faint croak announced a party of a dozen greys gliding in to pitch into the next hollow. A short crawl to the edge of the depression put the birds up. They were close and I neither saw nor heard anything drop from both barrels as they jumped into the black backdrop of a wood.

But at least I now knew where to secrete myself in the hedge and two more lots left behind three birds. Later, as I gathered my gear to head for the vehicle, something made me abandon my load and I walked to where I had taken my first shots of the day. There, lying breast down, wings outstretched as though still in flight with not a feather out of place and no sign of damage, was a big goose. It must have dropped beyond my vision and would never have been retrieved but for an afterthought.

Richard was pleased with his only kill – a bird out of a high skein which Henry had retrieved from a long way out as though his new companion had been a friend all his short life.

This ability to relate has been a feature of all my gundogs. Perhaps because they met so many shooters during my shop years, they were used to strangers. Very often customers would call in to borrow them when they needed canine help.

Sally, a yellow Lab, who came later, was 18 months old when I had my spinal injury and was probably the most versatile of all in this direction. Because my hands were so inept after the injury I would instruct her to accompany another Gun at flight times. All the handler had to do was call her after I had told her to go with him and she would obediently follow to his hide. She would work for him only for the remainder of the flight and then rejoin me when it was all over.

On my last visit to greylag country I was to come across a party of three Guns from Leicestershire. I was on my own on this occasion and knew not of their presence until after the first evening's flight. I was combining the trip with a day stalking in Glen Lyon and had returned to the hotel bar where the three were already ensconced.

It had been one of my better, nay it had to be my best, start to any visit there. A strong north-easterly was blowing when the first party of greys came in high. The Olt call drew them across my front and I dropped the outside bird with one shot. Five more times this happened and I did not send the dog because the birds had fallen a long way out and my ageing companion would have had great difficulty in making a retrieve among the steep waves in very poor light. They could be picked after dinner in the far bay.

The only black mark was the fact that I had lost my flute after the fifth bird and was forced to call by mouth – tiresome and a strain on the larynx. Foolishly I had not attached a neck lanyard and it had slipped from my grasp into two feet of water.

When I walked into the bar after flight I was greeted by handshakes from all three of the Leicester party. I could see they were obviously keen to strike up a conversation.

'Do you mind our asking what you were using down by the loch this evening?' one of them asked. I was nonplussed.

'How did you know I was there?' I asked.

It transpired that the three had arrived shortly after I had made my way down to the water's edge. The hotel owner had seen me settle into a willow bed from the hotel terrace and had suggested they stay clear of my bay.

'That was a remarkable bit of shooting and what on earth was that call?' they persisted.

When I recounted the unfortunate loss they asked if I minded if they searched for it the next day. I told them that, unless they had wetsuits and shrimp nets, they were wasting their time since the loch bottom was thick in silt at that spot.

Had I being staying longer than three days I would have telephoned my shop and got them to put a new call in the post. As it was I gathered an order for three of the items from the Leicestershire trio – paid for there and then!

The six geese were retrieved, as anticipated, after dinner, all within 50 yards of each other.

The next morning I was away after an early breakfast for my Glen Lyon rendezvous and, by the end of the day, had the antlers of a fine 10 pointer in the back of my 4WD.

My three new-found friends did not, however, have such a happy tale to tell on my return to HQ. They were still gooseless and had some good news and some bad news. They had found a party of greys feeding on a potato field a half hour's drive away and the farmer had given them permission to shoot. He had also informed them that many more geese were feeding under the moon and they were to go back that night.

I had already been asked to view the trio's weaponry and found one of them to be sporting only a light open-bored English game gun. It would have been of little use on geese and I pleasured him greatly by offering him the use of my Lewis and a belt of cartridges. The team had invited me to accompany them but I had been up well before dawn and a day on the hill had spent my reserves.

At breakfast the next morning it was easy to spot who had scored. Only Harry, my gun user, bore a happy countenance. It transpired that the geese had arrived at a goodly height in the still air and had been reluctant to drop in. The inexperienced fowlers had probably not been properly concealed. Harry was the only one to bring birds down – four times with the Lewis.

John, the team leader, was desperate to buy the gun. I had to explain the history of the weapon before he would desist and I told him I could provide an almost identical weapon from my stock in Blackpool – a Stensby in excellent condition and just as tightly choked. I subsequently despatched the gun to him and the sale was completed by return of post.

FORBIDDEN LAND

Some years later I played the tape, recorded on that earlier visit, to Lytham Wildfowlers at one of their meetings. The saga begins with a stealthy rise from hotel rooms and follows the gravelled road out of the grounds in darkness to the field gate. The latch clangs open and we motor across stubble to the lee of the wood bordering the loch.

There are no 'stands' in goose parlance although the great Bill Powell refers often to them in his two books on Solway goose shooting. But on that morning there really were stands as we lined out at 50-yard intervals.

The recording is still cherished, one of the prized trophies. On long hot summer days it is as efficacious to the soul as a large gin and tonic. Out come the gems from 40 years past; 'Bloody 'ell Edward, if I could gallop like that I wouldn't bother with an 'orse on my farm,' after I had sprinted for a runner dropped by the ageing Albert.

The young fowlers listened enthralled and I was approached later by four of them completely consumed by the experience. One of them was Geoff.

'Would you please tell us where to go?' he had pleaded.

They explained their impecuniosity. There would not even be sufficient funds to stay at a B & B never mind an hotel.

'Where on earth will you sleep? Its damned cold in them there hills in October,' I told them.

'In the car. We intend to get so pissed each night we will be able to sleep on a clothes line!'

After I had bored their pants off by explaining that 'sleeping on a clothes line' would still entail them being indoors they said they were sure that I had got the message. (Sleeping on a clothes line was a genuine method used by the doss houses of old. A rope would be stretched across the room and, for a penny a night, one could hook both arms backwards over the rope and sag into slumber. That way many people could be accommodated in a small space.)

How could I deny such enthusiasm? Have we not all been young and daft?

'I'll tell you what I'll do. Get a map and I'll show you exactly where some of the geese feed. You will have no chance of getting onto the land. Don't even attempt to. It is strictly keepered and I have already tried. These will be birds which flight from the estuary and, given a fair wind, you will be able to get under them on Crown foreshore – real goose shooting. None of this feather bed stuff.'

The stories they brought back were epics and would be worthy of a book in their own right. Sleep in their car they did. Well anaesthetised they were. Geese on the foreshore they got – and the geese, too, on the 'forbidden land'.

Exactly as I had predicted, the grey hordes were on the Laird's stubbles. Notwithstanding my warning not to disturb the nobleman they had driven their battered carriage into his estate yard. There they had encountered the factor and requested a stalk.

As this kindly man was explaining to the four that the geese were never shot, up rolled a Land Rover to decant the Laird himself. 'What do these fellows want?' he had demanded.

After the factor had explained he added his own decline and, as he turned away, told the lads over his shoulder that they would 'never get near them anyway.'

Nothing gained, nothing lost. One of them had called out, 'But sir, would you please just give us a chance to show you we can?'

The Laird halted. 'How long do you think it would take you?' Obviously ready for some entertainment.

'Less than an hour,' said Geoff.

'You've got three quarters,' replied the Laird.

The lads reckoned the first of their eight shots was fired on 40 minutes. Seven geese fell dead.

'We picked them in as quiet a way as we could and were strolling back to the car when we saw the Laird standing on the bonnet of his Land Rover in the lane,' said Geoff. 'He didn't speak. He just gave a very slow hand clap. We walked over to thank him but he drove off.'

Enthused by their initial sortie the lads were back the following year, exactly 12 months later. This time their first call was the Laird's estate, for the geese were in the same field.

'It was quite extraordinary,' said Geoff. 'Exactly the same thing happened. As we got out of the car the factor was there and up drove the Laird.'

'It's the boys from last year sir,' said the factor. 'They want to know if they can have another go at the geese?'

'Last year was a mistake,' was all they were to hear as the Laird strode away.

These Scottish sorties became the norm for an increasing number of the Lytham club members. All kept their destinations secret but such is the craft of the fowler, that they always came back with geese, though in lessening numbers as the professional guides moved in. A survey by the Wildfowl & Wetlands Trust from 2005 did, in fact, show that, by then the greylag had moved its main wintering grounds to the far-off Orkneys – a fact I have already disclosed.

In other words, this Icelandic breeding species was touching down before it reached the mainland. The proximity to frost-dispelling sea winds keeps the sheep-cropped grasslands – the greylag's chief food – available all winter and, because of the islands' inaccessibility, there is a fraction of disturbance from commercial gunners. I plead with those in authority to ensure sanctuaries are speedily established.

Pinkfoot at Dawn *(detail) from a painting by Ian Phipps.*

CHAPTER 5

Richard's Utopia

We had been driving along a narrow upland road for some time. Well-kept grouse moors stretched away, endlessly, on each side and, occasionally, there were neat rows of butts.

'Stop after the next bend,' ordered Richard. 'We could find geese.'

Geese up here. How come? He had to have his bearings wrong.

Not so. The scene suddenly changed. Below lay a fertile plain. Heather gave way to rough grazing and, next to that, fields of barley stubble. Small shelter belts of mixed hardwood and pine made up the patchwork and, in the distance, a firth showed white horses whipped by a stiff westerly.

We climbed out of the shooting brake and soon, true enough, there was goose talk. My dog would have shown us where they were. She was a veteran at the game and you would only have to point the binoculars in the direction of her gaze. But Richard had said no dogs. We would be on keepered land and he would never have got on in the first place had he taken one.

High powered optics soon found them, a small party of around 40 pinks resting where the clumpy grass started half a mile away. A sudden boom echoed down the valley. It sounded like a gas gun but the birds did not move.

'They put them out to keep the geese off the new grass,' explained Richard. 'That's why we are here. They'll take them off when we call tonight and then we give the geese a bit of attention to move them on.'

It sounded as though my new found goose hunter had it well sussed.

All this happened a long time ago and is an important part of my goose chasing. You could, in fact, say that this valley plays the major part.

GLASSING THE STRATH – *Whenever the journey to Ponkey's was done in daylight the approach was made over a grouse moor to unlikely looking goose country. The strath marked the western boundary and parties of geese were often spotted, by careful glassing, feeding or resting on the sheep-cropped turf. Runnels and peat hags made stalking hard work but often rewarding. Richard and Ken with the silver Subaru, easily hidden alongside the zinc shepherd's huts then common in the area.*

And it was Richard's account of his first-ever goose, from this same land, that did much towards the writing of this book.

A glance at the watch. 'Time to go. Mustn't be late for Miss Jane.' What other surprises were there?

After a few more miles we turned into a long farm drive. Well-trimmed hedges and neat fences led to a row of workers cottages and the farmhouse.

'Miss Jane will see you in the conservatory,' said the maid and we settled into the big, comfortable cane chairs. Richard looked like a Laird himself. His brogues always had a guardsman's gloss and he told me he never went goose shooting without a tie. Was this how he had opened so many doors where others had failed? I was about to find out over the next two days. A lesson in commercial travelling diplomacy.

Miss Jane, white haired and tweed clad, appeared with the cakes. She always, I was to learn, baked a fresh batch for Richard. The maid followed with the silver tea tray.

The conservatory faced south and commanded a wide vista of the estate. Miss Jane tipped her aristocratic brow towards a belt of pines half a mile away. 'The geese are in the top stubble. Rab has dug the hole where you asked, on the crest of the hill and 40 yards out from the wall.'

Rab? Hole? What was afoot? I was to learn that holes in Rab's stubble field were not his favourite subject. They were to be the source of much consternation in subsequent years and gave us the secret name (Ponkey's) for this anserine Utopia. As goose hides, the holes had no equal.

Later I asked Richard how the hole idea had happened. It had been his spinster host who had suggested it. 'I had been unable to get near the geese in a big field the first year I had gone there and she told Rab to take a JCB, tractor and trailer. It takes two men, one to dig and the other to cart the earth away. It stays on the trailer and is later tipped back into the hole but not until after the geese have been cleared from the field. Apparently the method was used on the farm many years ago.'

The audience over, we sped towards HQ, a cosy hotel close by. Today, sadly, it is boarded up and marked for demolition, a reflection on the lack of clientele in the remoter parts of Scotland.

'We'll book in and then I'll introduce you to Bobby.'

Bobby turned out to be a retired farmer whose wife ran a small cosy café slap bang in the middle of our 20 square miles of goose shooting. Mrs Bobby's stock pot was always full when Richard was due in the area and there was, I found, a very good reason for our second hostess's attentiveness.

Among my companion's many lines was a niche in exotic female cosmetics. It had opened a new door in the life of a humble café operator.

'You are looking very well,' Richard had beamed.

'Perhaps it's the eye-shadow,' said Mrs Bobby, wondering what might next land on her counter from the treasure chest.

There were more revelations. Bobby turned out to be a registered counter for the British Trust for Ornithology. With his pal Macgregor, a retired solicitor, they monitored the grey goose population in the area.

'They came early this year. September 15,' he told us. 'We reckon the number of pinks has gone up from 3,000 to 3,500 and there seem to be more greys. They came later as usual.'

How come a bird watcher was willing to impart such knowledge?

'I knew Bobby long before I started to shoot here,' said Richard. 'I began among the pigeons, years ago and as a farmer, he labels them a pest. He knows I only take the odd goose home. Sometimes I go with them on their counts.'

Richard had told me he had some rough shooting in the area. It lay behind the café. Sixty acres of land that Bobby had allowed to go fallow. It held pheasants, partridge, rabbits and hares. On the boundary was a mature pine wood that was, over the years, to yield fair bags of pigeon. Richard never took home more than a brace of pheasants, or partridge, but Bobby was glad to see the hares and rabbits thinned.

Time to leave the café and Mrs Bobby's soup. There was still groundwork to be done before the sun set. The remaining five farms, all keepered, were visited. More cakes were digested and tea quaffed. Obligatory. Sometimes there was a parcel for the farmer's wife or whisky for a keeper.

THE HOLE

The next day pre-dawn found us back on Miss Jane's farm. She and her maid were the sole occupants of the house. Her brother farmed the land but he was away, on the other family estate, 100 miles distant.

We parked in trees at the foot of steeply rising stubble. Richard had two pinks he had stuffed himself for decoys and I carried a sack of 24 flat silhouettes – twice the size of the real thing and quite weighty.

Richard was a few inches taller than my 5ft 11-inches with rangy legs to match. He sped up the hill so fast that I had to keep breaking into a half trot. Not so good when you had shared a bottle of claret at dinner not very many hours before followed by pints of bitter and scotch chasers!

'This is the last time I do this,' I gasped.

'What's wrong?' asked Richard. 'Don't you approve of shooting geese from holes?'

Of course I did not mind his cunning covertness. It was the slog on a rebellious gut. Why had we left the 4WD at the bottom of the hill? 'To save time. We are a bit late.'

My new goose partner was a hard man and I liked that.

Finding our subterranean hide was not as easy as I had anticipated.

The gear was left by a low crumbling stone wall and torches were employed for a slow, careful search. Rab dug his holes five feet deep and, in the inky blackness, they would be decidedly unfriendly.

Richard had insisted I took the hole first, while he tucked in behind the wall. It hadn't taken us long to fashion him a hide in the long grass at its base.

Only my head showed above ground in my lair and a shooting stick provided the perfect seat.

The first bunch came in when there was barely a hint of light. They pitched 100 yards short of our position, with barely a croak, and hadn't seen the decoys. Richard was quickly out of his hide to put them up. They would have pulled in the next batch and I noted his know-how. Their low calling proved this early lot to be greylag. Not as garrulous as their pinkfoot cousins.

Plenty of music announced the next bunch at about half light. The Olt goose call had just made it onto the British market and our duet pulled 20 pinks in to perfection, straight over the decoys, and between our two positions.

This was the first time I had shot with Richard and didn't know what to expect. He proved to be no slouch. I was hoping that he would take them early and so he did. Three birds dropped stone dead to our four shots and we quickly set them up close to the stuffed pair.

Richard's only gun was an Aya 3-inch side-by-side 12-bore, bored half and full choke. I had my deadly Lewis and had let the birds get well out before pulling the trigger.

In this half light the game-gun, still in the car, would have been better with heavy shot but, when full light came, full chokes were ideal. The birds stopped coming when we had eight between us. The greater part of the flight had gone out to the east, towards the coast.

Richard explained that the geese roosted over a wide area in the territory, on inland lochs or the coastal sand bars, a 10-minute flight away. Had we not been successful we would have waited until the stockmen and shepherds moved out to check their charges later in the morning. Geese, feeding on the neighbouring land, could lift and be attracted to our decoys. This was to prove a profitable strategy over the years when dawn had been negative.

I quickly realised that here was, indeed, a veritable goose paradise. The birds were hidden from roads by the rolling, empty landscape and were left alone most of the time by the landowners.

Richard went on his last goose trip to this same territory six years ago and filled the void with flyfishing. It was while he was clearing out his shooting paraphernalia that he came across a neatly typed account of the first geese he had killed, aged 30.

When his words landed on my doormat I knew I had to write about this land. In the end it was more an epitaph, for he died two years before this book was published.

SERENDIPITY

How Richard came to discover his secret place was, indeed, serendipity in its truest meaning: 'The faculty of making a fortunate discovery by accident.'

He had placed a shotgun into the boot of his car (well before the days of paranoiac security) in the hope of a go at the woodpigeons he had noted in large quantities on his last visit to the area. Nor, at that time, were there queues of hopeful pigeon-chasers knocking on every farmstead door. Now land owners charge to shoot these pests. (And rightly so, say I.)

Richard found a lordly farmer saddling a horse – he turned out to be one of those rare Scots who rode his boundaries Australian style. (It was also pre quad-bike days.) He was delighted to accede to Richard's request and added, 'Have a go at the geese if you get the chance. I can't keep them off my new grass.'

Not only had Richard never been close to a wild goose, he also had no idea there were any in the area. Such is the topography of this part of Scotland that the flocks feed hidden in the folds of huge rolling fields. Rarely were they disturbed – nor still are – and, if a stockman happened to put a flock up they merely hopped on to the next inviting field. For generations they have been tolerated. Thanks to this treatment I have, personally, seen their numbers build from around 1,500 in the 1960s to sometimes 10,000 in this locality. Only last season I watched a column of geese, at dusk, stretching as far as the eye could see from their protected feeding grounds to their guarded roost – which just happens to be a mile over our boundary.

I am quite happy now to pay a lot of money for the shooting rights on my goose grounds. In the early days it was all courtesy of the landowner and then the game rights were held by the occupant of a neighbouring castle. With his passing I was able also to acquire all the shooting.

On the day that Richard took me there I had no idea where we were bound. I, too, had passed the area on my way to the many recognised goose grounds over the years without knowing of its presence.

PONKEY

Our second visit to these goose grounds was in early November during a spell of almost balmy weather. We learnt, then, that there were to be no more holes. It transpired that a farm worker, who sported the fine nickname of Ponkey, had been ploughing the field with the hole and had continued towards the late evening. He had forgotten about the pit and, in failing light, had driven into it.

Though Ponkey escaped without injury there was considerable damage to the tractor and Miss Jane's brother John, all-powerful in the running of the estate, had declared no more holes.

We were to shoot many geese on this same field over the years, using bales as hides. It was immediately christened Ponkey's field and we eventually gave the same name to the farm, thus also lending it an air of secrecy.

On this second visit we first spent a couple of hours reconnoitring further afield and discovered a large party of pinks 10 miles away. The farmer was already known to us and said they had been there for several days. We elected to return at dawn.

The extensive acres on Ponkey's were known to Richard but, for me, they were uncharted waters and, while there was still daylight, we agreed that I should walk its extensive boundaries while Richard turned his attention to the pigeons on a field of newly-sown winter wheat.

There was carte blanche among the pigeons and rabbits and overseer John would particularly like to see a reduction in the extensive population of the latter. Walking from north to south, through a gully full of gorse bushes, I soon pouched four bunnies in spite of being dogless.

The land began on a rich fertile plain at 400 feet above sea level and rose gradually to rough grazing at 1,000 feet. The gully led on to rough pasture, full of rushes, and pheasants clattered noisily out of these beds and back into a keepered pine wood next door.

Over the top boundary was a heather moor and, turning due west to walk this march, the occasional grouse jumped ahead calling in protest. Half way along the fence, with not a shot fired in 15 minutes and the wind beginning to freshen, there came a distinctive clap-clap of wings followed by the chatter of geese. The sounds were dead ahead where the ground sloped slightly upwards.

THE POND

Leaving the unloaded gun behind and moving forward on hands and knees, I followed the goose noises which grew louder. Three-foot wings were hurling water, skywards. There appeared to be around 50 pinkfoot engaged in their daytime ablutions.

Trembling with excitement at the proximity of the object of our visit to this wild place I rapidly backed off. Surely I must have wandered off our land. Why hadn't Richard told me about this wondrous oasis?

With empty gun in one hand and bulging game bag steadied by the other I broke into a steady lope downhill. Nothing, apart from gates and cattle grids, barred the route back to the farm and I felt sure I couldn't possibly have strayed.

When I reached Richard's hide I was breathless, more from excitement than exertion. My discovery was, indeed, news and we hurried off to find Rab.

'Aye. The Major used to flight it for the ducks and I still tip all our waste grain there. Sometimes its black wi' geese!'

Next call Miss Jane. 'Oh have you come to finish the cake?' she beamed. We hadn't come to finish the cake but felt obliged so to do. Of course we must shoot the pond. She would tell the Major. (The Major lived at the aforementioned nearby castle and had rented the game shooting for the past 30 years.)

We couldn't wait to investigate the find and immediately drove up a rough track that stopped a field away from the moorland pasture containing the watering hole. By then the geese had gone but a pack of around 20 teal departed, followed by half a dozen mallard. The water's edge and the pasture down one side were covered in goose feathers. The close cropped grass was also thick with droppings.

Since we were on a three day visit it was decided to leave our discovery alone until the last night. If we hadn't by then, reached our agreed quota of 10 geese maximum, we would be in place for evening flight. There was a further problem – we had no dog and were reluctant to shoot over water without one.

VALLEY FLIGHT

By now it was late afternoon and the freshening wind was reaching gale force. The grass field, where the birds had been feeding further up the valley, indicated that they were probably roosting on a loch at the head

Top Pond – My sketch of the Top Pond at Ponkey's under a full moon. The fence hide was Richard's favourite position. The geese were lightly shot but it yielded good bags of mallard and teal. Sometimes wigeon and pintail made it from the coast.

of the strath. Richard had watched them flighting that way before and, if they did head for the loch, they would be facing directly into the wind. We decided to try flighting them as close to the roost as possible on the extreme edge of our land, but still half a mile away from the water.

We were, however, barred by recent ploughing and had to contend with a mile-long walk through a narrow strip of hardwood – mostly elm, for the dreaded Dutch disease had not then struck. By now the gale had reached epic force and with the branches crashing overhead like demonic giants thrashing their arms, we took to the field in its lee.

After half an hour crouched in the comparative comfort of a wall, darkness had wrapped its cloak over all the land and we decided that the birds must have abandoned the fight against the tempest and chosen the easy option of heading for the coast. As we were about to unload there came a 'wink wink' directly overhead and we could just make out a skein no more than 60 feet up.

The birds were almost stationery and we probably shot too far in front for only two fell, blown back over the wall. Keeping an eye on the barely-visible outside bird in the skein I slipped in another round of 1½ ounces of BBs and tumbled it straight down.

DAWN FLIGHT

Next day dawn saw us back at the field where we had found the birds the previous day with the storm still raging but, by 10 o'clock, there was no sign of geese. Such is goose chasing.

On our way back for breakfast we spotted a thin dark line approaching from the direction of the coast. Then two more lots behind. Most of them had, after all, done as we suspected and let the gale carry them to the sand bars the night before.

January on Ponkey's – January trips to Ponkey's were hard work but rewarding.
Left to right: Ken, Richard and the author, in 1965.

We pulled in and watched as they dropped in to the southern area of our territory and then made a quick call at the farm to get the all-clear before reaching HQ for a very quick on-schedule breakfast.

We soon found 500 pinks feeding in a grass field on the side of a wide plain and, after the toss of a coin, Richard elected to stalk into them while I took a sackful of decoys to set up in the valley bottom half a mile distant – in the direction we hoped they would take when they lifted.

Half an hour later, on zero hour, two bangs put the birds into the air and they headed directly towards my low hide on the edge of a newly planted pine shelter belt. As they banked towards the decoys, a long way off, I pulled out the nearest bird.

The wind had not abated and, after my shot, it looked as though the flock was making for their normal water over a hill when they suddenly wheeled and disappeared behind a mature pinewood. Leaving the decoys I set off in pursuit, via more low planting, and had reached the far side of the field when there were more shots from Richard's direction.

HEDGE HOPPING

Whether the cluster of geese flying low over the middle of the field I had just traversed were what Richard had shot at, I know not. They gave the impression they were hedge hopping to get out of the wind, would soon spot my abandoned decoys and veer off.

However, the first blast on the goose call produced an instant reaction and the bunch of about 20, headed directly to where I hid behind a 10-foot pine. As they passed immediately overhead I had to let them go before taking an easy right and left.

No sooner had I wedged both birds by the neck in the vee of a branch and trunk than yet another call announced a singleton following exactly the same path. Again the call worked its magic but this time the bird landed in the field 40 yards from the fence. An easy enough target, one would have thought, for a full and full choke 12-bore but it escaped untouched.

I set off once more, on my search. I had been too far off the feeding birds to disturb them on this wild morning and, on nearing the field, several more lots pitched in. The noise was considerable as the parties greeted each other and I guessed my early birds had joined a flock already using the winter pasture.

I was correct. From the edge of the wood I could see around 1,000

LEUCISTIC GOOSE – *A leucistic pinkfoot shot at dawn on Ponkey's. It was a first-year bird in good condition.*

pinks contentedly feeding in a calm upland meadow completely sheltered from the prevailing wind. They had probably been using the field undetected for some days.

My only way in would involve a long belly crawl through two fences and over a rushy field to a hawthorn hedge – a rarity in those parts. This was, of course, new territory to me but Richard had pointed out the boundary earlier and it was atop the sheltering hill.

Ten yards from the hedge, while I was taking a breather, a single bird appeared to my left, a perfect right to left swing and I took it at maximum range – about 65 yards out and at treetop height (a favourite Solway shot). Better a bird in the hand... The sky darkened with 2,000 wings and this time the army did disappear over the hill.

When I finally met up with Richard I found he had accounted for three geese one of which was leucistic. This made our total 10 for the trip and a dogless visit to the pond unnecessary.

So anxious, however, were we to spend an evening on our new-found waterhole that we arranged a return trip for the following month under the moon.

THE THIRD MEMBER

We had discussed adding a third member to our goose-hunting team and decided on Ken, an all-round excellent shot, our age, fit and a dog-man. The union was to last for many years. I had already shot with Ken on marsh and field and as I write this, 50 years after our first meeting on the tideway, he and I still shoot together. A little stiffer in the joints we may be but the heart still beats as fast when we hear the cry of the wild hounds of heaven.

HQ had only three bedrooms but, on these out-of-season winter days they were quite happy to give us a room each. Why do all goose shooters snore?

Because of the moon we hadn't expected much at dawn and, in fact, drew a blank on Ponkey's. We had finished the regulation 10am breakfast and were about to climb into the 4WD when a quick scan with the binoculars found a skein of around 200 pinks heading in from the sea. There then followed an extraordinary happening. The birds were two gun shots high and beating into a force four wind. Two fields away they wheeled and pitched into grassland within walking distance of where we stood. Ken and I reckoned we could reach the birds by bellying across the first field bordering the road and up to a low dry-stone wall.

Richard felt we would not be in range from the wall and volunteered to watch from the car. If we signalled he would motor round to drive them over us.

The stalk was probably the easiest either of us had ever done. In quick time we had reached the wall.

'What do you think?' I whispered.

'In range,' said Ken. 'You take two to the left and I'll go for two to the right.'

On the count of three we stood up and each got our right and lefts. I had a runner and, with the dogs in the car, caught my bird without needing a third barrel. (We had, incidentally, by now secured permission to use our well-mannered dogs on most of the territory.)

Richard had kept the flock in his binoculars after our shots and reported that they had gone down a mile away still on our land. We soon found them on another grass field which sloped steeply up the side of the valley. From the farmyard I again felt a stalk was on. The other two reckoned not, so we arranged that they get into ambush in a ditch along the field's bottom edge.

Again the stalk was an easy one and this time with no crawling. Long ago the territory had been opencast-mined for limestone and, after a short stroll, I was in position behind another stone wall 10 minutes ahead of zero hour. Through the chinks in the stones I could see the birds less than 20 yards away. Listening to the feeding buzz, and watching some bad tempered squabbling, I was so carried away that I overshot the time. I had swapped to number threes in both barrels and, rising in a gap, let the birds go before allowing two to close and squeezing before switching to another. Three birds fell together, dead in the air.

Four shots rang out from the bottom of the field but the birds were high and just two more made the total nine inside an hour.

We had taken with us two dogs, Ken his 10 year old Labrador Heide and myself the ebullient Gemma, a four year old springer spaniel. That evening, on this our first visit to the pond, we had no hides and, being the only wader-wearer I opted to crouch by its edge under a shallow bank. Ken and Richard were in the rushes by the fence.

Rab had told us that the birds would flight in over the moor having spent many evenings on the pond when it was shot by the Major. What we didn't expect was that they would all be greylags. Nor did we realise how many ducks there would be.

Rab had fed the pond for the previous two weeks and there was a steady stream of mallard and teal. None circled, coming in at head height and confirming that they had been unmolested for a long time. A bunch of wary wigeon called and circled, no doubt used to the attentions of fowlers on the nearby coast, and made off. But we were after bigger fry and the ducks were left to come and go.

Richard had only occasionally seen greys in the area, and during the day, we had seen only pinks. The full moon had just topped the hills when the first small party came in against a light wind and two were dropped onto the grass – easy retrieves for the dogs.

The next proved a problem. The bird slanted out, winged, into deep heather over the fence and I sent Gemma. She was small for a springer and struggled with the big bird. The ageing Heide had rightly refused to face the rough cover.

I took the bird from the little dog over the fence as it thrashed its mighty wings about her body. The next bird fell into the same area, also wounded, but this time the goose was inert when the dog brought it in. The torch revealed that she had neatly nipped its neck close to the breast.

Gemma was, however, saved from any more thrashings. We had enough in the bag and, as we quietly retreated, more geese were dropping in.

From that day forward Gemma never delivered any fowl alive. If they were runners they would have their necks expertly nipped. Rarely was there a mark on the breast skin. Nor was she hard mouthed (for the uninitiated to this term, she could deliver a fresh egg unmarked to the hand). To all other game, whether fur or feather, she did not deliver the coup de grace.

Gemma was special to me in many ways. I had bought her at six months old, partly trained, for the price of an eight week old pup. When I got her home I discovered why – she was gun shy! Her breeder had demonstrated her retrieving skills on firing a starting pistol and I was warned to, 'Be careful with a 12-bore.'

I took her first to a claybird shoot and she had tried to jump into the nearest car – any car – when she heard the initial shot. She was, however, cured on her first day on game at the age of 12 months.

We had surrounded a small tarn near my Lakeland home. Gemma was on a thick rope round my waist and tugged when I downed a tufted duck. Then, at the end of the drive, she watched the other dogs retrieving. She wanted to join in and, from that day, forgot her gun-shyness, but only on live-bird days. At clay shoots she could never master her fear.

Gemma had a sad end. At nine years old, and still capable of a full day's work, she succumbed to liver failure thought, by the vet, to have been from rat poison.

WEE JOE

The following account well illustrates the value of a good dog on one's goose hunts. It involves a tract of land that was once a lowland grouse shoot. Perhaps it was, in fact, too low to be a success for it is now abandoned and has become a truly lonely, fearsome place at night.

Ken was unavailable and overseas business for Richard had forced us to move our annual trip to our Scottish goose grounds back to mid-December. Often, in the past, the pinkfoot flocks had departed for easier feeding but we had no alternative – roll on retirement when we could pick our moment.

The afternoon was dull and still when the Subaru 4WD pulled up at Mrs Walker's cosy quarters. Bobby, she said, was in his workshop and it was this chance visit to the old chap's inner sanctum that was to solve a mystery which had baffled us for years.

Though Bobby did not shoot there was often a prime cock pheasant hanging by the neck in one of his airy out-buildings. Never was there a mark on these birds, immaculate in their undisturbed feathered regalia – too untouched to be presents from a gamekeeper, though keepered shoots abounded in the area.

Bobby had announced, the previous year, that he would soon be retiring to a small bungalow a few miles down the road from his farm and what he had sitting on his work bench would, he said, continue to provide his regular supply of pheasants.

The neat three-foot square cage, solidly built of three by two timber and wire netting, was his new trap. The one he used on his farm – and which we had never come across – was too old to move. His new home adjoined a local shoot's coverts and the new cage, discreetly stained, would be secreted amongst his raspberry canes. Bobby never, he told us, killed a hen bird. This must have been the salve for his conscience.

We had been sorry to hear of our host's imminent departure – it would be at the start of the following winter – but on this day the rascally old lad had some news to cheer us. There were plenty of pigeons roosting in his wood and that morning, he had seen five lots of pinks flighting at dawn from a loch at the head of a nearby strath. There would, he said, be time for an hour's shooting amongst his firs before taking off to see if the geese returned to the loch that evening.

No one else shot Bobby's wood and the pigeons came in thick and fast at tree top height, with none of that out-of-range approach and a spiralling down into the centre of the firs, as birds are wont to do after they have been under heavy, regular fire. That winter black Labrador bitch Jess was with us and we had accounted for around 20 birds when it was time to head up the valley.

We would watch from a narrow public lane, at the head of an unpopulated area, where the sides are bounded by steep hills. The valley bottom had once held the previously mentioned grouse shoot and, when I was first privy to the land as a young man, the birds flew over neat butts mostly of timber construction. A few were of solid stone foundation and these were still more visible than their rotting wooden counterparts. Now the heather was either gone – replaced by grass where the grant-aided draining scheme had done its job – or had grown into dense, straggly clumps. In other areas there were steep peat hags and treacherous deep bogs which no drainage would tame.

Sometimes the geese fed on these sheep cropped areas of turf and, over the years, we pulled off some successful dawn ambushes. Bobby said the birds had not been using these patches of feed during the daytime so far that year, but if they roosted on the loch that night we would wait for them there at dawn.

Dusk was gathering fast when we stopped under the short, wind-bent beeches by the edge of the water. The loch was a good mile across and we expected the geese to come in high and glide down to its far side. The area had long been a sanctuary and sometimes was host to many thousands of the grey hordes.

The dog was the first to hear the advance party. She had pricked her ears and cocked her head well before we detected goose music. The wind was at force four and up their tails as they topped the beeches. They were moving at great speed and well within shot.

Five lots came – probably the same birds Bobby had witnessed that morning – and all followed the same pattern. Though they could have been no more than 40 feet up each lot was only just discernable in the almost pitch darkness. The birds settled well over the water, each party noisily greeted by those already at rest, then there was total silence. They would, no doubt, be fast asleep within minutes, bellies well filled from a day on the barley stubble.

On the way back to HQ we called on the friendly Old Man Fraser to get clearance for a dawn flight where his land began a mile from the edge of the loch. We had shot his two farms for many years and Mrs Fraser was cross that she had not been alerted to our visit. Richard here, too, was made as welcome as a lost son and she knew how much he appreciated her baking. We had to promise to call again later in the week when, no doubt, there would be a sponge cake awaiting.

The road that ran alongside this strath would, that night, have been above the flighting geese. We had stood on its edge in the past and listened to the bunches of birds passing below us in the blackness.

At dawn the next day we left the vehicle in a lay-by and descended the steep slope onto flat pasture below. There was plenty of cover behind the clumps of overgrown heather and peat hags. The black Lab was invisible, too, against the dark earth. The birds flew early, as is so often their wont during the short December days, but they were nowhere near the height they had taken on their passage the night before. Through binoculars they could be seen topping the beeches as they lifted from the loch but, by the time they had flown the few 100 yards to where we crouched, they were two gunshots high. They all headed for the coast, 10 miles away, and, with luck, would be back on the same path that evening if the laws that dictate a goose's behaviour still applied.

To avoid a long and arduous trek from the road to get into the position for evening flight we decided to look for a way in by vehicle via the flat farm land. Old Man Fraser had told us 'it would be tricky' but if we called on Wee Joe, his shepherd who dwelled in a cottage on the edge of a large wood, he would, if we were lucky, show us a route. A bottle of Black Label might, he said, do the trick.

Later that day we found Wee Joe's tiny abode hidden at the end of a grassy track and neatly surrounded by a well-clipped privet hedge. There was an equally neat lawn and a vegetable patch and milk cow in a small pasture.

Our knock brought an aged lady to the door, her heavily lined features topped by snow white hair tied in a bun. We were told Joe would be late home, would be taking his dinner and would have no time to guide us anywhere. With that the door closed. We learned later that both Joe and his wife were in their mid-eighties and had lived in their home for over 50 years. They never went on holiday and Joe worked among the sheep six days a week.

Dusk was falling as Joe appeared – two sheep dogs at his heel. He was less than five feet tall and sported a fore and aft deerstalker. A shepherd's crook aided his brisk step and, as his wife had already explained, he wouldn't have time to show us where to go for the geese.

Then Richard produced the Black Label. 'Follow me,' he ordered. 'It will be quicker by foot,' and was off through the wood as fleet-footed as any deer. Richard's long legs coped with the pace but I was forced to break into a trot.

After five minutes Joe stopped abruptly at the edge of the wood. 'Follow that track,' he ordered, 'and don't stray off it. There will be plenty of cover after half a mile. You will be under the geese but let your dog do the retrieving. It will be boggy and I don't want to have to rescue you.' With that Joe – and the whisky – were gone.

By now it was almost pitch black but we had heard no geese. Perhaps, in the fickle way that wild geese have, they had changed their minds and would be roosting elsewhere tonight.

I left Richard on the edge of the first cover and carried on another 100 yards. There was no need to hide, the night was black enough to cover a platoon, and I sat at the edge of the track with Jess at my feet. Again the dog cocked her ears and, immediately, I heard goose talk. They were passing to my left and two bangs came from Richard's direction. There was an audible thump and I ordered the dog to 'get on.' She was quickly back with a pinkfoot.

More geese were on the move – many more parties than the previous night but few were visible particularly those to my right which were against the black of the nearby hill.

Richard scored again and, for my four shots, I also had two birds. The second was a runner but was retrieved far quicker than my first which had probably dropped deep into one of the dense growths of ancient heather.

Without a dog I doubt, however, if we would have found a single bird. In the past, when dogless, we had returned on more than one occasion to search for birds the next morning in this part of Scotland and never found more than a few feathers. Mr Reynard was, no doubt, the benefactor.

When we later passed the cottage we were tempted to hang a bird outside the door but I had given up years ago offering geese to Scots. They were amazed to find that anyone would want to eat one. Perhaps we should have knocked on the old green door but were apprehensive of the female tongue.

This was the only time I had shot that wild empty place at night though it was the venue for plenty of dawn sorties. Now the trek is beyond me and I wonder if the geese will ever be disturbed again at night on this passage?

ROE DEER

There is another spot where we regularly intercepted the geese on their way to this same roost, but much further down the valley where they fly high, other than in a fog or against a strong westerly. One late afternoon it was the scene of an unusual happening.

The route to the ambush led along a tall narrow deciduous wood. On this day, accompanied by a young fellow in his twenties, a violent gale thrashed the branches. As we neared the end of the plantation the dog moved alongside, stopped and pointed towards the far side of the wood. Two roe deer, a buck and a doe, were feeding, heads down and oblivious to our presence.

The buck was a yearling and the crashing timbers, plus the roaring of the gale, had deafened them to our approach. I motioned to young David to stay close and moved stealthily forward. We would see how close we could get to these beautiful timid wild creatures.

At 20 feet I felt we were close enough and coughed. Heads jerked round and the startled duo were off. After what was no more than a 30-yard amble they halted and looked at us again, as though in disbelief, before trotting quietly out of sight.

FOX STEALING

I have just mentioned foxes and it is extraordinary how cheeky they can sometimes be at stealing. I move the clock forwards a while to illustrate my meaning.

I was returning from a Scottish goose trip not too long ago when I called on a friend near St Boswells. He had promised a session decoying pigeons if the birds were still using a harvested rape field.

His keeper installed me and my five-year-old son Jago in a hide adjacent to a sparse wood with thick undergrowth. The birds were not showing a lot of interest in the field but the keeper knew that we were on a flight-line and the shooting was regular if not hectic.

Jago retrieved the odd bird which fell in the open, but we left two which plunged into the wood's thick cover. The keeper could send the spaniel for those later.

Then I dropped a bird at the foot of a sycamore and, since it was easily marked, sent Jago to collect. I expected him back reasonably quickly but, after several minutes, there was no sign of my willing helper.

It transpired that he had found the drop point – marked by a patch of bloodied feathers – but there was no trace of the bird. Then he observed a few feathers leading around a nettle bed. Following the evidence he quickly came upon a fox earth.

With the arrival of the keeper Jago led him to the spot and a close sniff confirmed Reynard's presence. Nor could the other two birds be traced. It had been a productive afternoon for the four-footed raider but I heard he paid the penalty dearly the following day.

The keeper told us he knew a fox was operating in the area but had, until then, been unable to trace the freshly dug earth.

INLAND FOG

Five years after we had first teamed up as a goose hunting trio, Richard, Ken and myself arranged a five-day trip in early November – our first visit of that season. We arrived at HQ in the middle of goose territory, at noon, to find it shrouded in a thin mist. At tree top, however, conditions were decidedly murky. And all this was in spite of a southerly force five – freak conditions only once encountered in the 35 years I have shot there. We were in unison in deciding to man the top fence. This should put us under the flightline to the pink's favourite roost. Rab confirmed the geese had been using this path all week.

The vehicle was left by a fir wood. An uphill mile-long slog took us to the fence, where visibility was down to around 30 yards, as dusk approached. It was to be an evening flight of all flights. I was manning a favourite corner on the extreme eastern boundary. Richard and Ken elected to find cover a quarter-mile along the same fence. We could all move if the birds did not conform to routine.

Glued to my heel was Briodie, an 18-month old black Lab on her maiden goose sortie. She had performed well enough on grouse and ducks in this her first season. Did she think we were on another duck flight and how would she react if, and when, a hefty goose thudded to earth?

The murky land was eerily quiet. Always at this hour, and at this location, one would hear cock grouse going to bed, their calling so evocative as they settled into their snug tussocks for the night. Not even an owl hooted in the thick firs by my right shoulder where they could guarantee to be preparing for their night time killing.

Lone fowlers are permitted to talk to their dogs and I had just informed the tyro Lab that the geese had more than likely headed for their coastal roost when a single call sounded. It was so close by that I assumed it to be some strange contortion of the imagination. But there, 20 feet above the nearest fir, the end bird of a small skein was slipping sideways in the headwind. A snap shot, before it disappeared into the gloom, brought the bird spinning down a mere yard from Briodie. As its mighty wings thrashed the rushes in its last rigours the dog had never seen anything like it and she barked!

Time only to lay the bird on the edge of my hollow and longer calls announced the next bunch, this time immediately ahead at eye-level. Another snap shot with the 32-inch Magnum dropped a bird 30 yards in front before the skein was overhead and too close to shoot. Briodie was out in a flash and, without hesitation, brought the bird perfectly to hand. Praise would have been more profuse but now geese were in the air calling incessantly. A right and left dropped two more as far out in front as I could see. Range was dictated by the failing light. Four shots and four birds but I was way over-gunned.

Birds were passing only feet above my head and I was confined to taking shots only to my left and also well ahead in case Richard or Ken were somewhere out there retrieving. To my right the wood hid yet more birds making their clamorous way to their roost.

Richard and Ken were in action but it was obvious that I was in the hot spot. Briodie was in constant movement and I resolved to stop at a bag of 10.

As I proceeded to pack as many as I could into my copious bag, late bunches still came over no more than double the height of the fence posts. Never was I likely to be so close to so many wild geese in a shooting lifetime and it felt good to be leaving them in peace. With the bag bulging and two brace over each shoulder the tally reached 12 – I must have miscounted but a recount confirmed a dozen. The dog must have spotted two that had dropped beyond my vision. The kills to cartridge ratio was one bird per two shots.

The final pair were carried by the neck in one hand. Unfortunately I had left the gun cover in the vehicle and, as I strained eyes to find the track through the thick reeds, I dreaded stumbling. So cumbersome was my load that I did not like to dwell on what might happen if I were prostrated.

The situation was not improved when, as we reached the territory to the rear of where Richard and Ken had been shooting, Briodie appeared out of the dark with another bird. Fortunately she was happy, nay proud I think, to carry her find all the way back to the vehicle.

Richard and Ken had accounted for seven birds between them including the dog's retrieve. We had reached our expected bag for the entire trip within three hours of our arrival.

Such, however, are the vagaries of goose chasing that our fears of an over-kill were completely unfounded. Dawn produced a blank with the birds feeding well off our territory and the remainder of the stay brought the total to a modest 24 with not a dawn or dusk flight missed. We left the boundary fence in peace and were gratified to hear the skeins using the same path the evening after our onslaught. They were their usual two gun shots high and it was to be many years before we shot that same spot again at dusk.

Chapter 6

Scottish Safaris

The part of my Scottish safari business involving the guiding of rich gents in pursuit of anything from stags to ptarmigan from pheasants to grouse, geese *et al*, began by chance.

While still in my early thirties into the shop one day came two Lancashire high fliers – one already a customer, the other a complete stranger. They were of similar age to myself.

'We would like you to organise a week's shooting trip to Scotland – pheasants, grouse and perhaps some stalking. We would also like you to accompany us. Please give the idea your best consideration,' and, with little else said, off they went.

This was a line of business I had never contemplated, though I had come across several sporting agents in my shop tenure. The idea had, I could see, its plusses and its minuses. A profit and a good time there would be but was absence from the counter a good idea when business was at its peak?

The angle which finally swung it was the fact that I could include days at the Scottish geese on estates hitherto closed to a goose chaser. Various exploratory enquiries produced encouraging responses. These were the days when Scottish estates were suffering severely from the swingeing inheritance tax rulings. Here was a welcome input to the coffers, if perhaps a little off-beat, when they learnt of my desire to hunt their geese.

There was an interesting aside to the second visit from my new client. Both men were delighted with my plans for the trip but, as they were leaving the shop, he turned back and, almost inaudibly growled, 'If I find you ever try to take me for a ride you will be in trouble.'

I was staggered, but not too much to riposte, 'Touché. Let me down once and, as far as I am concerned, YOU are finished.'

'I think,' he smiled, 'we are going to get on alright.'

And so we did. He did let me down – probably on half of the 10 trips I was to eventually organise exclusively for him – but he had an ace to play. With his apologies would always come the rider; 'I would like you to fulfil the arrangements yourself. Take a friend and give me the bill!' Always there were generous tips, sometimes by the simple expedient of doubling my account. The ultimate lesson in diplomacy. Small wonder that today – almost 40 years on – he is in Britain's 'Rich List'.

Probably the most exciting of all our safaris, involving this particular client, was a December one I had organised in the north-east. I had sought an estate where pheasants were heavily stocked – we would thus be guaranteed to burn plenty of powder and there would, if we so wished, be the services of a gamekeeper each. This time there were to be no stags on the list – the Scottish stag season ends on October 20 – but hinds were available if any of us were inspired. And, of course, there were geese aplenty.

There were five in the party, including myself, and two of them would definitely need a guardian in the form of a keeper. Though some of my paying guests on these ventures were tyros, I never presented a Gun who had not passed my own high test standard. Sometimes this would involve concentrated sessions on clays until I was satisfied my men would perform one hundred percent safely. There was rarely a pre-safari failure.

The Bentley Corniche was large enough to accommodate all of us, its capacious boot more than adequate for the array of armoury, paraphernalia and clothing – much of it new from the shelves of Entwistle Guns.

STRANDED

Un-forecast snow blocked our route and we found ourselves stranded in the ski hotel at the head of Glenshee on our first night. This was to prove an instant, and unexpected, bonus for Top Client whose response to his unscheduled stop was to, 'Bring out all the female staff and buy them all the champagne they can drink!'

Once more: what now, BB? who, in his emotive book *Dark Estuary* resolutely declared that petticoats had no place in goose shooting.

I was getting to know Top Client. He smiled all the way to our destination after they had cleared The Spittal of snow by the following noon. Nor was he at all concerned that the six foot snow fall had cancelled the first planned pheasant drive. We would have to move HQ to the coast where there was little more than a sprinkle.

The snowfall was bad news, too, for my goose shooting. The parties of greylag, which roosted on nearby small lochs, had moved. Their presence on the coastal plain would be a lottery.

The ensuing first afternoon produced a series of mixed drives which more than made up for our late start. The pheasants came thick and fast but only the odd one was to fall to my gun on that day. Instead, on each drive, I had a profusion of redleg partridge scattered around my peg. Redlegs were in their infancy as a game bird in Scotland and I had never experienced the delight of these little rascals that out-flew their large cousins, the pheasants, with ease.

No mention had been made of their presence on the estate and, at first, I was nonplussed. What were these spitfires exploding from the coverts?

'Will ye no be bothering with the pheesant's then Sirr?' enquired the head keeper. I told him I would when the pheasants became harder. This gave birth to a wide grin on his weathered countenance and he proceeded to lay on a drive which made me wish I had never opened my big mouth!

The birds came off a high escarpment and crossed a wide glen to a distant wood with wings set. Not only were they at extreme range but curling also. With a string of misses to my discredit a voice whispered over my shoulder, 'Same lead, Sirr, but a yard under them.'

The next bird crumpled. My mentor was the head keeper. 'They fool everyone Sirr. It's the curral but ye'll be reet the noo,' and off he strolled.

Our sudden presence on this part of the laird's vast land had come as a complete surprise to the head keeper of the territory and he proved to be an expert at conjuring the unexpected – as he had just proved.

That evening we were instructed to report the next day to a lochside castle an hour before dawn – game guns and, 'No fewer than 200 cartridges apiece'.

There was no moon and a stiff northerly sent flurries of snow over the ghostly lights illuminating a heavily studded oak door. Steps led to a 20-foot motor boat, its engine already ticking and filling the underground cavern with its choking carbon monoxide. The place was like an ogre's bedchamber. All five of us stepped aboard as the craft eased slowly away from the quay, the white beam of its navigation light stabbing the blackness. We passed beneath a low portcullis and felt the sting of snow on our cheeks.

One by one we were dropped off on tiny round islands no more than 10 feet across. Each had a dense box hedge neck high with a bench seat and table for cartridge bag. Heavy snow clouds gave no hint of dawn and I tucked myself under the lee of the hedge – game bag insulating the backside from the damp turf. As the sky grew lighter a whicker of wings had me heaving myself onto the seat. With back to wind I still felt snug inside the hide and I hoped the rest of my party were as excited as the increasing wind sent the spindrift past in fine clouds.

We had been told there 'might be a chance of geese,' but our main quarry would be diving ducks – tufted, goldeneye and pochard and there was soon an incessant barrage from the other four guns.

Ducks came from every which way. Usually, at flight time, one quickly establishes the approach route and can prepare oneself but, on this wildest of wild dawns, there was no pattern. Some battled into the tempest, some rocketed down wind and others side-slipped into the sheltered bays. But my gun lay still across my lap. I had heard geese at first light and it was geese I had travelled 300 miles to find. Let the other guns disturb them with their battery and perhaps they would home in to the only quietude.

The cunning plan worked. First a party of around 40 greylag pitched in 100 yards upwind quickly joined by a second lot. They covered a 30-yard front and, if undisturbed, they would drift down to surround my island in a matter of minutes.

A cackling from behind warned me of yet another bunch. They were heading for their wave-riding friends and would pass right over me. Geese to the left – geese to the right!

At 30 yards I took a right and left out of the airborne party, reloaded and as the floating flock took wing, they came broadside on in their struggle for height. The easiest of chances. As two birds converged I dropped them both with the first barrel and another with my second.

Time to shoot the duck. Full light was still only half made and my barrels quickly became hot. I was grateful for the rest when the flight finally ceased and began to search the loch for the boat when more ducks appeared, this time in dense flocks. They were followed by the whine of a high-powered motor and, from the lee shore, there appeared a long white wake as two keepers steered their speeding dory from bay to bay. This second flight was short-lived. After 15 minutes the skies emptied as the birds found sanctuary on the numerous small lochs around the estate.

As the boat neared the tiny island, that had been my home for two hours, I could see the keepers scooping ducks from the water with a landing net. I was told that the 'big boat' would be collecting me in 'aboot five minutes. And could I be congratulating ye, Sirr? We picked five geese in yonder bay doon wind frae your hide.'

VALUABLE CONTACTS

With each visit to Scotland the contacts built up. When an estate realised my passion for the geese, then free, unescorted invites were often proffered if, and when, I would like to make a personal sortie. This was my sort of goose shooting. The outings with a keeper at one's side were alien to the true fowler be it on shore or inland.

One fascinating package, organised for another client, contained a most rare ingredient – pigeon shooting from tree-top platforms. This time I had a party under my wing who seemed as keen as I was to get under the geese and the grey birds were at the top of our list.

The Guns were also fit enough to climb the ladders to the pine-top pigeon platforms and willing to scale steep sided moorland, for I had also been promised a day of driven grouse.

Though the pigeon shooting proved extremely exciting it was far easier than at first anticipated. The pigeons were not on the same estate where the remainder of the shooting was to take place and we had to travel a considerable distance to reach them. The lengthy journey was worth it. Once safely on the platform there was a chest-high rail. We were in a forest of mature sitka spruce and, although some 40-feet from the ground, there was no feeling of vertigo. The growth was so dense all sight of terra firma was obliterated and one felt as though one was standing on green clouds.

This was a roost wood and the birds came in unwarily from their afternoon feeding at eye level – like driven grouse but considerably slower and with no kinking provided one kept still until the last second. Kills to cartridge ratio was high and sport was fast and furious for most part of an hour. Below the keepers quietly went about their business of picking up, totally hidden from the flighting birds.

The afternoon on the grouse moor remains memorable to this day for one extraordinary shot. We were late in the season and most of the birds had packed. On one drive, however, a singleton crossed the valley so high that it appeared to be well out of range. Probably, I mused, an old bird who had taken the same escape route for many seasons. There was a picker-up close to my butt and we both gasped when the speck turned from a speeding missile into a plummeting bundle, which seemed to take an eternity to fall far into the glen below.

The marksman was even more of a surprise – the poorest shot in our party and his first day on grouse. He must have taken in the old

COCK GROUSE BY RODGER MCPHAIL – *Clients knew what to expect when grouse were included in the quarry list. It was obligatory for them to practice on simulated clay birds well in advance in order to deal proficiently with these difficult birds.*

adage, 'Give it three bus lengths.' Never before, or since, have I seen any gamebird killed at such a prodigious height and, once retrieved, I carried it home and had it duly stuffed and mounted for the fellow. The sad thing is that he probably never appreciated his feat.

As I have already said, the estate had promised geese but the method they used to 'guarantee birds' was to teach me a lesson. The five of us were taken by Land Rover to a mountain loch on the fringe of a pine forest in late afternoon. I assumed we would be flighting the geese into the loch and was mystified when we were placed in a tight line below a grassy dam wall.

Our host was the hotel proprietor, a keen and very proficient shot. 'There won't be any shooting until it goes dark,' we were told. 'The geese come in high and, when they have landed, the keeper will flush them over you.'

The ploy worked well – too well. Although the sky was almost black, the birds could be killed easily with game guns and, after the first two drives, I called a halt telling our host we had 'got enough for our needs.' He probably sensed my feelings for he made no protest.

I never used the hotel again, made discreet noises about the practice and later heard the unpleasant procedure was discontinued.

PETER'S GOOSE

In The Solway Years chapter I tell of solicitor Peter missing out on his first trip to goose territory – Rockcliffe Marsh – in the presence of head keeper Arthur Mills. Success was to come several years later when I nurse-maided a team of high-flying Fylde businessmen to Perthshire.

Peter was among them and, on the first morning he and I headed, pre-dawn, for a tattie field where towards 1,000 pinks had been feeding for a few days. I had chosen January because my hotelier host reckoned he could guarantee a build-up of both pinks and greys at that time of the year.

Floodwater and frost had turned the surface spuds into mush and the birds seemed to be on a gourmet feast. I have never been able to decide if diet has much adverse effect on the flesh of a goose. Certainly, over the years, I have detected none. In other fowl, yes. Before curlews were put on the protected list, their flesh turned from sweet to rank after they had been on estuarine mud for a while. In the spring and summer they feed on sweet invertebrates on upland pasture where they breed. And a teal can turn from good to utterly succulent when fed on maize. I know, too, that the Solway gunners coveted the barnacle goose when it was on the quarry list. Their theory was that its flesh was made desirable via its preference for young, sweet grass.

But back to that January morning when a freezing light mist dropped in as we decanted from our vehicle in the shelter of a wood. There was a hint of light which produced a stage-effect iridescence in the mist. The geese could fly early and I instructed Peter to load his magnum but to leave the weapon open over the crook of his arm. I did the same, with the sack of decoys over the left shoulder.

We had crunched our way along a rutted track towards our hedge when a faint croak announced a greylag flying at tree-top height from left to right across our bows.

'Shoot!'* I cried, dropping the sack, closing the gun and swinging through in one movement.

The bird had hit the earth and lay inert when my guest, his gun still over his arm, declared, 'I thought I was supposed to do the shooting.'

Peter was, actually, a lightning shot. On walked-up grouse he was one of the fastest guns it has been my pleasure to shoot with and, the following season, made a point of wiping my nose on the moor. Perhaps, that morning, it was the Glenfiddich from the previous evening which was to blame?

His goose was expertly taken out of the first party of pinks to home into our decoy pattern not many minutes after we had arranged two hides in a convenient thick hawthorn hedge. An outside bird had given him his chance and it fell to the first barrel at 50 yards.

I purposely broke the end flight feathers on both wings so that the bird could be identified at the end of our stay. It would be made ready for the table by Peter's excellent wife cook, Vivienne, and honoured with a bottle or two of his French Margaux. I smiled at the thought but it was not to be. The game dealer came early and Peter's goose went into a can of Campbell's Highland Soup.**

JURA & ISLAY

On a trip to Jura, when I had become one of those favoured enough to be put on to a Royal stag, I had seen the huge gatherings of both barnacle and white-fronted geese on Islay – one has to cross Islay to reach Jura by car.

A party was duly organised for the following year to fit in a dual-quarry trip – stags on Jura followed by the Islay geese. Top Client was accompanied by two business associates. He would be footing the entire bill and the schedule was tight – only four days to fit in both species.

This time the roads were clear of snow but Lady Weather played her hand again in the shape of a force nine wind, enough to cancel the ferry.

*Had we been covert shooting my call would have been 'Over' – the recognised way to alert a game shot to quarry. However in the world of fowling, the first expletive has proved, over the years, to produce the necessary re-action.

**This was in the days before the sale of wild geese was made illegal.

ORWELL'S COTTAGE – *When stalking parties went by boat via the northern tip of Jura, to reach the Atlantic seaboard, the passage took them past the cottage where George Orwell wrote '1984'. This futuristic novel was composed here in 1949.*

After 24 hours storm-bound I hired a helicopter and flew my party into Jura. We were met by Lord Astor's butler on the lawn of his shooting lodge. My men were impressed.

In Gaelic Jura means 'Island of deer.' The place has a unique charisma and, the following day, after a boat trip past the cottage where George Orwell wrote '1984' and through the Corryvekin whirlpool to the raised pebble beaches on the Atlantic seaboard, my party opted to remain on Jura for the remainder of their already shortened trip.

We killed our 10 stags but there was, of course, the goose part of the deal to be honoured. A phone call to the Islay hotel easily reorganised the schedule. My stay with them would be extended from two to four days and I arranged for two goose-chasing pals to join me there. They would travel up by car and I would arrange to fly Top Client and his two friends back to their car on the mainland.

The Islay hotel was a winner. An absolute gem. It had been recently acquired by a young couple who were intent on building it up. They had secured shooting rights over vast tracts of the island where their guests were free to roam at will.

Highland Red Stag by Rodger McPhail – Stalking was often the main attraction for my clients on their trips north of the Border. A party of three would normally book 10 stags.

Besides a profusion of both varieties of geese (barnacle and white-fronted) there were ducks, grouse, pheasants, partridge, woodcock, snipe, hares and rabbits. This was their first year and the few Guns who had been early guests had obviously not plundered the territory.

Bruce, the proprietor, was not a shooting man and was greatly relieved when he learned we preferred to go it alone once he had shown us his boundaries. He had led us up a blind alley for our first roost flight but the next day we soon organised ourselves. Dave and Alan were outstanding wildfowlers. They had brought their dogs, fat Sally, a Lab, and the dynamic and incredibly well behaved Meg, the tiniest springer it has ever been my pleasure to shoot with.

Sally was too badly behaved to take into a goose hide, or on a goose stalk, but little Meg was totally unproblematic. Her only minus was the fact that a large whitefront gander was a bit much for her to carry far and she was sometimes forced to resort to dragging by a wing.

More misfortune was, however, to rear at the end of our second day. Alan's wife was rushed into hospital and he flew back home leaving Meg with us. The following day is, I feel, worthy of recounting in detail.

Pre-dawn found the remaining pair of us in a deep, steep-sided ditch alongside a grass field where we had spotted a large party of whitefronts the day before. The territory, on the westerly edge of the island, was ideal for goose ambushing – a patchwork of small fields each surrounded by the six foot ditches. With our silhouette decoys placed 30 yards out we waited in weather conditions definitely on the side of the geese – hardly a breath of wind but under a cloudy sky. At least the sun would not be out to make our presence too obvious in the bare culverts.

The faintest of calls announced a small party at first light but they were over the top of us and down to earth beyond the deeks before we could react. When I suggested crawling out of our ditch and inching slowly towards the bunch David's nod indicated that he was already contemplating the strategy. The springy, snuff dry turf felt like a luxurious carpet under our bellies as we took our time.

To shoot geese with someone who was so much in tune to one's own thinking is a real joy and, as soon as the feeding buzz abruptly ceased, we rose as one to our knees.

We had crawled to within easy range and the four shots rang out simultaneously. Four birds crumpled. Two to the right and two to the left. Without a word we collected our birds and slipped quickly back into the ditch.

The next party, in half light, chattered loudly and, as they swung directly over the decoys, we took another right and left apiece. This time there was a broad smile and a nod from my companion.

One more small bunch came to the field but, by now, it was full daylight and they were suspicious of our silhouettes. David dropped the nearest bird, still a long shot, as they wheeled away. Nine shots nine geese. Time for breakfast.

But there was more to come. As we reached the vehicle a party of 12 whitefronts pitched into the middle of a field about half a mile away. A stalk and drive looked favourable and the toss of a coin elected David to take to the ditches. I would give him 20 minutes and then motor round to put them up. There was no need to suggest where my companion should take up his position. He would know exactly where to be.

A light southerly breeze had sprung up by the time I started the engine. Stopping directly upwind I alighted and a slam of the door and a wave of the arms sprung the small bunch 200 yards away. Two birds dropped straight out coinciding with the bangs. Climbing into the passenger seat I was given a huge smile. 'Miller,' he declared, 'You and me are like gold and silver. And I am not telling you which you are!'

The afternoon found us on the extreme westerly tip of Islay sheltered from the increasing wind by a long rocky outcrop. Time to hunt the roe deer. We were looking for a beast each, a third for the departed Alan and a fourth for the hotel larder. David, eyes as sharp as the proverbial dung house rat, sighted an old doe moving up a long crag that separated moorland from the sea. A half-hour stalk took us almost within range when the beast crossed the march* off our territory.

Below, on a rocky promontory glinted a pool, no more than 20 yards across, black with duck. The binoculars revealed around 100 birds, mostly teal but with a sprinkling of mallard and pochard. As we made our way down the bare crag the birds exploded en masse and, after a brief circle, disappeared over the ridge.

The pool was in a hollow and totally sheltered from the prevailing wind. Its water was brackish and proved to have been filled by storm-lashed waves from the tidal sea now 20 feet below. There was nothing but ocean between this secret resting place and North America, 3,000 miles over the Atlantic. We lingered in this sheltered hollow listening to the surf pounding the rocks and soon small parties of teal reappeared trying

* March – an oft used term in Scotland to indicate a boundary. It is rarely used in England.

ISLAY WHITEFRONTS BY RODGER MCPHAIL – *On Islay the whitefronts had no set pattern – apart from dawn and dusk from and to their maritime roosts. During the day parties moved at random, feeding on the close-cropped grass.*

Mixed Bag on Islay – It was obligatory for all the Scottish safaris to include geese. The author shot barnacles (normally protected) and Greenland whitefronts on Islay in 1980. A year later all geese were protected on the island. Pressure from farmers had allowed the birds to be shot but now the tenants are paid to accommodate them. Left to right: the author, Dave Smith and Alan Latham.

to regain their cosy haven. We departed quietly and, by the time we had reached the ridge, the pool was already half filled with dark blobs.

AUDACIOUS STALKING

As we headed for the peat bogs, closer to the centre of the island, we found an old doe with a yearling calf. They were upwind with the low winter sun at our backs. Between us only flat featureless bog.

'If Alan were here I'd bet him I could stalk and kill both of those without even stooping,' David goaded.

'You are on for a bottle of Bruichladdich,' said I feeling totally confident that I would not be paying out.

There then followed an extraordinary display of the most audacious stalking. At a steady pace David merely approached his quarry totally upright, the low, glaring bright sun behind him. When one of the animals raised its head from grazing he would merely freeze until the feeding resumed. At 100 yards he dropped the doe. The younger animal ran only a few yards before halting and it, too, was despatched. He had used his staff to steady the aim.

'Its all about wind and sun,' grinned my remarkable companion. The Bruichladdich just happened to be in the motor and the top came off in an instant.

We found the group of five does an hour later after a hike into an area of hillocks. A crawl took us to within 120 yards when cover gave out. David told me which beast to take and we squeezed the trigger on the count of three. It was more than gratifying to see the supremo take two rounds to despatch his doe.

This was the last time I shot with David, this most talented of countrymen. While still in his forties he died suddenly. Not only was he an outstanding fowler and stalker but also an expert fly fisherman and taxidermist. I hope the preceding tales of his prowess are a fitting tribute to his memory.

The stirring sketch by Rodger McPhail of a party of geese heading low inshore (see page 141) epitomised the sort of chances that were to be offered on this most magic of islands. Dawn and dusk provided the greatest concentration of birds but just as stirring were the hours we spent in wild places during daylight.

We were the only shooters staying at the hotel and, throughout the week, we saw only one other party of Guns. The birds were little disturbed and flitted about continuously in search of feeding/resting grounds. We spent many hours on the sand dunes, in the far north of the island close to the shore, where there was an erratic flight line. There were regular sightings of the giant white tailed fish eagle that had been re-established as a breeding species a few years earlier.

An added bonus was the number of rabbits inhabiting the dunes. It was amazing how far 1¼ ounces of number 4's out of a full choke barrel will kill a bunny! Though we were stoked with 1⅞ ounces of BBs it was a quick enough job to swap cartridges when a rabbit appeared from a distant burry. Sometimes a stalk after the four legged rascals was necessary and the odd *Lepus lepus* met its end after a 20-minute crawl. Sometimes they escaped their doom when their pursuit was interrupted by the appearance of a skein of geese.

Into the bag that week went a great variety of game. I know that none of mine found time to go into the freezer. On our return we headed straight to Alan's home and presented him with a third of the bag. The remainder were gratefully accepted by friends.

A JURA ROYAL

I was once asked to name my favourite red stag stalking venue and it didn't take long to proclaim Jura. Its charisma is such that, once visited, the aura it exudes never goes away. The allure is born of so many facets. The dramatic naked Paps. The raised pebble beaches. The sinister Corryvekin whirlpool. George Orwell's romantic hidden cottage. The grave with its 126-year-old incumbent. The remote empty friendly caves and bothies where you make sure you replace the firewood you burn. Its rank wild goats with their yellow staring eyes. The sea trout in its tiny lochs. And not forgetting the malt whisky distillery.

Granted this book is not about stalking – but the pursuit was so much a part of many of my adventures that I make no excuse for including the dramatic incident where my professional stalker was hurled through the air by a wounded beast intent on killing him. It could so easily have ended tragically – and since we do dwell on emergency medical aids it serves to illustrate the efficacy of whisky as a wound dressing.

On this visit I was with long-time shooting companion John Tomlinson. John had been a part of my rough shooting team during my gun trade years. This was a hassle-free five days with no clients to nursemaid. Since the incident was so embarrassing for its protagonist I use fictitious names.

We were to take three stags each and the trip had a perfect beginning. After spinning a coin to decide who would go into the first stalk, I had won.

Less than an hour after leaving the Land Rover we had reached a plateau on the north-eastern edge of the island when Colin, the head stalker, sank to his knees behind a peat hag. A quick scan through binoculars brought a nod.

'We have a beast directly ahead but he's too far.'

Colin, then in his sixties, was a man of few words. I had been on many stalks with him and we followed, bent double, as he moved slowly behind a ridge parallel with the stag and its group of 20 hinds. After no more than 100 yards he stopped and crawled up into a vantage point. I awaited Colin's signal and wriggled into position on his left.

The stag appeared to be close on 300 yards and carried an unusually wide spread of beam (antlers).

'We canna get any closer.'

'How far?'

'275 yards.'

'I won't miss.'

Colin said nothing for what seemed like an eternity. After my glib statement it did not do my nerves any good at all. It was true that all my stalks with Colin over the years had produced clean kills but there is always a first time.

'Take him, but aim high.'

I was using a .270 Mannlicher and 4x40 Khales scope – a calibre with a very flat trajectory. When I took the shot the beast went straight down and as we rose to walk in John enquired, 'Is it a Royal?'

'Aye.'

Thank God Colin hadn't told me. I am sure the knowledge would have brought on the worst attack of buck fever I had experienced since my first kill long ago.

The bullet entry hole was exactly where I had aimed – directly over the heart. The soft nosed round had both ruptured this vital organ and also destroyed the spinal cord. Hence the beast's immediate collapse. After the gralloch Colin patted the stag's rump.

'Did you know him?'

'Aye. Since he was born. He was one of my best beasts but he's going back* and would have died in a hard winter.'

Later John killed a 10 pointer and the next day with David, the under-stalker in charge, I was again first in line. The morning was one of high wind, low mist and intermittent showers. It took three hours to get on to a beast and I was forced to shoot through swirling cloud at a mere 75 yards.

This time the stag sank slowly down where it stood. The stalker immediately ran forward ahead of John and me.

'Is it another Royal?' called John.

'Could be.'

Approaching from behind David grasped the antlers and instantly

* Going back – a stag regressing in physique.

A Royal Stag *– My last stalking trip to Jura resulted in my first, and only, Royal – a 12-pointer red stag.*

was hurled past me high off the ground. John's reaction was fast and a round through the neck killed the animal instantly.

By now David was back on his feet and unfastening his breeks with shaking hands. On the front of a thigh was an ugly puncture wound but worse than that his genitalia dripped blood. I thrust a full hip flask into a trembling hand and the hapless fellow lifted it towards his mouth.

'No. Pour it on the wound,' I ordered. That done, David gulped down the remainder and we headed rapidly for the all-terrain tracked vehicle. David limped only slightly and, after loading the kill, we sped downhill to one of the strategically placed first aid boxes. There a little dusting of penicillin powder was applied and a dressing strapped on the thigh.

On the way back to the lodge David revealed he was to be married in three days time. We refrained from offering help with his nuptials! Medical attention was quickly sought and the doctor declared that the whisky application was, 'the best thing you could have done'. Three days later both the wedding and the honeymoon proceeded as arranged.

The remainder of our stay went according to plan. The weather behaved and we dallied for a goose flight on Islay on the way home. I was unaware then that this would be my last trip to magic Jura and that, some 30 years later, my 12-year-old son and his school party would land on its shores only yards from where I had slain my Royal.

Jago was spending an outward bound week on tiny Rua Fiola, between the Scottish mainland and Jura when an overnight trip was made by boat. The group of 10, plus instructor, was dropped off on one of the raised beaches and trekked for three hours to sleep in a cave past the whirlpool. Breakfast was cooked on a driftwood fire before they were collected after their 24-hour sojourn.

Fittingly the mounted head of the stag graces the stairwell to Jago's bedroom. Perhaps, one day, he too will be privileged to hunt those same hills. Little will have changed on that timeless landscape.

RULES & REGULATIONS

To give the reader an idea of what faced me when I took on the challenge of educating novice Guns for my Scottish safaris, I reprint below a typical set of instructions issued by a formal driven shoot.

They were compiled by John Wilkins, shoot captain of the Winmarleigh Estate, near Garstang, Lancashire. Both John and his brother David are featured in Chapter 10 and both are just as keen as I am when it comes to goose chasing. Winmarleigh attracts its own often-considerable show of feeding geese from nearby Morecambe Bay and there is a policy of controlled shooting. Most are pinkfoot and do not feature in a driven shoot day when bags comprise mostly pheasant, partridge and ducks.

All Guns are instructed to read and observe the following:

SAFETY

When standing at peg:

a) look behind you and know exactly where beaters, cattle, sheep, buildings, roads, etc are, and never shoot towards any of them.

b) if you shoot behind, always take your gun over the top, and not across the line.

c) never shoot forward towards beaters and guns at an angle below 45 degrees, including of course ground game. Below 45 degrees, ricochet pellets can cause serious damage.

d) do not allow your shot to hit trees. This has an unsettling effect on people below the trees or inside a wood. Such shots are often dangerous with an increased chance of ricochet. (See page 152))

e) do not shoot at dropping or falling birds. It is highly dangerous to follow them down with your gun.

When walking gun

a) never shoot forward it is a driven shoot and such shots will be much more sporting for the standing guns. (Subject to alteration where necessary.)

b) never shoot ground game unless specified.

c) assist in keeping guns and beaters in line.

Never raise your barrels until you have decided that it is 100% safe to do so, count to 3 if you are not 100% sure.

If you send a guest, be responsible for him observing the above.

Sometimes, when I undertook the onerous crash courses for my new pupils, I had as little as two months to lick them into shape before we headed for our week in the Highlands. I refused to undertake the task in less time but these men were usually entrepreneurs and fast learners. On the actual trips there were few crass errors and most of them seemed to enjoy their experience. For some it was to start a sporting career with either gun or rifle.

Much of John's regulations do not, of course, apply to the goose shooter but it does help to outline what stringent rules the shooting man has, these days, to obey.

It is also an obligation of the shoot captain/manager or organiser to deliver a safety talk to Guns prior to a driven day. John pointed out that should these aforementioned shoot controllers fail to undertake this task they could be held liable and sued should an accident occur.

This is how John instructs his Guns as soon as they are assembled: he stresses that all must read and digest the 'Safety' list (already outlined above.) He also offers spare shooting specs and earplugs and indicates where the first aid box is kept. On John's shoots he aims to have two qualified first-aiders present all the time.

The following has also to be signed by all participating Guns.

NOTICE TO GUNS

Before shooting, please read the following notes:

LEGAL REQUIREMENTS

You must:
1. Hold a current Shotgun Certificate.
2. Hold a current Game Licence for shooting game.
3. Use non-toxic shot when shooting ducks, geese and other listed species.
4. Transport your gun in a slip on public roads.
5. Abide by all the other laws and legislation regarding shooting.

INSURANCE

You must have your own Personal and Liability Insurance (BASC or similar).

SAFETY INSTRUCTIONS

You must:
1. Conduct yourself in a safe and responsible manner at all times.
2. Ensure your gun is broken and unloaded between drives.
3. Never take a risky shot that may endanger people, property and animals.
4. Ensure adequate trajectory and avoid shooting at falling birds.
5. Never shoot into trees. This can have an unsettling effect on people below or beyond the trees and increases the risk of ricochets.
6. Avoid spent shot falling on roads or property.
7. Never swing your gun through the line.
8. Observe where pickers-up are prior to the commencement of the drive.
9. Remain on your peg until the drive is complete.
10. When you are a Walking Gun, assist in keeping Guns and Beaters in-line.
11. Never be under the effect of alcohol/drugs etc. when in charge of a gun.
12. Wear EYE and EAR protection.
13. Read the copy of the 'Risk Assessment' and 'Health and Safety Policy'.

GENERAL GUIDELINES

Please:
1. Act in a sportsmanlike manner at all times.
2. Be prompt on shoot days.
3. Wear suitable clothing and footwear. Camouflage clothing is unacceptable.
4. Be polite to fellow guns, beaters and members of the public.
5. Respect farmers' property:
a) Use stiles and gates wherever possible. Do not spring off the wire fences.
b) Remove empty cartridges and litter.
6. Keep shot game out of the public eye.
7. Report anything untoward to the shoot captain without delay.
8. Assist the pickers-up in making every effort to retrieve shot and pricked birds.
9. Be responsible for the conduct of your guest guns.

ANYONE WHO BEHAVES IN AN UNSAFE OR INAPPROPRIATE MANNER WILL BE ASKED TO LEAVE THE SHOOT IMMEDIATELY.

I have read and understood the above.

SIGNED................................ DATE ....
ADDRESS

All Guns are asked to collect their empty cartridge cases and mobile phones are to be used only in an emergency. (Hear, hear, did you say?)

THE SWEEP

In case all this sounds rather serious, John tells me it is appreciated. And there is, of course, a lighter side to the day: all shoots have, since shooting began, encouraged a sweep when guesses at the day's bag total are made.

Here John reveals his impish sense of humour. He is against excessive swearing and, to curb such social errors, anyone erring is precluded from the sweep and their contribution forfeited. One can only imagine the ensuing ribaldry.

After ingesting all John's vital conditions I congratulated him for so thoroughly addressing this side of a shooting day. In fact, there is only one point I would challenge – item 8 under General Guidelines.

Over the years I have been on some shoots when dog handlers have complained about Guns with over-zealous dogs. Sometimes they find the job they have gone there to undertake has already been done for them. It can and does cause unnecessary friction. But by all means help out if needed and if there is a pricked (wounded) bird and no picker-up is available, do send your dog.

John is a perfectionist in so many aspects of shooting. I tell later of his addiction to clay bird shooting (he has represented England in the Veteran's classes and it was he who coached my son at the age of 12. Though I was a professional clay bird coach myself, injury now precludes me from this pursuit and John was most willing to spend a considerable time helping knock Jago into shape.)

No one can be too careful with a loaded gun in their hands and safety is a vital part of clay bird training. It is then automatically transferred to live shoot days.

Soon after I came to live in The Lakes, before my youngest son was born, I joined a rough shoot and was horrified by the virtual non-existence of safety. I laid out a set of rules especially for the shoot but they were largely ignored and I left in dismay. The alarming thing was that the shoot organiser was a member of Her Majesty's constabulary!

RICOCHETS

John's warning of the dangers of shooting into foliage is, I feel, extremely pertinent and cannot be too strongly stressed. Unfortunately, I have first-hand experience of this, resulting in a hospital visit. It happened a long time ago and occurred thus:

Four of us had gathered on a rough shoot in the Fylde, near Blackpool, to walk up a series of duck ponds used by mallard as daytime retreats. Late September foliage still heavily clothed the trees round one pond in particular at the end of a wood.

I was to do the flushing and I gave careful and precise instructions where the other three Guns should stand in the field, where the birds would go out. At the given time I approached the pond, which contained around 30-40 birds. The main body flew out, to order, over the treetops and were greeted by the waiting Guns.

My chance came when one small bunch took off to one side, well away from the reception party. Maximum range was at almost treetop height and I tumbled a brace just before they lifted over the trees.

There followed urgent shouting. Someone had been hit! Unfortunately one of the Guns had decided not to stand where instructed and it was he who had been hit by ricochets from the leathery sycamore leaves. (I know they are leathery at that time of year. Boy Scouting tells you they are much kinder as emergency bum wipes in spring!)

The Gun had been hit in the face, fortunately missing the eyes, but a visit to the Out Patients was necessary to confirm there was no danger from shot that had penetrated the skin.

John Wilkins, very wisely, covers himself by offering shooting specs to his guests should such a million-to-one event occur.

The following diagram indicates the acute angle at which the offending pellets must have been deflected:

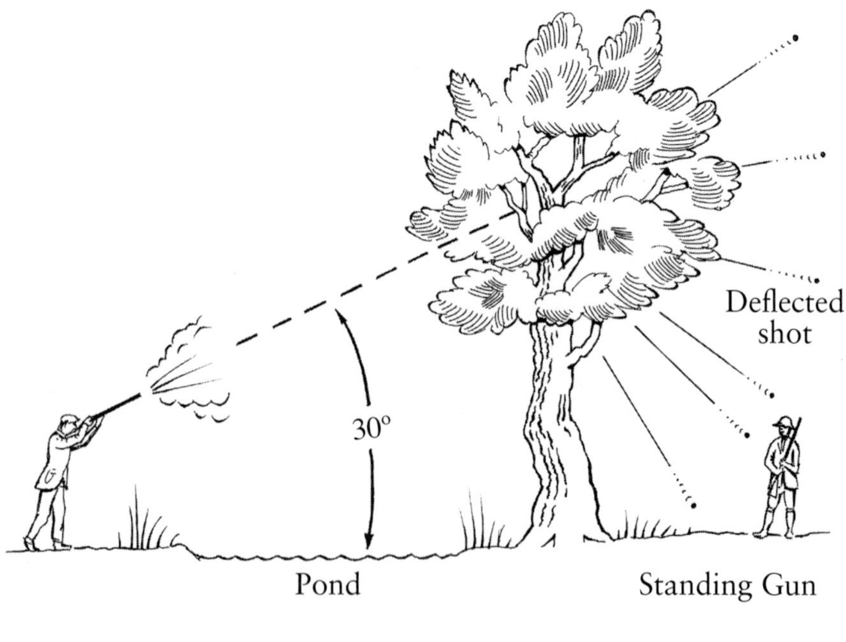

RICOCHETING SHOT – *this diagram shows how violently shot can ricochet.*

By now the reader will have deduced that I am an advocate of clay bird shooting as an invaluable aid when it comes to educating the shotgunner. My third son, Jago, began his tuition on clays four years ago, and, since then, has done plenty in the field also. I asked him to place the shooting disciplines he had experienced in order of preference. His reply was most significant and revealing.

Top of the list was wildfowling on the marshes, particularly when the geese are there. Next came flighting geese inland followed by rough shooting and pigeon decoying as equals. Equal in last place were driven pheasants and clays.

I suspect I was somewhat to blame for a youngster to place the inanimate and live quarry on one level. Perhaps he had listened to my scornful remarks about those whose only pleasure derived from shooting was to stand on a peg and have half tame birds pushed over them by someone else. Though I have shot more driven reared game than most, it has never really been for me. Now grouse (always a wild quarry) are, of course, a very different matter. My son still has this to come.

One must not, however, deride driven shooting out of hand. Is it not because of covert shoots that much of our countryside is preserved and the vermin kept at a sustainable level?

Happily, more and more we are seeing a divergence from reared shooting with the upsurge of wild bird estates as in Sandringham, Holkham and Barnard Castle to mention only a few thousand acres.

SHOOT CAPTAIN

It can be argued that the post of shoot captain has no part in goose shooting. I suppose, strictly, it is an appointment found only in the world of coverts and moor. And yet if you are lucky to be part of a syndicate renting inland goose shooting, or a private marsh, there has to be a gaffer. Since we goose chasers consider our sport to be on a far superior plane from that involving the pursuit of reared targets, perhaps our troop leader should have the title of brigadier instead of captain!

Whatever your preference it does not, of course, alter the fact that a shoot captain must possess a mixture of qualities. Foremost he has to be a diplomat. He must command respect and be able to impress on his team that his word is law.

Likewise every team member must accept and carefully ingest his delivery. Many Guns will be used only to handing out instructions in the course of their businesses. In the shooting world he must accept the status of a pawn and strictly toe the line in each and every respect. He who would refuse to be subservient must be sent home. I have seen it happen and have inwardly applauded.

MARKING

Marking fallen birds is a subject already brought up and is one of the most essential crafts every shooting man should do his utmost to master as quickly as possible. Once you have practised the routine of 'photographing' your marks, it will soon become second nature.

I must explain the terminology 'photographing'. First, establish where your quarry has fallen by using a landmark. It could be a tall tree, the end of a wood or a church spire. Do not, for God's sake, choose a cow or a sheep! Then, using the mind's eye, imprint where it is in relation to the chosen landmark.

Years ago I used to shoot with one of those natural countrymen who was a master of the art. He would direct the picker-up to the spot, perhaps 80 yards off, instruct him to stop and cry, 'If you bend down now your hand will touch it!'

It was not, of course, quite like that but the bird was never far off.

Remember, also, that it is not only your duty but also etiquette to mark fallen birds on a formal driven day. It is unlikely that you will be given a second invite if you do not remain on your stand if you have anything to pick until a dog man reaches you. And if there are likely to be any tricky retrieves remain until the bird is in the bag. It must be added, however, that on any prestigious shoot there are likely to be plenty of dog handlers behind you.

There are times, also, when you must leave your position if you are able to retrieve a wounded bird quickly. Nothing, be it vermin or game, should be neglected if it is not dead. A shooter's number one duty is to alleviate suffering as quickly as possible.

If you are on a rough shooting day and cannot effect the retrieval of dead game without a considerable delay there is a ploy I have often used to enable a more thorough search later. You may, for instance, be an outside Gun on a walked up grouse moor out of sight of the line. Roll a tissue handkerchief from corner to corner and tie it to a shoot of tall heather. It is the sort of retrieve any dog man will delight in when he returns with his pair of spaniels.

The epic retrieve is, of course, the goose that has collapsed stone dead when nearly out of sight. It cannot be too often stressed that it pays to watch a skein for as long as possible through a pair of binoculars if you or a companion has hit a bird. Marking at these sort of ranges can be a lottery but it is surprising how often diligence and tenacity is rewarded.

The earlier pages of this chapter will have given the reader some idea of the sort of pressure I was under when organising these safaris which often included raw beginners. After 10 years I gave them up. Happenings like the loch-roost incident, last minute cry-offs and the fact that I liked to share my precious time away from my shops with the likes of David Smith convinced me that life was too short to invite hassle.

The following few lines are more of a tongue-in-cheek postscript to safaris.

THE LODGE

There was a certain hunting lodge in wild Scotland which would rank as one of my all-time favourites as a retreat. Lie abed at night (and they truly had the most comfortable beds in the Highlands, as would befit Lords and Ladies of the realm) in late October and listen to the surf crashing onto the tide-worn boulders below your window. No sweeter music was ever composed.

I was careful who I took there for those last five days of the red stag season. Should I suspect that my charge would not be able to fully grasp the privileges to which he had been introduced, then I would select another venue.

Top Client was one of those privileged. In fact, such was his bearing that he would have found the wearing of ermine as natural as does a cock pheasant in all its finery.

On our journey north I always asked my chief guest (the financier) which bed chamber he preferred – the Christine Keeler or the Mandy Rice Davis room?

Inevitably back would come the query, 'Which has the more comfortable bed?'

Another titillation were the whisky all-ins dispensed by the butler in our peat water baths. Top Client always called for a third, but I would not allow over-indulgence on precious stalking trips. There was wine to be quaffed at dinner and a sore head was definitely not the recipe for total appreciation of the occasion when my companions were faced with a tricky belly crawl the next day.

The reader will, I hope, by now be grasping some idea of how difficult it is to answer the question, 'Which do you prefer: stalking or goose shooting?' There is an ethos or culture surrounding both. Suffice it to give both 10 x 10!

Chapter 7

'Retirement'

My so-called retirement merely marked the withdrawal from my gun dealership. The decision to sell up had come two years earlier than anticipated.

Plan A had been to head for the Lake District at the age of 50, there to go into the holiday cottage letting industry. This, I reasoned, would give me all the time I needed to shoot, fish and keep fit logging. Two marriages were behind me when, over a pint after a day's rough shooting, a close friend with an equal love of the outdoors asked what I planned for the future.

Roy was 15 years my junior, with a background in accountancy and computers. When I told him my thoughts he said he, too, was disenchanted with his current employ and fancied heading for the USA to explore its potential. 'Why not,' he suggested, 'make it a joint venture?' He reasoned that, between us, we would have a fairly hefty wedge of capital to impress our brothers on the other side of the Atlantic.

Great-winged Canadas, blue geese, snow geese, Ducks Unlimited, Alaskan salmon. They could all be my neighbours. My only first-hand experience of North America had been in the 1960s, when Mohammed Ali fought Joe Frazier in Madison Square Gardens, and I had nipped over with a bunch of pals. I liked what I saw. I met Ali after the fight and had him crying in pain when I shook the hand that had pounded his opponent for 15 rounds!

However, the realisation that, before one indulged in the niceties of life, one would have to start to again apply ones self to creating a viable business had me prevaricating.

'Why not buy an airbus ticket, fly around the States for a month and then decide?' suggested my entrepreneurial young friend.

So it was that October of 1980 saw us aboard a big silver bird bound for Florida. From there we city-hopped to Texas, to southern and northern

California, through Nevada to Boulder, Colorado.

Having established that an easily-funded sum would buy us a motel, a bar or anything in the leisure business, Roy's accountancy brain made it clear that failure would only be down to over-borrowing. We would not have to do this.

The US embassy was pleased to give us our 10-year visas, with an option to renew, and, in July '81, we were back in Denver, Colorado. Here the red carpet came out when the realtors saw the size of our account.

But it was not to be. After four months, and car journeys that took us to far away places in the Sierra Nevadas and The Rockies, we were heading back for Blighty. I missed Britain's countryside and understood why our USA cousins who loved field sports have such a passion for Scotland. Roy had plans to marry.

On the day we made our declaration to depart there were three days to go to August 12. The next day we were on a plane out of Denver and, 48 hours after that, I was once more flank gun on my brother's Scottish grouse moor!

Plan B swung quickly into place and, by the autumn of that year, I was the owner of a property in seven acres of hillside and woodland in my beloved English Lake District where red deer, roe deer and badgers shared my garden.

Plan A, for letting cottages, was shelved two years after meeting Annie – who was to become Mrs Miller mark three. Annie would occupy herself operating the house as a B & B while I would create the Lakes Shooting School.

I was to enter into partnership with the owner of a large South Lakeland estate and we intended to open one of the biggest clay grounds in the UK. Planners duly arrived with their decibel meters and, such was the topography, no readings were recorded, even at 100 yards.

However, fortunately the far-seeing planners gave a firm NO to the venture and, though initially miffed, I was later to be grateful for their foresight. Viz.; Sitting alone one early summer evening on the shores of Rydal Water, intent on watching a considerable flock of resident Canada geese honk their way in to roost, my reverie was most irritatingly disturbed by a sudden, and then incessant, distant popping. It was a long-established Lakes clay pigeon club going about their weekly shooting programme five miles away over a mountain range! Such were the quirky acoustics in that part of the world that gunshots travelled vast distances along the most tortuous routes and, innocently, I could have been a perpetrator.

My observation of the honkers had not been out of idle curiosity. I had been appointed an official National Trust goose controller and had the right to roam over an area heavily visited by both Canadas and greylags, of which there were several hundreds. A poor substitute, maybe, for the real thing – following their migratory cousins – but it was a chance to be at close quarters with the great birds.

Nor were my Scottish goose grounds too far for lightning 24-hour visits. The guest house proved to be a huge success and I was well occupied lending a hand tending the grounds and cutting enough timber to keep a giant wood-burning boiler ticking throughout the year. It gobbled six tons of four-foot logs a month and was a wonderful excuse for spending many hours in the forest with tractor, trailer and chainsaw.

A regular place in the village cricket team, the establishment of wonderful duck flighting on a two-acre tarn, plus regular invites to fill in on a prestigious driven pheasant shoot, made life blissful. Little did I know that, at the relatively early age of 57, it would be transformed so drastically. But, before that incident, there were many happenings to make life interesting.

STABBED

In the chapter Lancashire Geese I tell of how I was able to return a favour to a farmer who had let me fish in his carp pond while I was still a schoolboy. I now recall another good turn I was able to do for a friend who provided me with some goose shooting when I went to live in Lakeland. Unfortunately it was to lead, albeit indirectly, to my friend's near demise.

Rafe (*fictitious*) had introduced me to a Cumbrian farmer who had permanent goose trouble. Resident Canadas and greys were taking a large slice of his precious sheep pasture and it would be down to me to keep them away. This was besides my similar commitment with the National Trust. It was an all-year round job (but with shooting* seasons strictly adhered to) and I only added the occasional bird to the freezer. Little charisma surrounds these home-bred residents but they are certainly a welcome addition to the wildfowl population when they flight on to nearby Morecambe Bay.

My chance to repay Rafe came with a call from Bruno, an Italian trophy hunter who had been one of my more affluent clients in my gun dealing

* Canada geese are now classed as pests and DEFRA encourage their shooting all year.

years. Ever alert to the possibility of a new opening, Bruno wondered if I might have a contact who could find him some roe stalking in The Lakes. Aware of his generous monetary reward for outstanding services I put him in touch with Rafe, who had access to a great deal of stalking.

To say that Bruno and Rafe jelled would have to be one of the all-time understatements. A high-flying Italian business magnate and a Cumbrian stalker would not appear to be the ultimate mix. But it was. Both were passionate when it came to deer and Rafe was soon travelling the world with his new Latin soulmate in search of exotic species.

It was while involved in a moufflon hunting trip in The Alps that Rafe almost met his maker – not high on the face of the Eiger but in the not-so-friendly streets of Islington! On his way home he had missed the shuttle from Heathrow to Manchester and, rather than hand his benefactor a hefty airport hotel bill, he went to seek more modest quarters. I let Rafe tell his own story:

'It was around midnight and I was on foot, heading for some digs I had used before, when a blow to the back of my head knocked me to the ground. I instinctively kept hold of my suitcase and, as I rolled over, a youth kicked me in the kidneys trying to make me let go. Another youth was pulling at the case and I could see a knife in his hand.

Then the first one, who was holding a baseball club, made his second mistake, (the first was to hit the Cumbrian iron man) he tried to kick me in the same place. I grabbed his foot and a quick twist dislocated his ankle. He was screaming as I rolled up his leg and did the same to his knee joint. I was wearing heavy shoes and, for good measure, I stamped my heel on his face and gave it a good screw. It stopped the noise!

I knew the knife would be coming from his mate but I wasn't quite quick enough. It sliced my cheek and sunk into my shoulder as I deflected the blow. By then I had reached his neck with the other hand and smashed his head into the wall. (I learned later that it had fractured his skull.) Then I felt a hand on my shoulder, 'It's all right sir, it's the police – we'll deal with it,' a voice said.'

But Rafe's troubles were a long way from over. The pair were rushed to intensive care and Rafe was locked in a police cell.

'The police suggested I should have used less force so I asked them if that's what they would have done if someone was trying to stab them. They then found my gutting knife in my suitcase. There was a trace of blood and when they asked what I had been doing they didn't seem very convinced.'

Rafe was in his cell for four and a half hours. What desolation he must have felt so far away from his cosy hillside cottage. Then his gaolers made contact with their police colleagues in Cumbria.

'When they let me out they said they had been told to be 'very careful' how they handled me and that was it. I didn't even get a lift back to the airport!'

One cannot help thinking that if more law breakers received the same sort of treatment meted out by Rafe, there would be a lot less crime on our streets. It is pretty damned certain that there will be at least two who will never attempt it again!

ROAD CASUALTY

Not long after this affair the same Rafe was involved in another incident concerning the law and a miscreant. This time it happened here in The Lakes.

Breakfast was long finished in our B & B and I was feeding the hens on the leftovers (if our friends from the USA are in town there are always heaps on the plates) when a guest nipped back to collect something from his room. He bore a bewildered expression. 'I've just witnessed an amazing thing in your village, Edward.'

He went on to tell me that he had been at the petrol station when a car pulled up and a man jumped out. 'He was well dressed but before he had moved a couple of steps a Land Rover pulled up and out sprang another chap who seemed very angry. He grabbed the first guy by the front of his jacket and with one hand picked him up and sat him on the Rover bonnet. Then, after a few angry words, he just tucked him under his arm like a bundle of laundry and marched off to the police station over the road.'

From the description my guest gave me, the chap doing the bundling had to be Rafe.

I could have phoned the station. The sergeant was a shooting pal but this was a Sunday and Rafe would be in my local come evening.

Word had got round by the time he arrived and there was a fair crowd, but we had to wait for Rafe to down his first pint before the tale unfolded. It transpired that he had been called out to a road casualty (a wounded deer) three miles beyond the village and was in a hurry.

'I came up behind this chap dawdling in the middle of the road and flashed and pipped. He just gave me the 'V' sign.'

The act went on for a mile until the two vehicles reached the petrol station. 'I would not have stopped. You get to an injured animal fast, but the idiot gave another 'V'.' The next scene we know until Rafe found the sergeant behind his desk.

'Dennis (the sergeant) knew about my call-out and after I told him about the silly b******s' driving he told me to get on with my job. He would deal with the problem from there.'

It transpired that the errant motorist was let off with a warning and no more bad driving incidents were reported. Off the record the sergeant told me later, 'The poor fellow was scared stiff and I had to sit him down with a cup of water. He spilt most of it and was glad to get off with a caution!'

The 'road casualty'?

It was a roe with a broken foreleg. After despatching the unfortunate creature with a humane pistol Rafe dressed it for auction at the next village cricket club fund-raising jamboree.

A STALKING HORSE

Knowing of my all-consuming passion for goose chasing, a long-time friend once asked me to compare red stag and goose stalking. We hear of both goose fever and buck fever and, if I were asked which was the most overpowering I would instantly have to say the latter – just.

I have known tyro deer stalkers to shake so much at the moment of truth, when a stag is in the telescopic sight crosshairs, that they have been unable to squeeze the trigger. Forehead has lowered onto arms and I have even been obliged to take the rifle quickly from their grasp and do the job. If the stalker, who has led you to the beast, says shoot: you shoot.

But the intoxicating thrill of being on the hill, perhaps on some remote Scottish island, and giving advice, is for others to write about. I would never pretend to know enough about deer stalking to commit any guidance to paper.

There is, however, just as much satisfaction in pulling off a difficult crawl up to a bunch of ever-alert geese as there is in moving close enough in to a stag to despatch it cleanly. That both 'fevers' remain with you forever is fact, if you are a true countryman, though their effect is lessened by the years.

With geese there are many disappointments. It would need both hands to count the number of times I have stalked a single goose, for perhaps up to an hour, to find it had departed without sight or sound when I have reached the vantage point. But never is there despair. The thrill is in the chase and when success does come it is sweet.

Certainly one of my most memorable stalks happened with Richard in the 'retirement' years. It is memorable, I suppose, for the outrageous method employed.

We had drawn a blank at dawn and, after a wholesome but hurried breakfast, had returned to the field where we had left the decoys. A small bunch of pinks were feeding close to the silhouettes and departed noisily.

There had been a hard frost and, after we had spent half an hour crouched in a bare ditch, a singleton appeared from the direction of the moor at a great height. Our calls brought a quick response and the bird pitched in 100 yards away. Now we had the ultimate in pulling power – decoys and an animate goose. But after an ever-more chilling wait, knee deep in freezing water, the sky remained empty.

The singleton was still feeding contentedly, albeit now further out, when a herd of bullocks in the field behind us, decided to check us out. That was when I suggested we might try the stalking-horse method. I was wearing a copious overcoat and, in whispered tones, persuaded Richard to drape the back end over his head while we exited in stooped mode out of the ditch.

Obligingly the bullocks remained in a bunch and we headed towards our quarry, all the while pausing and issuing the occasional low 'moo' from beneath my face veil. The hapless bird did no more than raise a quizzical head once and was despatched by 1⅞ ounces of Remington BBs as it jumped at around 45 yards.

I suppose an equally bizarre event occurred on the morning when Richard thought I had finally flipped. Yet again a vicious nor'easter crucified the extremities when we arrived, pre-dawn, at our bale hides.

We were still in the days of the easily handled rectangle bales of straw and, even though it should have been cosy enough in my tiny lair, I was so frozen I feared it would put me out of combat. With dawn a good way off I gathered a bundle of straw and, in a deep rut where there was no danger of stubble ignition, I lit a jolly blazing mini-inferno. The conflagration was out of sight, I hoped, of Richard behind my hide and in no time I had cast off my convulsive shivers. Then came the bellow from behind my sanctum.

Alerted by the smoke Richard had scurried over thinking I had set fire to myself while stoking my pipe. 'Now I know you have flipped,' said my bemused long-suffering companion as he stomped off.

There was more to follow. Now thoroughly warmed I concentrated on the job in hand and was rewarded by the faintest shadow pitching in 100 yards down the field. Knowing I had the dark background of a wood behind me I moved cautiously and silently towards the bird. It was the dimmest of blobs on an ever-lightening stubble.

With around 20 yards covered the bird jumped and I fired into the blackness a yard above its head. The response was instantaneous and a large pinkfoot lay stone dead on the stubble. Richard, however, had not seen my covert exit from my hide and again thundered, 'Now what the bloody hell are you up to?'

'Goose shooting,' I called smugly and carefully paced out the distance – 94 yards. Later inspection revealed BBs through the head.

BULL FIELD

That morning was to provide another mystery event. We collected three more geese between us and were about to pack up when a bunch of around 30 pinks appeared over the Scots pines and set their wings for the decoys. Unfortunately I was caught out in the open and, though I lay quite still with my face in the stubble, they took alarm and Richard was able to connect with only one barrel at extreme range. The bird swung out of the skein and, half a mile away, collapsed with a thump into the middle of the bull field where three of Scotland's finest specimens were in residence. A quick scan through the binoculars confirmed that the bird was totally inert. We would discuss its retrieval later.

After gathering the decoys we made a quick detour to report our efforts to Rab, who was ploughing nearby. Then we headed for the bull field, en-route to breakfast. The plan was for Richard to attract the three gentlemen from over the fence while I drove into the field to make a hasty retrieve. But nowhere was our goose to be seen – not a feather and, by the time I had done several sweeps of the territory, the bulls were on to me. All I can remember is that I did make it back to the road unscathed.

But what of the goose? After breakfast the mystery unravelled. Rab's aunty had seen our bird drop on her way to feed the hens and, realising the problem we might have, had kindly walked into the bull field and collected it. She had hung it in the shed next to the rest of the morning bag. (It is a contention that a bull will not attack the female of our species. Aunty had very kindly proved it again that morning.)

TEA OR COFFEE?

Throughout my association with Ponkey's I had, up to this point, been only once on my own for the geese. It was in the early 1980s soon after my arrival in The Lakes and I was on a special mission.

Running a cricket team then, as now, is a costly business even if it is merely a village eleven. I'd had a brainwave – a disco night in a local inn where the food would be largely free. A friend had promised a saddle of venison and I would provide the fowl to make a game terrine. The law says that geese cannot be disposed of for profit but, of course, I had first to embark on a successful hunt.

The old sages said we should wait for the fowl part of the dish to arrive before the tickets were printed. My confidence touched about seven out of ten in favour of success

Richard was happy for me to make my lightning raid and, by mid-morning, on October 1, I was free to climb into the Subaru and head north across country on empty roads. Rab was baling near the road. He pointed towards the belt of Scots pine. 'They are in the field below. About 3,000 and there's more arriving by the hour.'

Those were the days before stubble burning had been rightly banned. Rab had torched the field in a high wind and the flames had spread so rapidly that they had left the high grain spillage in long piles between the furrows. 'They seem to like toasted barley,' grinned Rab.

The pinkfoot were feeding close to a dry stone wall below which I knew was a convenient bed of thick nettles. I parked the vehicle 200 yards away, behind a spinney of beech trees, and, as I rounded its corner, the whole pack lifted with a deafening clamour. As one, they made off to the moor above, where there was tundra-like short grass to be cropped.

I had half expected the birds to have been feeding on the moor as they arrived from their northern breeding grounds. This was their normal procedure but the grain was lying in such copious quantity that they had chosen this easier and abundant option.

I settled between the nettle bed and the wall with the sun and a stiff westerly on my back. It was cosy on the dry bank and the dog was well hidden. There were three hours to go to dusk and the 12 shell decoys should pull the birds in to range.

Black Lab Briodie warned me of the return of the first bunch. Around 50 pinks were topping the firs half a mile away. They were at extreme range as they came directly overhead and I deliberately picked two old birds. The skein held a high proportion of young, easily detected by their extreme undersize.

Briodie had them back in a trice, fine birds in the peak of condition.

Within five minutes another party had repeated the procedure before the wind swung suddenly round to due south and increased considerably. This altered the flight path and the next bunch of eight swung wide off the moor and came in low past the beech spinney. I had to stand to take my shots over the wall and, after dropping the lead bird as it crossed over the decoys, my second barrel succeeded only in clipping another. The wall was high at this point and the ground on my side sloped sharply.

There was no way over for the dog and I sent her 80 yards to the gate. She looked back for directions as soon as she had leapt the five bars and I directed her with a straight arm and a loud, 'Get on.' A three-year-old long-limbed slender Labrador in full stride is one of the finest sights a shooter may behold and Briodie was on to the strong runner in seconds.

I deliberately left her to sort out the gate and wished I had a camera as she cleared it, bird in mouth, with a good foot to spare.

As I sent her back for the first bird I stood on tiptoe to peer over the wall and was amazed to be greeted by TWO dead pinks, two feet apart! Six shots and seven birds. All that summer pigeon shooting had paid off!

I was looking for a dozen geese to take back but, with the wind change, the pattern had altered. The birds were now in much smaller lots and some in singles.

They were dropping in further out and although Rab had left three lots of bales in the centre of the vast field they were of little use. The birds were preferring a hollow out of the wind. My only hope would be to lie full-length against a wire fence where tussocky grass grew a foot high.

Briodie was left in the vehicle and I was thankful I wasn't lying out there in December. I was on a hilltop and there was zero protection from the wind. Four more birds were added to the bag in the next hour before they stopped coming. The kills-to-cartridge ratio had, however, plummeted. I was well concealed but each time I took a shot I had to gain a kneeling position,

Dawn saw me back on the field, tucked into one of Rab's bale hides. There was enough room for Briodie and now the capricious wind had swung to a chilly north. It was still strong enough to keep the birds low and the first bunch of five swung straight in to the decoys at first light. Two more lightning retrieves were none too soon, as another small lot followed the same path as the first.

With 15 birds in the bag for the two flights I stopped. There was just time to nip to the next farm to look for a brace of pheasants before heading home.

As I reached the edge of a wood, bordering a stubble field, a tractor appeared through the gateway. It was Rab and, as he dismounted, he was growling like only Rab can growl. He reckons to like we Sassenachs about as much as a Rangers fan likes a Celtic supporter.

'I had a job catching ye. I thought you were awa. Tea or coffee?' He held a giant flask, a box of tea and coffee bags, plus two hot bacon rolls wrapped in foil.

'Tea please. The finest drink to pass an Englishman's lips.'

'F*** the English.'

'Thank you Rab. I suppose you'd piss in it if I weren't looking!'

That pleased him and he spilled half the mug with his convulsed laughter before it was brewed.

But how true that we English regard tea as the elixir of life. The other day I phoned a long-time keeper pal soon after winter dawn. Isobel answered.

'Have I woken you?'

'No. I am up at six thirty every morning to make a cup of tea.'

'Surely you get Norman to do that for you?'

'He doesn't get it right.'

'Ah. Are you like me. Very strong but with lots of milk?'

Her reply had me feeling very sorry for my old pal Norman. 'It all depends on what mood I am in!'

GOODBYE BRIODIE

I have related the remarkable prowess of Labrador Briodie and I feel she is worthy of a few more lines. She joined the Miller family because it had become evident that springer Gemma needed a companion. She became bored and even dejected when not in action with the gun. I put the word about and soon Briodie arrived, partly trained and only needing experience.

It meant that the diminutive Gemma could watch as her new long-legged pal retrieved those winged ganders. She could, indeed, clear a four foot fence with a goose in her mouth.

Her remarkable nose was demonstrated one night towards the end of that fateful season that was to mark my sudden, albeit temporary, retirement from shooting – I refer to my cycling accident. In fact, it was probably the last time Briodie was to retrieve a duck.

We were on my home shoot and had finished picking up after an excellent evening flight when a guest Gun said he felt he may have a bird down in the valley below the pond he had been manning. His dog had drawn a blank but I sent Briodie out in the direction he indicated from the edge of the water. It involved the surmounting of a high dry stone wall, crossing a road and then another tricky wall to descend into a steep rough pasture. We had a five-minute walk back to the vehicles and had almost reached them when Briodie padded up with the inert mallard drake.

But, perhaps, her greatest asset was her understanding when I needed her to do a special task. Scattered over around 100 hundred acres, we had a series of ponds, four of which were fed for ducks. They were situated beyond various hillocks and could be shot without disturbing the others. Sometimes a great clamour would come from one of these other waters and, if the bag was poor, I could point Briodie towards the racket and tell her, 'Get on.'

She never failed to flush the pack even when she may have had to travel a quarter of a mile in total darkness. By employing a duck call, it guaranteed more sport and sometimes resulted in six to 10 extra ducks in the bag in the space of a minute. The ploy was to allow the first wave of birds to settle before shooting those still coming in. There was then time to reload and often take another right and left. I hasten to add that this was a practice rarely employed – only undertaken when guest Guns had seen poor sport. They were always well impressed.

Though Briodie was fated to retrieve no more ducks, her life then took an interesting turn. Four months after the end of that season I had my crash and my second son William, then aged 26, came home to see me back to fitness.

His duties were not inconsiderable. They included the extensive grounds to be tended and tons of logs to be harvested for the winter. He took over the log cabin which was tucked behind a belt of trees in the garden, but he rarely slept in it. His bed was a blanket under the stars next to his campfire unless it rained. And his companion? Briodie.

The pair became inseparable. Will caught trout from the hillside tarn and Briodie shared them grilled over their wood fire.

There was no shooting for me the following season as I underwent intense physiotherapy and, after 12 months Will was heading for the USA.

He was then building classical guitars for a living and was told that Santa Fe, New Mexico, was just about the best place in the world to care for his fine veneers. There was no humidity in Santa Fe and they had warped for fun in Cumbria's damp climate.

For a short time Briodie remained in the UK but it was not long before Will had shelled out £350 to fly her over the water. 'He wouldn't have done it for a girl,' cried his mates!

Will did not follow his father down the shotgun trail, nor did my first-born, Jonathan, whose passions instead are rugby and running up Lakeland fells, but his early training had turned him into a fly-fishing addict. The hills of New Mexico were full of trout and Briodie rode in his pickup with the canoe on its roof.

Eventually Will turned his skills to making bespoke furniture and Briodie languished in the cool of his workshop as she grew older. When it was too hot she ambled over the field and swam in a cool stream.

When she was 15 Will had some bad news. The dog had a malignant growth on her neck. It had been removed but her end was near. There was more to follow. She was then bitten by a black widow spider and was in a coma.

Two days later Briodie was running around, recovered her appetite and lived another two years. How and why no one knows. Her end came one day when she had gone for her swim. She didn't come back and Will found her, as though asleep, in a hollow half way to the stream.

As I write these lines, 14 years after his departure, Will still resides in New Mexico for part of the year and spends the rest of his time in the Caribbean, taking out parties of Americans in his charter fishing boat. (Alright for some eh?)

NOVEMBER GEESE

I give you now an extract from my records towards the end of Richard's shooting days.

By the time he reached the age of 50 his attitude towards his much-loved geese was leaning heavily towards conservation. He had been making his excursions to Ponkey's for 20 years and now steadfastly refused to visit during the 'easy' period.

I am positive that this policy helped to swell the numbers using the terrain. No other gunners were permitted on to this land which had become sacred to the visiting pinks and greys. Meanwhile much of the remainder of Scotland was harried relentlessly by the rapidly swelling pool of professional goose guides and independent visiting fowlers. Such were the huge rents proffered to landowners and estates that it was difficult to say no.

Richard's Utopia remained at peace and the Icelandic flocks grew fat on the spilt barley. Most were obliged to depart only when the last stubble was ploughed in, usually by the beginning of November.

'Time for a trip,' Richard had announced on the phone. The date 6-11-83. I had been longing for the summons to reach my Lake District home during every week of what had been a gale-torn autumn. Trade in that area of Scotland for Richard meant he could do a 24-hour recce before we met at HQ.

I had found my companion hard on closing time in the bar of the cosy inn close to our lodgings. As I had hurried along the country lane to the hostelry, under a fast waning moon, I could swear I heard the faint sound of feeding geese. Was it merely a wound-up imagination playing tricks, for the direction from which I felt I had heard the chatter was not from a quarter which normally held geese?

Richard detached himself from a huddle of farmers in the corner of the smoke-laden bar. His beaming visage told me he had extra good news even before he spoke. It was revealed that I had, indeed, heard geese not far from the front door of the inn. I was also to hear a confession.

Richard had arrived on schedule and had spotted around 500 pinkfoot feeding on land which had become forbidden territory following the purchase of the 1,500 acre farm by an English family three years ago. The new tenant had quickly established a keepered game shoot on land which had, over the years, yielded many productive dawn sorties. In spite of past rebuffs Richard had called at the farm and received consent. 'Provided you remove them immediately. They are on stubble which I have under-sown with grass.'

It meant Richard had to plan his first ambush the following morning – the day I was to arrive. Richard told me he had been in position early but the birds had flown late in one flock – they were feeding both under a waning moon and during the day – and he had collected only a pair. They were, however, keen on the sweet field and he had seen them go back there later. The owner had agreed to two visits and we therefore stood a chance at dawn the following day.

Richard had discovered that the birds were using a loch well inland from our territory and, because of the disorganised feeding pattern, reckoned they would not come again until well after dawn. That did not deter us from being in place before first light. We had merely to traverse only one field in front of HQ to reach the spot and my companion insisted I use the spilt heap of straw where he had hidden himself the previous morning.

My hiding place was conveniently sited 100 yards from a low stone wall and Richard tucked himself into the thick undergrowth at its base on the flight line.

The day was almost windless and misty and, with barely a chink of light in the sky, there came a warning honk from my companion. It was enough for me to be ready for a snap shot at two pinks before they disappeared against the backcloth of a nearby fir wood. Only one bird climbed back into vision a good 60 yards away, and another hurried swing saw it tumble stone dead onto the stubble. I was on form!

For the next hour the sky remained empty. There was only the merest zephyr of a cold northerly and the odd snowflake drifted down as we were contemplating breakfast. It looked as though the battalion had found fresh pastures but then Richard's glasses picked out a long black line coming in from the direction of the distant mountain range.

The breeze was up their tails and the birds were overhead in quick time. It looked as though the whole 500 were in the clamouring horde and, after two high altitude circles, they didn't like the sprinkling of snow on our decoys and headed off. Richard was able to pull out a low singleton as they departed and we watched them through the glasses in case they settled inside the considerable compass where we had permission to operate.

Our luck was in. When almost out of sight the party made a 360 degree turn and headed back in our direction. Three fields away – they are 100 acre fields in that area – they wheeled several times and pitched in behind a fir wood.

We agreed there would be little chance of a stalk on the bare grass where the birds were feeding and I volunteered to make a wide detour to hopefully push the geese towards Richard. We had collected the decoys but posted the three dead birds near the straw heap where Richard buried himself in its cosy layers. By now it had stopped snowing but we felt we stood a better chance in full daylight by using the genuine articles as decoys since the birds were well spooked.

The plan worked to perfection. The pack lifted with a deafening clamour as I came up behind them, and a minute later two black shapes detached themselves from the sky followed by a double report.

MUSHROOMING

On our way back we filled two upturned decoy shells with a bounty of fresh mushrooms – another regular bonus in this land of plenty. What joy there is in mushrooming if one is a true countryman. If you are lucky enough to live where this delicious fungi proliferates, mushrooming is something that comes as naturally to an infant of the soil as suckling at a mother's breast!

Mushrooms were, of course, a highly favoured feature of our Solway days. There they were in great profusion but the trained eye can spot edible fungi at 100 paces in the most unlikely of places. On one occasion we were heading for goose territory along a remote Highland road when I yelled 'stop' to the driver. To the right, in the sheep cropped verge, I had spotted a giant white dome.

'Reverse please,' I requested. 'I have just found tonight's first course.' I was staying with a friend and there would be 10 for dinner that night.

Through his rear mirror my host saw the dome. 'It's an old football.'

But it was no football and the huge horse mushroom made soup for all with seconds to spare. I am sure it would have been a record, for I reckon it weighed in at over a pound and was by far the biggest specimen I have come across in a lifetime of hunting these delicacies.

But back to our November geese. With permission to tread the sacred turf now expired we decided to set our decoy pattern in the adjoining mushroom field, which was part of Ponkey's, on the next morning. Cover was sparse. More snow had come in the night and made our shell decoys visible from a great distant. We had toyed with the notion of taking the six dead birds across the field in the 4WD but the ground was extremely soft and we would have caused an unnecessary and unwelcome scar on the pasture. No farmer appreciates thoughtless abuse of a grass field when it can be avoided. I have always preached the adage, 'Come and go as though you had never been! Damage nothing and remove all traces of your visit.'

The only easy place for concealment was on the edge of a low fir wood, where I elected to go, while Richard took his chance in a shallow depression in the middle of the exposed field, where the sheep had scratched out a banking in their search for soil minerals. Our cammo netting was too bulky for the sparse cover and Richard used a small piece of sacking propped up at eye level with a short stick.

In my snug den, sheltered from the biting northerly, I marvelled at my companion's devotion to his task as dawn broke. Experience told him a sharp-eyed goose would spot him easily against the white back cloth and he remained motionless in his shallow pit. Gritty determination paid off. A party of five pinks stole up from behind the covert figure and passed over his form without wavering. I had seen them coming and even when I employed my call as a warning Richard remained inert. The episode should have been filmed to demonstrate the art of concealment!

As the tough old warrior rolled onto his knees there was time only for one hurried shot and the bird folded up dead among the decoys.

Under these conditions undoubtedly the ideal decoy would have been a set of silhouettes. Later in the season I would have included a sack full but November snow, even on Scotland's severe east coast, was the last

SNOW AMBUSH – *This shallow hide proves how the merest of cover can work provided the Gunner remains still. Richard retrieves a November goose. The sacking was essential as a wind break. The force of the nor'westerly is indicated by the bent rushes.*

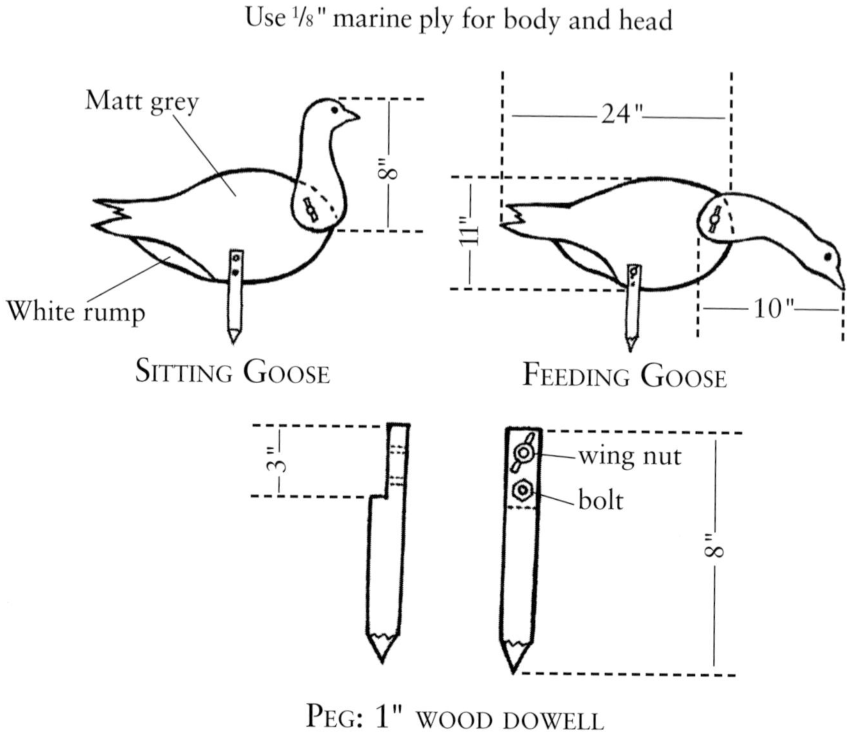

Silhouette Goose Decoys – here are the measurements and instructions for making a simple silhouette goose decoy.

thought I had in mind. They are useful in rain too, when the backs of the shell variety glisten unrealistically.

Only when the white stuff is driven horizontally by a cyclonic blizzard is it sometimes necessary to nip out from your cover and give the weather side of silhouettes a wipe. If, however, you use round single pegs to plant your decoys it should keep them in to the wind. At a time like this the white coating can even enhance the colouring when the lower parts take on the appearance of a white rump.

If you do decide to add to your decoy bank by manufacturing a quantity of these sometimes deadly aids, do make them slightly larger than life.

I have found that ⅛-inch marine ply (the waterproof variety) to be the best with around 18 in the feeding position and two with head up. They also work out at a fraction of the cost of the imported shell jobs.

The bird was to be the last goose from our short trip – more snow fell later in the day and the grey army went in search of greener pastures. We indulged in a productive pigeon session over a field of neeps where the tops still showed, then we headed for the Border with a haul of seven pinks, 20 pigeons and a carrier bag apiece of mushrooms.

LAKELAND PIGEONS *by Rodger McPhail – When there is a bumper crop of acorns in the Lake District woodpigeons invade in their thousands. The fruit of the oak is also a favourite food of the mallard. If you have an oak tree on your flight pond you are in luck.*

At this juncture the reader may appreciate my recipes for mushroom soup and pigeon paté:

Mushroom soup

Fry a couple of rashers of dry-cured bacon until crisp (avoid supermarket bacon which is full of moisture). Then lay them twixt a crust and trough down as a chef's perk. Sauté an onion in the bacon fat until soft. Add fresh garlic and the washed, dried, but unpeeled, mushrooms. Cook for several minutes to intensify the flavour with freshly ground black pepper. Add milk and liquidise until desired consistency is acquired. Correct seasoning.

If, like me, you are a garlic addict you can add a few more cloves crushed and lightly sautéed in butter. You can, of course, freeze the soup in thick polythene bags if you are lucky enough to have an excess. Powdered milk can also be used without losing any flavour.

Pigeon paté

After that trip I would doubtless have added pigeon paté to the freezer too. I use two preparation methods – long and short versions.

The easiest is to fillet off the breasts and sauté until pale pink in oil, garlic and black pepper. Cook a chopped onion in the juices until brown then add chicken stock. Simmer for 20 minutes with a bouquet garni. Chop breasts and pass through liquidiser using the stock and contents to correct consistency.

The longer method is to casserole a quantity of whole dressed birds after sealing in hot oil. Use a slow oven with a liberal helping of onion in the dish. A few wild mushrooms give an extra dimension.

De-bone the meat and liquidise into paté. A shot of brandy and cream gives this dish a supreme touch.

Geese can also be treated in both of these ways to produce a paté reminiscent of rich beef.

ROGUE BADGER

Life in the Lake District was never dull. My marriage was bliss and Mrs Miller encouraged my shooting/fishing expeditions, which were many. Every Saturday in summer I played cricket.

Roy, of the USA era, had kept in touch and I was best man at his Cheshire wedding. A year later he rang to say he was a father.

'Guess what we are calling him.'

'Clint,' I replied. We had met the unforgettable man (Clint Eastwood) socially in Carmel, California.

'No. Edward. I want him to have as good a life as you.'

I was mightily touched.

Six weeks later he brought young Edward to meet us and we celebrated in the usual manner, from morning to night on a balmy May Sunday.

Roy's wife collected him from the pub, appropriately named *The Drunken Duck*, and I set off home on my pedal cycle.

The rest is hazy. I remember a hill and I remember a badger dashing across the road out of the night. I swerved. There was a sensation of flying as my cycle apparently hit the bank and I was thrown over the handlebars.

I know not how long I had lain in the road. First there were car headlights and then the sound of running feet.

'It's Ed.' They were pals from *The Drunken Duck* and one happened to be a paramedic.

'Can you feel that?' he queried.

Nothing.

'Don't touch him.' I was covered with a coat.

They tell me the ambulance took 20 minutes, but it didn't seem that long. Wife Annie arrived and, as they put me into the ambulance, I said I wouldn't be long.

Intensive care for three days and then, after 10 days, Southport Spinal Unit. During that time I had decided nurses weren't humans, they were angels. I was told I had dislocated my neck and probably would not be able to walk again.

There is reference in the Preface to hospital beds being great social levellers. During my three months in the hospital I was very lucky to be alongside John, an ex-Wigan miner. I am not trying to say that I am, in any way, superior socially to a Wigan miner but in order to appreciate the full benefit of his company I was obliged to learn another facet of the English language.

Very quickly I realised how lucky I was to have, in the next bed, a fellow incomplete tetraplegic (restricted in all four limbs but not paralysed). John had suffered his trauma three weeks before me and it was he who explained the electric shock-like strikes which were to emerge in my arms and legs as the nerve system began its slow mending. Nothing the learned neurologists could do to my nerve network would hasten the recovery. Only time would announce the final score.

But how does a man reared north of the Ribble understand such a declaration as the following uttered from the ever-helpful Dorothy, wife of John? 'Want me fot do that you?!' Would you like me to do that for you? I was trying, at the time, to reach my drinking tube.

John, of a similar age to myself, was discharged a few days before me. As I waved my goodbye from my wheelchair by the front door I wept a little. It was the first, and only, time I did so over my new physical state and I suspect it was more my feeling of the loss of a friend than of despair for myself.

MONSTER PIKE – *I would like to have taken my Wigan pal trolling on Esthwaite. This monster pike (returned, unharmed) was boated by Bob Rhodes of the Ross and Cromarty trips.*

John and I kept in touch and one day, two years later in June, he arrived unannounced at my Lakeland home with two of his Wigan pals. They had been fishing on nearby Lake Windermere for trout since dawn and drawn a blank.

The Wiganer is supreme at luring monster brown trout using the ledgered hypodermic inflated lobworm (and maggot but that is illegal) method.

'Nah then yer owd bugger. Wheers them trout yer towd me abaht?' Inside their boot the three jolly lads had a crate of ale and a bucket of maggots. Grasping a bottle apiece they followed me to my small tarn in the seven acres surrounding my home and proceeded to hurl in hands-full of their very active grubs. My rainbows, up to 6lbs in weight, had never seen anything like it and the water boiled.

They must have caught and returned the entire stock over the next two hours. I know the fish were very hook-shy for a long time afterwards. John and his pals returned home happily with a brace apiece.

UNCLE CHARLES – *After moving back to Lytham we made many trips to Scotland where my third son Jago went duck shooting with his uncle Charles at his home near Ponkeys.*

Chapter 8

Back To Lytham

I had been in the Southport hospital for about a month when my old pal Colin Sephton, ex-Olympic clay shot, heard I had become a forced neighbour of his and was at my bedside within minutes of the news. He farms a considerable acreage of the fertile Lancashire vegetable mosses only 15 minutes from the hospital.

At that stage of my recovery I was convinced I would be playing cricket before the summer was out, never mind participating in the relative sedateness of shooting. Colin and I had lost touch after I sold my gun shops and, though work meant he had no time for clays, I was to learn that he was just as keen on his goose shooting. His land borders the Martin Mere sanctuary and geese flight over its boundaries for six months of the year come dawn come dusk.

Colin told me how he left the birds undisturbed during the day and maintained a strict no-shooting rule after 10am. He has succeeded in persuading all the landowners surrounding the sanctuary to do the same and it has resulted in excellent relations between farmer and the sanctuary staff.

I related to Colin how keen I still was over my goose chasing and, as he left, his words rang in my ears. 'Make sure you come to see me as soon as you are fit. We'll knock a few pinks down together at dawn.' It was, however, to be quite a while before I took up his offer. In fact, 18 months after Colin's visit, I decided to retire from the shooting scene because of my restricted limb movements.

It happened during a November trip to Ponkey's with Richard – the first attempt to shoot since my accident. At the time Ken was out of commission and Richard was loth to take anyone else to the land he had so carefully guarded for 27 years.

The crunch had come when I had attempted to walk through a wood. Dawn had been and gone without any geese showing an interest in our decoys and we were looking for pigeons. Richard strolled manfully ahead with my cumbersome swivel chair but, after only a few paces, I knew it was a no go. The journey home was a muted affair. I had made up my mind to call it a day.

Soon afterwards I got rid of my shotguns and moved back to Lytham – my home town. I had twice tumbled badly on the sloping lands of my hillside home in The Lakes and the medics had told me to 'live where it is flatter and preferably drier.' My spinal damage meant I would suffer more in the cold and wet of the Cumbrian fells.

In the meantime Jago Edward had appeared on the scene. The spinal unit physician had explained that my reproductive powers were likely to be severely impaired and I often wonder if my third son's arrival was nothing more than a gesture to prove him wrong. Whatever it was, he had already proved to be one of the best mistakes I have made in my life.

His arrival had come after my decision to pack in shooting and now I was beginning to think that, perhaps, I should try just once more so that I could introduce my son to its wonders.

MARTIN MERE

As soon as we arrived in Lytham we became family members of the Wetland Trust and made frequent visits to Martin Mere, an hour's drive away south of the Ribble. By the time he had reached three Jago could tell the difference between a pinkfoot and a greylag at 100 paces. Hours were spent on the Southport coast road at high tides when the pinkfoot were pushed off the marsh and flighted only feet above the car roof onto the RSPB sanctuary.

In my bedroom, which overlooked the estuary, I had a 60 power tripod-mounted scope. The view to the Mere, five miles away across the river, was helped by the installation of a ship's porthole fitted at considerable effort into a window. It convinced my wife, finally, that I was nuts!

On a December visit to the Mere I suddenly decided to call on Colin. He lived only 10 minutes away and I hadn't seen him, nor been in contact, since that day in the spinal unit.

We found him hard at work among his potato processing machinery. His face was a picture.

'This is a surprise. What brings you?'

'I'm thinking of starting shooting again.'

'Great. We have a day on the pheasants this Saturday. You are welcome.'

'No. I couldn't manage pheasants.'

'Come for the duck flighting in the evening then.'

'Can't manage that either.'

'Well, what sort of shooting are you talking about?'

'Goose shooting.'

'That's no problem. When can you get here?'

First I had to find someone willing to act as my minder. In spinal unit circles they call these kind folk 'carers'. Annie is my registered carer but I would need a shooting companion to drive me to the goose grounds.

A phone call to Robert had him enthusing. It was only a question of when. There was, however, the small matter of a gun. I would need a stock length of 12½-inch because of my disabled arm. (This is two inches less than standard). The weapon would also have to be easy to handle because of my weakened state. After much research I settled for an old Greener GP single 12 and had a detachable choke system fitted. With 1¼ ounces of threes it shot sweetly.

I had no shotgun certificate and carefully explained to Robert that he would need to put the gun on his certificate, until mine arrived, and that Colin was willing to accompany me in my hide – this covered the law's requirements that the landowner, or shoot owner, must be in my company while certificate-less.

Came the day. It was by then the end of December and I was as excited as I was on my first Solway outing. Colin was up and about when we arrived an hour before flight. These potato farmers don't appear to sleep much. We had time for a brew and to examine closely two of Colin's collection of fine old English large bore fowling pieces – a Purdey single hammer 4-bore and a Holland & Holland of the same calibre. He shouldered the Purdey when we headed out at the first hint of dawn.

SHOOTING SITTING

Colin posted us in a five-acre field of artichokes planted as pheasant cover. I chose to position my four-legged shooting stool close to a stack of hay bales as security in case I needed a back support.

First to move were the whooper swans, now becoming more widely known as tundra swans. Martin Mere is the winter home to something like 1,500 of these enigmatic birds at their peak. Their ghostly shapes, passing by at only around 20 feet up, got the heart beating faster, even though they were not a quarry bird. They were the precursors to better things.

Golden Plover by Rodger McPhail – After two bad falls on the precipitous slopes of my Lakeland home medics said I must live somewhere 'flatter, drier and warmer'. We moved back to Lytham on the Ribble estuary. A ship's port hole was fitted to my bedroom window and a high-power scope installed to observe the tidal wildfowl. Geese could be seen roosting on the sand-banks and flighting in and out of Martin Mere sanctuary. The estuary was home for numerous flocks of golden plover.

There was little wind and the main weight of pinkfoot moved out of the sanctuary high to our left and a field away. Colin had predicted this and knew that smaller lots could be slipping in low over our territory.

Robert was the first to connect, pulling a pink out of a bunch of five. Then Colin was in action behind me and a booming three ounces of BBs had a singleton tumbling from a great height. I had let it go!

My chance came with a party of three to my right but my stationary seat was awkward and I knew I was behind when I fired. The recoil, though slight, nudged my unbalanced backside off the stool and I was wedged against the bales unable to move.

We had arranged an emergency call – a prolonged blast on the goose flute – and with Colin busy retrieving his bird Robert was first over to ease me upright. It was obvious that a more stable form of shooting seat was necessary. A typist's swivel chair had to be the answer and we resolved to hunt Preston for a surplus office equipment saleroom as soon as flight was over.

I elected not to shoot again that morning and Robert stayed with me. With the flight just about over we were about to pack up when a single goose headed straight for us 30 yards up. Robert urged me to try again but my confidence had gone and he dropped it well in front. It served to whet my appetite even more.

A fiver soon secured me a substantial office chair with adjustable height and back. A nifty shove with either foot had me spinning to right or left with balletic grace. The five roller fittings were quickly removed from the feet.

The following morning found us in the same field in a freshening westerly. The wind would be directly against the geese and I felt a huge surge of anticipation. The format was the same as the previous morning, except that we retreated to the rear of the field of Jerusalem artichokes to get out of the wind. The birds were noticeably lower and, had Colin been under the main flight with his four, he would most surely have had a bag limit. I gathered that, these days, Colin is happy with no more than a couple of birds per outing.

This time I didn't feel the need for a hay bale backrest and had total confidence in my new throne. It meant, however, that my view was more restricted behind the seven-foot plants and I was almost taken by surprise by three pinks that swept past low to my left. This time I was able to swing well ahead of my bird and it crumpled and fell 50 yards behind into a stubble. Colin volunteered to make the retrieve but I insisted on going myself and what joy it was to reach down and pick my first goose for five years!

After those first two outings, because of my limited fire power, I resolved not to flight unless strong winds prevailed. There came, too, a body blow. Robert wasn't happy to put my Greener on his shotgun certificate – even though I had checked with the licensing authorities that this was the correct procedure – until I had been granted a fresh licence. He said he felt it was a grey area and he didn't want to tempt problems.

A SAVIOUR

Then enter, stage left, Paul, an early-retired builder. I had known this most ardent of shooters from my shop years when he took up the gun as a teenager 25 years earlier. When I moved back to Lytham from the Lakes he had been first on my list for the Morecambe Bay fishing trips out of Fleetwood. In fact, in those days, he spent his entire year either fishing or shooting. It is called 'being born of golden sperm!'

His reaction to my shotgun solution was instant and he became my new partner to the Mere territories. Paul's armoury was impressive. Perhaps his most intriguing fowling piece was a Hammond double hammer 8-bore proofed to throw 3½ ounces of shot from each barrel – a massive load capable of pulling geese down from a great range.

I remember this gun arriving in my shop via an old-time long-retired fowler. The new licensing demands had caused him to relinquish the weapon. 'I hope it goes into good hands,' he had said. It seemed as though he was parting with a dear friend.

I had immediately phoned Paul's older brother, Ricki, and it took him literally minutes to arrive at my door. The weapon was proofed for black powder only and Alan Myers, of big gun fame, would turn out the four-inch brass cases to order. Paul had prised the Hammond from Ricki's possession and used it regularly on the Morecambe Bay shores.

Two more outings in January also convinced me I had to increase my own fire-power before next season. My shotgun certificate arrived at the end of the month and I now had the chance to try out a variety of musketry, though stock lengths were the big problem.

ABSORBALL

By the commencement of the next season I had settled, finally, on a Beretta semi auto three-shot gas operated 12-bore with multi-chokes. Constant practice with the loading system convinced me the tool was the right one and the stock was duly reduced. Also fitted was one of David Nickerson's Absorball recoil pads to make me all the more inured from recoil discomfort on my hypersensitive frame. There came then the oddest of coincidences.

While the pad was being fitted at my old gunsmithing firm, which had moved premises from Blackpool to rural Pilling, I received a call from Ray Holden at Hy Fly game farm, literally round the corner from the smiths.

'Can you join us for duck flight tonight?' was the surprise invite. And his other guest – David Nickerson, all the way from Lincolnshire! The recoil was negligible and subsequent testing with 1¼ ounces of number threes for the geese was still agreeable on the shoulder.

The evening flight with Raymond, his son Leroy, David Nickerson and 'minder' Paul, was a delight. Mallard only were on the hit list and Raymond was quick to alert us to several bunches of pintail which were left unshot. It was a thrill, also, to hear a pack of wigeon so early in the season.

During the following year a phone call from Colin, in mid-October of that second season of rehabilitation, took Paul and myself back to the Mere territory. This time our cover was a field of maize. The pinks were there in great numbers and Paul was soon in action after moving under the flight line which was to the extreme northern edge of the maize.

I saw two birds tumble to the boom of his 8-bore and then silence. More skeins passed over his position but he had obviously decided that two out of the new arrivals was enough.

Anchored as I was to one position, my only chance came at half light. The lead bird of a sizeable skein headed directly overhead and I hit the bird hard with my first barrel. It turned instantly and a second barrel also connected. The bird went into a shallow dive, back towards the sanctuary, and was barely visible when it crumpled. Paul joined me immediately. He had seen my goose turn back but had lost sight of it.

Years of marking experience, begun under the careful tutelage of an equally passionate fowling parent, enabled me to issue precise directions and it was with great satisfaction that, 15 minutes later, I saw Paul heading back from his half-mile long retrieve with my bird. It had fallen three feet our side of the sanctuary boundary.

It was also the biggest pinkfoot I had ever shot and I knew where it was going. An old pal in gooseless, deepest, darkest mid-Devon loves a Christmas goose and I parcelled it up for him in the feather. Packed only in screwed-up newspaper and in a light cardboard box it tipped the Post Office scales at eight and a half pounds – which would have put the bird at around eight pounds. I gave my Devon friend careful instructions on the total need for at least five hours of steam roasting after its dalliance in the deep freeze.

RETURN TO CUMBRIA

I had three stirring seasons flighting the Martin Mere geese before moving back to the Lake District. My wife had been so miserable at my depriving her of the mountains, woods and tarns that I decided to suffer the pain of cold, wet winters and return. Coming back has been worth it. We have now been here for six years and it also brought my Scottish goose shooting a touch closer. I would exchange my Lancashire goose grounds for the much more enigmatic northern fields. Though I love the Lancashire dawns they never held, for me, the lure of geese north of the Border.

That last season on the mosses provided a memorable incident which I feel must be recorded. By then the crop system on the farm meant I could be taken by 4WD to one of the boundary hides constructed at eye-level in a drainage ditch. One morning I knocked a pink out towards the end of flight and it had dropped two fields behind into the middle of a potato crop still not harvested.

Paul and I drove to the edge of the field and I gave him the area of the drop, around 300 yards distant. There was a howler of a north wind and, as he reached the spot, I saw the bird dash away from behind him into thick cover. The wind took my shouts away so I gave him a long blast on the goose call. It worked. Paul turned round and reacted as well as a good field trial Lab to my arm directions. He had the goose in his fist after a hectic chase.

The frantic scamper over the clinging black peaty terrain did not, however, do much for Paul's well-being and he made a declaration. 'Unless you drop them stone dead we are going to have to get a dog.'

The quest was on and that is how Wally, a powerful chocolate Lab dog came to join our team. Brother Charles had heard about Wally in his Scottish neck of the woods. At two years old he had picked geese but was, we were warned, 'A bit headstrong on game.' Since the prime purpose was the retrieval of the first-mentioned, he changed owners and has proved to be first class at that job. The headstrong bit was also no understatement! Tether him to a fence post and there is a grave danger that he will uproot it in his lack of control! But as they say, 'Horses for courses.'

GOLDCREST

Before I conclude my lines on Martin Mere I also tell of a meeting I had soon after dawn one January among the Jerusalem artichokes. Neither the promised wind nor the cloud had materialised and, consequently, all the geese came off high over my chair hidden in the dense growth.

I was contemplating an early breakfast when suddenly a movement, only 18-inches away, caught my attention. At first I thought mouse, so tiny was it. The weather was certainly mild enough to have awoken one from its winter slumbers.

The eye was just as bright and beady as that of a mouse but it had a short sharp beak and feathers. A vivid gold slash on its crown and a black stripe above the inquisitive eye identified it as a golden crested wren – the smallest of our winter visitors. Its pale cream cheeks added to the exquisite markings.

I was transfixed by this extraordinary dainty creature which was obviously unaware of me. I hardly dared to breathe.

Goldie was in no hurry and nor was I. Unfortunately he got fed up first when he found nothing to eat on the bare stalk and flitted off into the tangle of vegetation.

IRELAND'S TERROR

While still with the chapter covering our four years in Lytham I must relate the story of a holiday in Ireland. Earlier in the book I tell the story of my flight to Northern Ireland to acquire a Holland 4-bore. This was by no means my first visit to the Emerald Isle. Many were the excursions I had enjoyed during the 1960s, when old friend Peter Waugh had been a tax exile in County Wicklow. Peter shot most days of the week – wood pigeons, clays and pheasants in that order.

Goose shooting I couldn't really tempt him to. He had been the victim of a near-death incident on the River Ribble estuary, at Lytham, years earlier and could not be coaxed again onto a marsh. However, in deference to my passion for the grey birds, Peter organised an outing to whitefront feeding grounds. We were to visit a bog, where they fed during the day, and would line out in a ditch while the territory was driven to our hidden positions. Not really my style of goose shooting but it would have been unfair to try to explain that to my kind host.

Besides Peter and myself there were three other Guns, who unfortunately did not grasp the plot. Before the beaters were in sight, great gatherings of snipe poured over. My three companions, all in the country for the pheasant shooting, quickly changed loads from heavy to sevens and soon had hot barrels.

The geese were there but departed sideways and only one fell to an outside gun.

Peter lived in the Irish Republic and my second visit to the northern region of Ireland was in the summer of 1998 – a bird watching week with wife Annie and five-year-old son. Strangford Lough, 15 by 10 miles of tidal wetland, is a magnet for all lovers of wildlife. It is, of course, a wintering resort for thousands of pale-bellied brent geese.

Our decision to take a holiday in that delightful part of the world was prompted by the 'Good Friday Agreement' announcing the blessed cessation of hostilities. How foolish we were.

It was a mere 30-minute journey from Lytham to the port of Fleetwood where we drove onto the Larne commercial ferry. We wept for the northern Irish holiday trade. In most hotels we were the only residents. Thankfully the excellent restaurants, within the hotels, were reasonably busy thus improving the atmosphere.

The bird life was no letdown but everywhere there was an uncomfortable police and Army presence. The RUC stations were surrounded by chilling security fences and every morning, on returning to our car, I found it difficult not to peer underneath for the dreaded bomb. Had I done so I am sure my wife would have driven straight to the ferry!

Frighteningly, only a few days after we had returned home, there came the devastating Omagh bomb outrage when so many innocents were slaughtered. My wife's sense of direction is, fortunately, bad and I hoped she would not realise we had stopped in the very street where the carnage had taken place.

However, the highlight was undoubtedly the discovery, in Bangor harbour, of the black guillemots. We were able to stand a mere few feet from their nesting holes in the harbour wall and observe their bright vermilion mouths. The downside, that day, was when we booked a sea fishing trip. We had misunderstood the directions delivered in rich Irish brogue the evening before. This was easily done and we could only stand and watch as the 40-foot sleek craft sped past our jetty. We waved frantically – and they waved back.

SIMON

After that excursion into bird watching there follows, I am happy to say, another tale with a strong 'goose' flavour.

I have already mentioned sea fishing trips out of Fleetwood with Paul but, prior to that and as soon as I was physically capable of holding a rod, I had been driven to east Devon as a possible area in which to settle. It was certainly drier, warmer and flatter than The Lakes.

Here, on an angling trip into the English Channel, I met, in the oddest of circumstances, a fellow fisher/shooter who was to become a close pal for many years. It happened thus.

My non-fishing driver had transported me to the dockside where the remainder of the party were already aboard the 35-foot vessel. Though I had carefully explained to the skipper, by phone, my physical impairment he had obviously not got the message.

'Step onto that barrel and then the box,' were his cheerful words.

Not wanting to appear a problem I did as instructed. Unfortunately the 'barrel' was merely a plastic dustbin in which was coiled an anchor rope. As soon as it received my 15 stones the thing toppled and I was hurtling deckwards.

'Here comes another visit to the spinal unit,' was what flashed through my mind. And then my plunge was, miraculously, halted and I was cradled by a hulk of a young fellow. It was Simon.

'I reckon I owe you one,' was all I could say.

Later I was to hear that Simon, then aged 28, and his party came from Blackpool, where I had manned my gun shop for 21 years. All six of them knew the shop and, as a boy, Simon had been a regular customer with his dad. He still had the double barrelled .410 purchased from me when he was 10.

He progressed to 12-bores but, currently, could find no shooting near his home apart from clays. Two trips to The Solway had been goose-less and he was still desperate to put one in his bag.

'Do you have a 4WD?' I enquired.

'No, but I'm thinking of buying one.'

I suggested he phoned me as soon as he had done so and I would guarantee him geese. What else could I say? I had already warmed to my saviour.

The remainder of the Simon story is told as the book unfolds.

FIRST HARE – *Soon after securing the shooting rights on Ponkey's I took Jago on his first outing with a .410 (the stock having been suitably shortened). Here he is pictured by the iron gate on the track to Top Pond.*

Chapter 9

Ponkey's Secured

A series of circumstances, in the 27th year of shooting Ponkey's, came close to ending the association with this most cherished of lands. I had only recently escaped from the delusion that my shooting days were over following my spinal unit sojourn, Ken was suffering from a blip in health and Richard was more and more turning to flyfishing.

Even in my immobile months I had kept in touch with Rab by phone and it was during one of my calls that he told me a syndicate was making noises about the shooting. The Major, who had rented the game shooting for many years, had died and most farms in the area were being rented out to local shooters who were syndicating them and then sub-letting as a money-earner.

The farm was then being worked diligently and efficiently by Hamish, nephew of the late Miss Jane – she of the sponge cakes and afternoon tea – who had not been born when I first hunted its geese. Both Ken and I were totally honourable to Richard and had never visited its pastures without first consulting him. A phone call explained to Richard the danger threatening our privilege and he kindly gave me the go-ahead to approach the young Hamish about rental. Ken was keen to chip in 'whatever it cost.' What spunk. He would surely recover from his maladies.

Rather than broach such a weighty matter on the phone I motored up to see Hamish and felt deeply touched at the warmth with which he accepted my offer.

Now it was essential to find two more to share the very substantial cost and they had to be fit and strong enough to put me back on my swivel chair whenever I fell off! Paul and Simon fitted the role to perfection. They were as devoted to goose chasing as both Ken and I were and they also had 4WD vehicles – or soon would have.

Although we had only shot geese there we already knew of Ponkey's bountiful larder. An idea of what it had to offer is illustrated by an extract

Woodcock *by Rodger McPhail*
Migratory woodcock usually arrive on Ponkey's by early October.

from our subsequent game register:

December 3/4 2003. Guns five. Weather cold. North-east wind – force three. Thin cloud. Snow on moor top. Bag; Geese six, Ducks eight (six mallard two teal), Pheasants six, Partridge two, Woodcock one, Snipe four, Grouse one, Pigeons three, Rabbits two, Hares four. Total 34.

Though the bags are mixed, the prime motivation among us all is, I am pleased to say, the goose shooting. By December, when the weather has been hard, the skies can be empty of geese – driven to the coast for softer pickings and an unfrozen roost.

On the day of the above bag the visit was split, as normal, between evening flight on the first day and rough shooting, following an early breakfast, on the second. We were heading for home by mid-afternoon.

Four geese had gone in to the bag in the evening with the other two being added in spectacular fashion around mid-morning on the following day. It happened thus:

As we entered the boundary wood three large skeins appeared, all trumpets sounding, from the direction of the coast. After two circles of a neighbouring estate's field of winter wheat the entire army of around 500 birds pitched in and got on with their guzzling. We had watched, transfixed, at the spectacular sight from the shelter of the wood. They had passed over, well up, and were now only two fields off. Though we were loth to disturb the horde we knew that they would be off in alarm at our first shot and we carried on with the drive.

I was the only standing (sorry sitting) Gun – at the road end – and, at the first report, the geese lifted. The birds were oblivious to where the shots had come from and, by a stroke of luck, headed directly towards the wood.

Two of the guns were quick to react and tipped their game sixes to the ground as they delved into their goose cartridge pocket for BBs. Each had time for only one barrel apiece as they shot through the lace of branches. Both connected and two birds crashed through the tree tops to the accompaniment of much splintering timber.

We make it a rule to shoot only as many pheasants as we need for our own use and the putting down of 100 ex-layers in the first year proved a great success. The only drawback is that the cocks have wised-up after a season of fire and are great sprinters! How much more rewarding, though, to put one of these wily old fellows, with their half inch spurs, in the bag than a June poult.

For me the snipe are a great bonus. Plucked and drawn and inserted into a jacket potato with plenty of butter and oven baked they are, as they say, orgasmic! As a reward for carrying out all the organising – and anyone who has undertaken this side of a shoot will understand what an onerous task this is – I am usually allowed to carry off these morsels.

BADGERS

The reader will no doubt have realised, by now, that I hold a slightly jaundiced view of the badger. It is a danger to all road users – particularly those on two wheels – and a pain on any shoot. Until the other day I thought we goose chasers were immune from its predations but now I have my doubts.

The incident was a strange one.

We had been out at dawn for the geese on the Ponkey stubbles and had put four pinks in the bag. A fifth, hard hit, had flown on towards our boundary then plummeted stone dead just over the march in dense reeds.

Rob walked the 200 yards to the spot, gun under arm and dog at heel. He sent Sam over the fence but from 10 yards into the reeds, and just about where he reckoned the drop was, there came a fierce growling and the dog dashed back, tail between legs.

The vegetation was not only dense but tall also, with a stream through its middle. At the top of the bank – well above flood level – there was an old badger sett and Rob's immediate reaction was 'Brock.'

He had told me he had contemplated taking his gun to investigate; he was wise not to do so. He would, of course, have been committing an offence. The law allows you to enter your neighbour's land to retrieve but not with a gun. It could be argued, under the circumstances, that he would have been justified to slip two cartridges into the breech and go boldly into the jungle but should he have done so who would have believed such a tale?

Later that evening, upon my return home, I reported the incident by phone to the next-door shoot manager. He promised to investigate and I subsequently heard that no goose remains were evident, though the sett did show signs of recent use. It can only be assumed that the creature had been in residence when the bird fell and was in the process of carrying it into the hole when Rob showed up.

The badger does have a wide diet and is especially fond of a nest of mallard, pheasant or partridge eggs whatever their state of incubation. The farmer also has many reasons to despise this animal, cute though it may seem to the city dweller.

The damage a family party can do to a field of grain has to be seen to be believed. Standing wheat, barley or oats are great places for a game of rough and tumble for a dozen juvenile Brocks. They do not go about their flattening of the crop on its edge but steal furtively into the centre and can leave a tennis court size area as flat as a cowpat. The crop may not be entirely lost if it still has to ripen but should it be on the cusp of harvesting such frolics can be a costly business.

This powerful predator doesn't stop there. So devastating are its teeth and jaws that it can tear holes in rabbit netting for fun with obvious results. He can also be a menace if he takes a liking to the grain in your pheasant feeders. Recently our resident family discovered they could dine in comfort by ripping off the spiral feeder nozzles at the base of the hoppers. We have been forced to fit anti-badger spikes. And, for good measure, also fenced each feeder with sheep netting. Time consuming and a drain on funds but, hopefully, it will work.

Finally, there is the wretched business of bovine TB. Cattle breeders live in constant fear of the disease being transferred from the badger to their stock. As a devoted listener to the daily farming programme at 5.45am on Radio 4, I hear regular debates over the argument for badger culling to check the disease. The jury was out on the subject when this was written.

I have explained that, for our little band of five, the main attraction on Ponkey's is, of course, the enigmatic migratory geese. Other globe trotting quarry, like woodcock, teal, wigeon and pintail, add to its charisma but we do our bit for the resident pheasant population by

A THIEVING BADGER *by Rodger McPhail. Besides being carriers of bovine TB, badgers can be great wreckers of standing crops and, on a recent visit to Ponkey's, a Gun had one of his pinkfoot geese stolen by Brock.*

putting down the ex layers each year.

They come from a game farm a mere half an hour distant and one of the unexpected bonuses from their crop is the profusion of eggs deposited by the predominant hen birds in their temporary pen.

In this year of the book Rab erected the structure in the middle of the shoot following the previous season's indiscretion when it was placed too adjacent to a lane. (My fault.) Unfortunately, the lane became a highway down which our birds strolled onto the next shoot, never to be seen again. Wise Hamish, our farmer, chose the site this time and he has been proved right – again.

The birds remain in their temporary caged home only for a few days and kindly deposit their bounty of eggs. Mary squealed with delight when she espied the gifts and carried them back to her cosy cottage where bright yellow sponge cakes soon emerged from her oven like a wartime munitions factory! What scrumptious eating and yet another reason for making the three-hour trail to attend the pigeons marauding the sprouting summer kale.

This year, to make our flushing task easier, Hamish planted his kale and turnips in strips. Instead of vast expanses of waist-soaking growth we have each variety adjacent in gunshot-wide tracts. There they will remain until January when sheep will be allowed to chomp their way through a nourishing diet.

Who, I ponder, will enjoy their fare more? Me with my fat-make sponge cake or the woolly cheviots with all those vitamins? Each to his own, as Grandma was wont to mutter.

Chapter 10

Fowling Quarters and Kindred Spirits

There are two aspects of our wonderful pursuit of goose chasing which demand much consideration and care – the choice of headquarters when far away from home and companions. Here I offer advice which I hope will be of help to those of lesser experience.

When Richard first took me north we stayed at a cosy country pub/hotel which was fine until winter sank into its icy depths. In those days the fourth season really did have a vicious kick and, with central heating still a thing of the future in that remoteness, we were driven to seek somewhere that did not necessitate dressing in extra clothing to go to bed!

At first we could find nothing better than a newly opened motel – then a concept not long arrived from the USA – on the outskirts of town involving nigh on an hour's pre-dawn drive to the goose grounds. There were plenty of state-of-the-art radiators over which to dry off damp gear and no one noticed, or bothered, what time we came and went.

The inner man was well catered for at the caring Mrs Walker's cosy eatery in daylight hours and there was a fine selection of bar food, take-aways etc. in town to satisfy young bellies in the evenings. What it did lack, of course, was rural atmosphere. The traffic and all-night street lights tried hard to destroy the ambience of the whole venture. We decided to seek something else.

A newly opened B & B was located only a 10-minute drive away, hidden in a wood, and, yes, they did not mind our going out in the early hours and returning mid-morning for breakfast. We agreed that dogs would be kept strictly in cars and, yes, they would be quite happy for us to leave wellies and waterproofs in the garage. No, they did not mind shooting.

Sadly we did not last the season. The couple were from suburbia with young children. They claimed we had woken one of the bairns on an early morning rising; the porch had to be redecorated because a dog's tail had brushed it, and a duvet cover had been discoloured with an 'oil spot.'

At first they were glad of the revenue but we suspect the crunch came when we left a brace of pinkfoot in the garage as a 'Thank you' and they were seen by the landlady who, more and more, we suspected did not approve of our pastime.

Rab's wife, Mary, then seemed to have found the answer – a nearby farm where we could have a room apiece. There was a dining room and the farmer's wife would be very happy to cook breakfast 'whenever'.

What a jolly, delightful, lady Linda turned out to be. Her breakfasts were epic and we could shoot the pigeons in the farm's roost wood whenever we wanted. Her charge was £16 a head but so good was the fare that we insisted on paying £20. (I know prices are irrelevant to the reader in five, 10 or 20 years time, but they merely offer a comparison.)

Then we invited Boris

His splendid yellow bitch performed in her usual efficient manner at evening flight. However, after stacking a couple of pinks and half a dozen mallard and teal on the bank, she had become transformed from yellow into a deep chocolate brown.

After flight and back at HQ the routine, already established by the other dog men staying at our new digs, was carefully explained to Boris. A good scrub down with dry shippon straw and kennel the hound in his vehicle.

As usual, I was first up next morning an hour before departure, for dawn flight, and tapped on Boris's door. Minutes later I was surprised to find a very clean yellow Lab wandering into my room bright eyed and bushy tailed. It wasn't like Boris to rise that early to give his dog a run.

'Where did she sleep?' I enquired.

'In the car,' and nothing more was said.

Two hours later, after flight and over our mid-morning breakfast, Linda did not seem to be her usual jolly self. The meal was a hurried affair since we had seen a party of geese dropping onto our land as we were heading off after flight and we wanted to spend the rest of the morning trying to get on terms with them before going home.

When I phoned to book the following month I discovered the reason for Linda's earlier depression. 'Will your friend be wanting to take his dog into the room with him again?' she enquired.

Horrified, I was to learn the reason for the canine's pristine condition on our last visit. She had left her coating of rich peat bog on Linda's carpet – and some of it on the bed valance and just about every piece of furniture leg in the bedroom. Commercial contractors had been able to remove all traces from the axminster but repeated washings of the valance had failed to return it to the immaculate condition which all of Linda's soft furnishings boasted. The extra £4 per head we had been paying all season had, after all, been hard earned!

Boris had not, thank goodness, been invited on our next trip and it was then that we learned that Linda and her husband were to retire from farming and move to a small bungalow next door. And she did assure me her unfortunate encounter with some of Scotland's prime peat bog had not precipitated the move!

She also had some good news. The shooting/fishing hotel down the road had been sold and the new owner was keen to encourage extra trade and would be prepared to do a deal on room rates. The previous owners had refused to budge from an exorbitant price, even though we had offered to book on days when they would sometimes have been empty.

The new owner was delighted to offer terms not much more than our B&B rates, breakfast any time up to midday and there was a drying room, kennels, game larder and a security gun room.

This set-up is, I stress, the ultimate in shooting quarters and if you can not afford it, take up another pastime! There is one all-pervading lesson. Go only where the host and staff are totally in tune with field sports. Gone are the days when men with shotguns were ignored by the public.

ALL IMPORTANT

There is another tale which serves to illustrate the need for a surplus of one particular all-important commodity in shooting HQ's.

We had discovered new goose grounds a long way from Ponkey's and it was up to me, on a summer jaunt, to find digs. With wife and child in tow we spent a morning recceing.

The tiny sign on a gatepost announcing B&B was so overgrown by foliage that, at first, we missed it. Only the sharp eyes of our five-year-old detected the notice and we retraced our steps.

A long, rough, wooded drive opened into a clearing. Domestic ducks played on a pond and a dog barked from purpose-built kennels. It was

FOWLING QUARTERS – *Always choose your fowling quarters with great care. Left to Right: David Wilkins, John Wilkins and the author head for breakfast after a successful morning on Morecambe Bay.*

certainly secluded enough to prevent prying eyes seeing us come and go with covert shotguns.

Olive was middle aged, twinkly eyed and yes, three of us could have a room each and breakfast whenever. The extensive dwelling included an old keeper's cottage, hence the kennels, and was in an L-shape. Our wing was the converted gunroom and game larder. We could have a key and free-range of the kitchen when Olive and her husband were out. It was the sort of trust offered only by gentle country folk.

There was only one draw back – a single bathroom-cum-loo. Not a problem, one would have thought, among three chaps. There wasn't, unless Arthur happened to be one of the party. Whether it stemmed from childhood I know not, but Arthur's toiletry needs were unusual. Unless he could have two visits (and on a bad day three) a morning, all in the space of one hour, he was as evil as Ghengis Khan on a bad piles day.

The warning light flashed on our first morning he was with us when he borrowed my Shooting Times and headed for the sanctum.

'We are due out in five minutes,' I told him.

'You carry on. I'll be along later,' was all he said.

We couldn't. He had the keys to the 4WD. As it happened it was a morning of heavy cloud and the birds were half an hour later than usual, so we missed nothing.

Then came the day we were in someone else's vehicle and Arthur had to climb aboard after only his second visit pre-dawn.

Half way through flight a small party of greylags was heading for my hide when they suddenly flared. A voice behind me enquired, 'Have you got any toilet paper?!'

Sometimes there were two Arthurs in the party and this is when he became Billy two Sh***.

They also say that, in every cloud, there is a silver lining and for Billy two Sh*** it came when Olive, who was a fanatically devoted horse-women, decided that she and her husband would move to Northern Ireland to be near their daughter and where they could buy a 50-acre farm for the price of their Scottish woodland home. I heard Olive filled it with horses.

That was when we found an hotel with en-suite facilities. Long drive to goose grounds or not, it was certainly worth it when Billy was aboard!

THANK YOU MR BUSH

It is an ill wind that blows no one any good. Thanks to the way President Bush has chosen to deal with the terrorist situation, US visitors to Scotland had, by the 2003/4 summer, all but disappeared. The dearth of the Macktavishland-loving Americans resulted in hotel prices tumbling to an unprecedented level.

Unaware of this state of affairs, I casually requested a brochure from the splendid and most prestigious hostelry that sits on the edge of one of our Scottish goose shoots and reeled at its new prices. Five years previously I had tried to negotiate another out-of-season deal to no effect.

Now they were offering all the world and his wife B&B at £30! And that included a whopping Scottish breakfast, plus en-suite and satellite TV. Brekkers after flight wouldn't be a problem if we wished.

It will be interesting to see how long this status quo lasts. Perhaps, we shall be there for a long time.

KINDRED SPIRITS

The reader will now have gathered that getting one's companions to toe the line on goose hunts can be a problem. Finding those who have the same passion for the chase is another. Now, as a septuagenarian, I choose my fellow Guns carefully and can afford to be fussy.

Occasionally one is tempted to take out an acquaintance who would 'like to shoot a goose' after he has spent all his years as a driven bird Shot. Ninety percent of the time it is a mistake. To get such a Gun to keep his head down and not to move is well nigh impossible unless you have him in the hide with you. Too many years on a pheasant peg have rendered him totally inured to the necessity for covert behaviour. In his type field-craft is non-existent – an alien talent. To him a pheasant might as well be an inanimate object – a clay bird with feathers.

Conversely, come across a keen youngster, or fowler, who has never had the opportunity to get under the geese and you have a kindred soul. The vibes are there on the way to the goose grounds, very evident when they head for their bed, and infectious in that hour before dawn when you gather by the vehicle. If they are lucky to bag their first goose it is a cause for much joy, cameras and phone calls home. Perhaps you have set another spirit off on that long, long trail hunting the grey battalions.

One such tyro was the aforementioned Simon, whom I had met in that most bizarre fashion, on the angling boat in the English Channel.

January had come by the time Simon took delivery of his Freelander. I had received a report that there were a few geese in an area not far north of the Border and plenty of pigeons feeding on newly sown rape.

We erected our hides in a belt of low birch trees bordering the field on a day of light wind and clear skies. The pigeons came on a steady line and Simon was in constant action retrieving both our kills. That was when he also decided to acquire a gun dog! He was learning fast!

We had been on the farm since dawn but there had been no sight or sign of geese all day. Then, in mid-afternoon on the pigeon field, there came a low gabble. Definitely greylag, but where?

I was scanning too high. A party of seven was heading across the field directly towards Simon 75 yards to my right. My goose call was in my pocket. I wanted to shout but feared I might alarm the birds. Had they been dropping in to decoys I would have shouted. In those days we had not got round to carrying the so-useful two-way radios and I had to wait, watch and listen for the bangs.

Nothing. The birds had to lift to clear the trees over Simon's head.

'What happened?' I yelled.

'I was lighting a fag,' came an anguished reply.

It was, without doubt, the main reason for Simon kicking his smoking addiction! He was distraught and it was no help when I declared that there was more chance of a Stuart sitting on the Scottish throne than there was of seven wild geese again flying over his head 20 feet up!.

October in the following season saw us on Ponkey's. This is when Simon met Boris for the first time. I must stress that I am indebted to Boris for all sorts of reasons and this is not his real name. Let me explain.

My initial shotgun experiences with Boris were on a marsh where he was, unquestionably, a supremo. What he did not know about fowling was not worth knowing. I learnt much from him.

However, coastal fowling is, essentially, a lone pursuit and it is difficult for a true born-on-a-marsh gunner to fall into line when it comes to goose chasing, be it on salting or stubble. This is why Boris would often do his own thing, like a maverick steer. Such quirks are fine on a marsh but, when it comes to organised shooting, it can have its drawbacks, as will soon be revealed.

Boris was waiting at the barn when we arrived at 10am after our long journey north on a wild morning. He told us that a low flying fighter jet had just disturbed around 1,000 pinkfoot from a nearby stubble and that they had headed back towards their moorland roost.

Rab had placed three single bales, each spaced about 100 yards apart on the field as hides, and the straw had not yet been baled. I posted Simon in the middle hide and asked Boris to man the far one where the geese should swing in towards the decoys. I hoped his experience would make him leave them for Simon to have first crack. If he did so Boris and I would get our chance when they spun back with the wind. Boris also had an excellent yellow Lab bitch and he drove off to tuck his 4WD under a belt of firs. That was the last we saw of him and his dog for the next two hours!

Within 10 minutes the first bunch of pinks appeared from the moor and swung in low, directly over the bale I had asked Boris to man. Unfortunately they flew beyond the decoys out of range of both myself and Simon and pitched in 300 yards past us. The second party did exactly the same and I urgently called Simon over.

'Walk towards where the birds dropped in and, when I lift my arm, bury yourself under the straw'. I told him to lie with his feet towards the flight path and to sit up when they were 30 yards in front.

Within five minutes another small party was heading straight towards Simon. He let them come too close and missed with both barrels. As they rocketed back, down-wind, I killed the nearest bird with a snap shot. They were gone, via Boris's unmanned bale, before I could get onto another.

Simon came scampering past to collect my bird and set it up among the decoys. A very fast learner I mused.

'Take them at 50 yards,' I bellowed above the wind as he was sprinting back to bury himself under his straw blanket. He was only just in time as another gaggle of around 20 swung down from the moor.

This time Simon shot his first goose – well out in front and a right and left. The bunch came directly back over my head and I had to let them go on before dropping another.

Four more birds were added to the bag before Boris reappeared. He had not fired a shot and did not say what he had been up to. There was a runner to be picked from the thick cover by the tumbledown wall at the bottom of the field and his dog was quickly onto it delivering an old gander impeccably to hand. Oh, I thought, that her master could behave so well!

Following my renewed suggestion to man his hide, Boris declared he would, instead, get under the straw at the top of the field. I was lost for words.

In the far distance, and atop the horizon, he proceeded to amass a huge pile of straw and perched himself and his dog in its middle. His silhouette was of Martello Tower proportions, visible for miles and it prompted the tyro Simon to come over and ask in bewildered fashion, 'Why is he doing that?' It was a question he was to pose many times.

Four bunches of geese built into flocks circling high over Boris's fortress, several shots out of range, before finally heading for pastures new. Fortunately we had shot enough.

DISASTER

Another memorable trip with Boris, memorable again for all the wrong reasons, was when John was the third member of the party; John who was awaiting two new knees.

At the end of a successful evening flight on Top Pond in filthy weather – swirling mist and near freezing heavy drizzle – Boris had gone off to fetch the vehicle from over the hill.

'Follow the fence and you can't go wrong,' I had instructed, though he should have known the land as well as me. Presently, through the fog, John and I saw headlights approaching. Suddenly they veered away from the fence at almost right angles.

'My God he is going to end up in the bog,' cried John. Too late. The beam dipped violently and the vehicle came to an abrupt stop.

In spite of his knees John had to limp the 300 yards to the scene. Fortunately he found a driver only shaken and the two of them came back to retrieve me.

We were in trouble. No mobile phone and a mile back to the farm for help. I began to shake with the cold and John was close to exhaustion.

Both John and myself normally carried phones but mine was on the blink and John had inadvertently left his in his car. Boris had always refused to use one. (I don't think he wanted his wife to bug him.) We left the guns and the evening's bag in the hide and Boris, strong as an ox in spite of his seniority by several years, half carried me, half marched me valiantly back to the warmth of the partly sunken vehicle. The rear-end rose high in the air and water was just lapping the sill. We silently hoped it had stopped going down!

By now John was in a bit of a state. Though I was the more disabled his three trips to and from the scene on dicky knees had taken their toll and he was gripped by a severe shaking. Fortunately the engine could still run and the Land Rover's efficient heating system soon had him warm again and out of his ague.

This was when our 'delinquent' went some way towards gaining Brownie points. He discovered his wife's mobile phone in the glove compartment and we were able to ring her at home for Rab's number.

The rest is history. The vehicle was slowly eased out of its watery hole with much sucking by a giant John Deere and proved to be undamaged.

The Boris's of this world are not, however, the worst category of shooter to have with you. They are, in truth, all heart and I would miss my Boris. As long as I have breath he will shoot with me.

SNAKE

Number one criterion is, of course, always safety. After that the deadliest, in terms of undesirability, is the avaricious Gun who covets the shooting you have.

In the long ago we did not pay for our goose shooting. And then beware the guest you so innocently invite who would try to steal in at the back door without you, once the contact had been made.

After Richard had first taken me to his secret place I warned him about the type – the ultimate definition of the proverbial snake in the grass. So many times, from the sanctuary of my shop counter, I had listened to customers bewailing how they had been so betrayed.

Richard was, at first, surprised that this creature even existed in the shooting world but, be sure, he is there waiting to pounce. And there was, in fact, one such acquaintance who cunningly invited Richard salmon fishing with the sole purpose of inveigling his way onto his goose ground. Fortunately I had already alerted him to this particular fellow and he carefully avoided his efforts to curry favour. Had he done so you could have safely wagered your Grandma's gold wedding ring that he would have been back there faster than Johnny Wilkinson's left boot.

TIME OUT

There can come a time in a shooter's life when he considers, rightly or wrongly, whether he should be taking lives, albeit of a lower strata than our own. It happened to me in my mid-thirties and when I told Richard and Ken I was taking a year off potting animate quarry they understood, so much so I wondered if they, too, had been down the same road.

A year later I rejoined them. I was still in the gun business and had merely increased my tally of clay birds. I am glad I took time out and I was able to resume my goose chasing with all the vigour of old.

During more than 60 years of shooting I have witnessed some remarkable examples of shotgun ability and, conversely, many examples of rank bad marksmanship. So bad, in fact, that one sometimes wonders why such Guns insist on pursuing the sport.

In my early years in the gun trade I ran a clay pigeon shooting school, and very lucrative it was too. Many sorts passed through my hands over the decade I operated. Some were naturals and it was easy to spot them. Others were so wooden that I was forced, respectfully, to suggest they try golf!

One fellow who fits into the first category has only just arrived in my long career involving guns. I was to discover his extraordinary skills with shoulder weaponry quite by chance.

AIRGUN ARSENAL

The story began with, of all things, a call from my GP. We are lucky here in our little Cumbrian village to have a doc who treats us all like his own big family. One of his patients, a widow sadly too young to have achieved that status, had, it transpired, asked the good physician for his guidance in the disposal of, extraordinarily, seven air rifles. Knowing my connection with the gun trade he had put the unfortunate lady in touch with me.

Susan, aged around 50 something, lived some way out of the village and I was shown a stack of boxes containing the highest quality air rifles, all apparently in an unfired state. They had been her late husband's and, when she had gone to a dealer she had not liked the figure he had offered. Hence her seeking advice from her doctor – like you do at such times. After eight phone calls, all personal approaches, I was quickly able to present her with a substantial bundle of cash and everyone was happy. It was also to result in a severe decline in the over-population of jackdaws in the valley.

The only fellow not to take up my offer of a superb weapon at a most attractive price, was probably the wealthiest of all those I had contacted. Could he try it first? Would it do what I claimed? Couldn't he buy one cheaper elsewhere? He was as sick as the proverbial parrot when he missed the chance and still bleats on. It pleased me greatly to inform him they had all gone.

The first sale I made occurred within minutes of my taking possession of the armoury. I was on my way down the village street for a bag of spuds when out stepped Jack, the new owner of one of our local hostelries.

'Do you fancy a powerful air rifle to stuff those jackdaws on your chimney pots?' I asked.

Jack's eyes sparkled and I suppose I should have wondered sooner at his intense enthusiasm. Within the half hour he had selected the most expensive of the bunch and had me ordering him a scope from my old Preston shop.

'You've done a bit then?' I queried as I watched Jack caress his acquisition.

'Nineteen years in the regular Army and the last seven in the SAS.'

Tales soon filtered back to my cottage that Jack was knocking jackdaws down in flight with his Weirhauch before the scope had arrived.

Bunkum, thought I, until I swept swiftly round to the nearby hotel on my disabled chariot to be given a private demonstration. No wonder, I mused, that we have the finest Army in the whole world!

More was to follow. Jack was from Welsh farming stock and had grown up with shotguns too. I took him to my Scottish shoot, and in the first season hardly ever saw him miss. He quickly acquired a 20-bore (one of Patrick Keen's delightful McNabs) with multi chokes, and then made a mistake.

He thought I would allow him to flight geese with the puny tool. It took me a while to make him realise my intense respect for the beloved goose. You might be able to down one through the head with a .410 coming into decoys at 20 yards, but I am afraid I am one of those who believes in according these magnificent creatures the ultimate respect.

Big guns, big shot for big birds to minimalise chances of wounding. It brought to mind the fervent altercation I had a few years ago with a certain sad area representative of BASC who tried to tell me a game gun was all one needed to dawn flight geese! The incident, is I feel, worth telling:

BAD ADVICE

I was in my old Preston shop, a couple of years after my discharge from the spinal unit, when in came an acquaintance, for some 'goose cartridg-es'. It transpired he had booked three dawn flights on the Lancashire mosses with a goose guide and had been using game sixes.

'Don't they fly a long way before they fall?' he had lamented.

Mike, the shop owner, was as horrified as myself and sent him off with a box of 2¾-inch threes to throw out of his game gun which was probably bored improved cylinder and half choke if it followed standard English choking.

I knew the guide was BASC registered and it prompted me to phone the organisation headquarters. Accordingly I was put in touch with the aforementioned representative who, alarmingly, thought it 'perfectly acceptable' to shoot geese with such armoury. My argument was, and still is, for big shot and heavy chokes but the misguided BASC man, definitely not a son of the marshes, was adamant.

But, back to my 20-bore friend. A dealer pal had recently told me he had taken into stock one of the mighty 3½-inch 12-bores capable of throwing 2¼ ounces of shot – an 8-bore load. I suggested he loaned it to Jack with a sale potential.

What was to follow served only to confirm what I already knew. The gun was a Browning semi auto, with interchangeable chokes, and Jack took it with him on our last Scottish goose shoot of the season. That evening we were on Top Pond when three geese came over, well high, with no intention of stopping on their way to the main roost. But one of them did stop.

'Too high,' called one of my regulars as Jack threw up the weapon – which was amazingly light and a delight to handle. I couldn't even see the birds but, after just one report, a blob appeared out of the heavens and smacked, stone dead, into the middle of the pond to the accompaniment of a mighty column of erupted water. Lead was still in and the full charge of BBs had wreaked their havoc.

GOOSE TALK

We had arrived on the shoot by mid-afternoon that same day and found around 500 pinks on a field of new grass on a direct level with Rab's open bedroom window where the land rose steeply. Our Scottish friend was in a bad mood. The birds were no more than 400 yards from his boudoir and moonlight goose talk had kept him awake most of the previous night. We had flushed them when we arrived and, with luck, they would be back at dawn.

Plan A was for Ken and myself to decoy the field at first light while the other three – the young ones – marched to the boundary fence. It would be the first time the fence had been shot for four years. We leave this route, to and from the main roost, unshot to give the geese the security they deserve.

We did contemplate trying the grass field under the moon but had a feeling that, with the lunar phase waning, the previous night was probably the last suited to moonlighting. All thoughts in this direction were also dispelled when snow began to fall on the way to the hotel after an hour with Rab and a bottle of Bells. The forecast had been for strong north-west winds and no mention of the white stuff.

Next day, an hour before dawn, saw us driving through a blizzard and an ever-thickening mist. Ideal for a fence flight but no good for this crock who could only reach there in a 4WD. Drifts barred the way and the four fitter Guns, including Ken and his new knees, set out as the sky was just beginning to lighten.

These days we all have two-way radios and, besides their huge communication advantage, they provide a sometimes fascinating insight to trawler life aboard the close-in boats in the North Sea. It appeared that haddock would be cheap that week.

A single shot soon had Jack scoring once more. Two shots and two geese with the tool he was reluctant to use!

He is, however, not the easiest of Guns to handle (something to do with the 20 years in the army I believe) and though, on the walkie-talkie, I rather forcibly suggested he should move out of the wood and along the fence to get under the flight line, he went in the opposite direction!

CAMOUFLAGE

Simon followed instructions and, with lesser artillery, downed two pinks and a bonus for me. The date was December 10 and, as he went to pick his first bird, in half light, an aged cock grouse jumped and was promptly downed.

Two weeks later, after a slow five hours of steam roasting, (it took that long to tenderise the old chap) it was totally and utterly so delicious that I urged my long suffering wife to dash to the village store to grab a bottle of claret to bless the whole affair!

After flight that morning I asked Jack why he had not done as I had suggested. His answer made sense. Combat training dictate was totally against the mixture of his wetland camouflage and blanket snow. Ingrained teaching precluded his embarking on what he felt would be a useless venture. He was, of course, right. Simon did only get the one chance, in half-light, the remainder of the birds veering off to one side on their approach to where he crouched in the all-white terrain.

Another lesson learned. Now four white smocks hang in the shoot's store cabin. And Jack did buy the Browning auto. Next season should, I mused, be interesting!

Though camouflage clothing is essential for a goose chaser he must quickly learn that complete stillness is the number one ingredient when it comes to concealment. Sometimes the pheasant shot, used to half-tame birds, will never comprehend this. Movement is a goose's greatest ally. Do not be fooled into presuming that, because a skein is still two gunshots away, you will be undetectable. One hundred eyes will be watching for that faintest of movement and, with plenty of alarm croaks, the big birds will be gone.

LOOSE CANNON

Another type of Gun to be watched for on one's sorties both north and south of the Border is the loose cannon – of the verbal variety.

One such was James, a game shot who accompanied us on a mixed shoot which was to include grouse, pheasants, ducks and geese. Fortunately his big gaffe happened on the last day of our four-day stay and I was able to hurry him away from our irate hotelier/shooting host. Until then the trip had been a great success with our predicted bag of each variety topping the estimate.

We had assembled, at 10am, on an upland farm on the edge of a grouse moor which our hotelier had been renting for the past 10 years. There were 10 Guns in our party and the format was that eight would stand and two would walk with the beaters on each drive.

Alistair McPherson, the shoot owner/farmer, had always been a walking Gun and it was he who gave the customary safety-guidance talk at the commencement of each day. Alistair was a no-nonsense straight talking Scot with a thick brogue. Even after my many years listening to him I had some trouble taking in all he said but, with some imagination, one should be able to get the gist. Unfortunately, however, our loose cannon chipped in the minute he had finished. 'Now could someone say that in English!'

Perhaps, had I been able to warn my colleague that the moor owner was not over-fond of the English, he may not have been as rude. But, knowing LC, he might have been.

The deeply wounded Scot turned crimson with fury and I feared what might happen next when our ever-tactful hotelier stepped in and quickly took the wretched fellow by the arm and guided him to the vehicles. He was given a father and mother of a dressing down and warned to stay well away from Mr McPherson for the rest of the day. Happily it diffused the situation at the time but I was to later hear that the hapless hotelier was never offered the moor again!

MUCKLE LYIN YONT

Local dialect is, of course, a big problem for we Sassenachs venturing north to tarry among the rural Scots. Visit the Inverness region and you will feel verbally at ease among what is surely the most beautifully spoken English in this fair isle. Elsewhere you might as well often be in a far flung corner of the Empire.

The phrase 'Muckle Lyin Yont' is taken from a Scottish poem and means 'much lying beyond'. Muckle can also mean big. It must be stressed that this comment on the Scottish melodious and fascinating rendering of our tongue is in no way meant to be derogatory. How I would love to have been born in that most beautiful of all lands. Indeed, had I got my way, my third son, who shot his first goose there at the age of nine, would have been born a Scot. And did not my paternal ancestors come down from Ayrshire to Lancashire some 300 years ago?

There was one occasion in a wee farm cottage, in a far away corner, when I thought I had solved my language problems. Accompanying me was Ken mark two, a Blackpool hotelier. Jamie was halfway through the bottle of Bells we had presented him with but a short while earlier when we got round to asking him how to reach the field where the geese had been feeding that day. We had spied them from a distant hill washing in a recent rain pool and cropping on the surrounding bright green pasture. The area was unfamiliar and I needed to know exactly how to get there in darkness the next morning. Jamie's directions came thick and fast with much gesticulating.

'Do you mean we should go through the gate behind the cottage and up the field by the stone wall?' I enquired.

Jamie began his verbal onslaught again. The trouble is that in Lancashire, where I come from, a dyke is a ditch while in Scotland it is a wall. The area was full of dykes, ditches and walls!

Seeing I was still baffled Jamie turned his attention to Ken, who was soon nodding his assent. Eureka! At last! Someone who must, indeed, be heaven-sent. A new and able shooting companion who also understood the lingo! I relaxed and left them to it though, strangely, Ken only nodded and never queried the directions.

Once outside, and on our way to HQ, I asked Ken to explain where we had to go at dawn.

'I haven't a bloody clue,' he told me.

'But you kept nodding,' I cried.

'Well he kept calling me Ken and I thought it would be rude if I said I couldn't understand!'

I then had to explain that the oft-used 'ye ken' in Scots parlance means the same as the ubiquitous 'Yer know' in England. We would, I declared, have to bring the starting time forward half an hour to compensate for the prolonged search we would surely be faced with next morning. We were to be joined by the aforementioned, sometimes wayward Boris, who lived near enough to journey over that morning, and he was given the new TOA by phone.

DISASTER

I had warned Ken that, 'We may have trouble with Boris. He is sometimes bad to manage.'

Boris was, however, never late for a shooting or fishing appointment and, next morning, we found him already sitting in his 4WD by the barn. To describe the weather that dawn as 'hellish' would not have been an overstatement. A gale raged out of the west and the rain, which had created the fresh lake, where the 1,000 pinkfoot had been frolicking the previous day, was now horizontal.

It was to be a morning of disaster. The evening before we had left our 24 shell decoys in the farm workshop. This was now securely locked and the key was not on its usual hook. We would find our way to the flood, set up the hides, and return for the decoys when Jamie's light came on.

'Follow us closely,' I instructed Boris. 'We will open the gates and you close them behind us'.

Up a one-in-four incline by the dry stone wall (dyke) through the first gate and all went well. Then, when we reached the second gate, Boris was not behind us. We carried on and eventually found the flood and set up two hides, one in a nettle bed, where two fences met, the other in a ditch. The ground was littered with fresh droppings visible only by torchlight in the inky black.

Suddenly the rain ceased and the clouds were swept away to reveal a clear dawn and the first party of pinks swept in low, saw something amiss and were gone. Had we posted our decoys they would, no doubt, have circled.

Then, with the wind still howling and in half light, we heard the incessant blaring of a horn. At the top of a ridge, 300 yards distant, we saw Boris's vehicle moving slowly along. It stopped at the top of the field, turned round and proceeded back in the direction from which it had just come, all the while with the strident horn howling like a berserk banshee.

The flight was now well and truly on but, at the sight and sound of this mad chariot, they quickly went looking for pastures new. Ken, being young and fit, legged it up the hill and cut Boris's charge short before the entire farm staff turned out to answer the siren.

Boris told Ken he had thought it better to go back for the decoys, ignoring my instructions and making a complete balls-up of the flight. Then he said he would stay at the top of the hill because he thought he knew where the geese would be feeding.

Half an hour later, with the sun well up and the wind abated, we packed up gooseless and went looking for Boris. Ken came back from another quick recce shaking his head. 'He is lying in the middle of a winter wheat field behind a small rock with his dog sitting next to him,' was the report. 'What do we do now?'

'Leave him there and go for breakfast,' I replied.

TOUCHÉ

I lament my inability to comprehend the Scots brogue but, conversely, I am sure strangers to my native Lancashire and to Cumbria, where I now live, are baffled by those rural dialects.

For instance, I had just arrived at a Lake District trout water with a born and bred Prestonian when a tiny child appeared from a boat clutching rod and bag of fish. The huge beam of joy surrounding the little fellow was turned to one of complete puzzlement when my elderly friend asked him, 'Are tar tut main mon then?'

'Pardon?'

'Are tar tut main mon?' delivered loudly and with great vigour.

To an equally baffled father I had to explain, 'My friend would like to know if your son is the main man – the most important member of the party?'

Likewise, shortly after arriving in my new hillside Cumbrian home, I was fencing with a helpful local (they are all helpful in this neck of the woods) when he asked me to 'passusyonpost ligginowertheer' – 'pass me that post lying over there' and later 'asta gettena stapple onthi?' 'Do you have a staple in your pocket?'

On that day my fencer was Tom and whenever he handed me a staple, they always bore a useful hint of grease – he kept them under his hat!

There is a footnote to this piece on regional dialect and it might easily bear the sub heading: Has the world gone mad?

The little gem appeared when I phoned the Scottish DEFRA office to register the pheasants we were to be putting down on our Scottish goose grounds next season in line with the bird flu regulations. The charming Ms on the end of the free-phone number was obviously not Scottish. I wrongly assumed her lilt was Welsh.

After we had concluded recording the required information I asked how easy it was for her to understand heavy Scottish brogue since she seemed to be from the land of the red dragon.

'I'm not Welsh. I'm from Sweden and I don't understand a word when it's like that!' came the shock response.

I had always put the Scots at the top of the intellect pile. Now I begin to wonder.

DOG'S BOTTOMS

The penultimate tale in this chapter also has a strong rural Scots flavour. There happened, in this beautiful village where I am privileged to live, an event which also sparked memories of a rather special place in these stories of goose trails. How my chance meeting occurred was most bizarre for it came about through, of all things, bottom sniffing. Before I am accused of pedalling pornography let me hasten to add that the participants were canine.

Bobbie, the 10-year-old family Jack Russell goes deaf when he is doing what he wants to do, like all his breed, and he was delighted to meet a pooch, of similar stature, to partake in this obligatory ritual.

'Do you know why they do that?' I enquired of his new friend's owner.

'No, but doubtless you will be telling me,' replied a tall polished Scots gent who would not look out of place at the heart of his homeland's rugby pack.

'Well,' I proceeded. 'Not many folk know that, before man arrived on this earth, the globe was ruled by dogs. Once a year they gathered, from all points of the compass, to form their rules. In this period of their evolution their rear ends were detachable and all had hung that part of their anatomy in the bottom room at one of the annual gatherings.

'Unfortunately some wag shouted 'Fire' and all of them, to the last dog, rushed out, snatching the first posterior they came to. Since then all species, from Chihuahuas to great Danes, have been searching for a correct match.'

'Ah,' said my acquaintance in his smooth lilt, 'You've heard Matt McGinn's recitation,' and launched into a much more hilarious rendition of the real version.

'All the dogs they had a party
They came from near and far
And some dogs came by aeroplane
And some by motor car

They went into the lobby and signed the visitor's book
And each one hung his a***hole upon an a***hole hook.
One dog was not invited and chose to vent his ire
He rushed into the meeting place and loudly shouted 'fire'
Now the dogs were so excited and had no time to look
And each one took an a***hole from off the nearest hook.
Oh this is a sad, sad story for it is very sore
to wear another a***hole you've never worn before.
And that is why, when dogs meet, by land or sea or foam,
Each sniffs the other's a***hole in hopes it is his own.'

The gent, on holiday with his wife, went on to explain that Matt McGinn was the Billy Connolly of an earlier era and died as Billy's career was commencing. My friendly Scot promised to send a print-out of Matt's recitation and it quickly arrived on disc.

But how did a poem, about dog's bottoms, evoke memories of goose shooting? Make another brew and harken.

Early one September, when young and fit, I was invited by Bob Rhodes, of the Ross & Cromarty chapter, to an abundant grouse moor in Lanarkshire. Its owner was a distant uncle of Bob's and we were required to report to his farm by 9am for a 10am start.

Bob was then farming and a further member of that vocation, the equally fit and youthful Jim Burns, made up our trio. After a pre-dawn start from our Lancashire bases we were sitting down to a sumptuous breakfast, by 8am, in a remote hotel not far from our host's farm.

Totally replete we entered Mary's kitchen on the dot. Atop her Aga sat a huge pan of sizzling bacon; Breakfast for the farm staff, I concluded.

'Sit yourselves down, you haven't long before you are off,' ordered Mary and three plates, groaning under mountains of bacon, eggs, sausage, haggis, fried bread and beans, were ceremoniously placed on the table.

Bob, sharper by far than either Jim or myself, re-acted faster than an adder's strike. A problem stomach precluded him from all food before morning exercise. His share was piled on top of the remaining two platters and, manfully, Jim and I did what justice we could to the humongous piles in spite of our already overloaded guts.

Bob received severe abuse from us both and we didn't care one jot when we delayed his slog up the severe climb while we left behind the undigested contents of our stomachs for the ravens to relish!

The grouse were there in great numbers and the three English incursors did more than their share in reaping a bounteous harvest. Nor was the day finished with our departure from the moor.

As dusk drew in we were led to that aforementioned 'special place', a hidden inland marsh set among rolling hills and reached via an overgrown track. It was obviously a much-used rendezvous for water fowl and I detected some pinkfoot goose feathers and heaps of old droppings. I was assured that the geese would be back 'later in the season' and our kind host, quickly detecting my keenness, promised to make contact upon their return.

There were no hides around this most tranquil of waters and I learnt that the wilderness was neither fed nor regularly shot. It was the sort of environment which teems with natural food. We huddled down among the lush vegetation and, that night, mallard and teal came in great numbers. We left before the flight had ceased with game bags bulging.

Twelve months passed before I heard, via Bob, from our thoughtful host. The geese were back and coincided with a fowling trip already planned further north that week.

This time my two companions were not those from my initial visit but, nevertheless, just as competent with the gun. Bob insisted I avail myself of the invite.

We settled in to the waist-high rushes as the sky darkened. Everywhere there was even greater evidence of bird life than on our previous venture. Where grass touched the water's edge it was as close cropped, by a 1,000 bills, as any bowling green. The results of nightly preening lay like a white carpet on the sward.

Mallard were, once more, the forerunners followed by arrowing teal and, a real bonus, packs of wigeon. Only the wigeon circled before dropping in. Perhaps it was their first sortie for it was comparatively early in the season for the species in those parts.

There is no record of the bag but I do recall that we stopped when our dogs had retrieved a tidy pile next to each of us. We were just preparing to depart, with no sign of the ever-elusive geese, when their chorus burst over the ridge of a nearby hill. They were only just visible, at around 30 yards, and we stopped at six, two each out of that first wave. As we hurried down the track more were dropping in and the babble was deafening.

We handed over our entire bag as thanks to our host. The norm would have been to accept a brace of whatever species we were offered, but we were to be away for several more days. He told us that, after

WIGEON *by Rodger McPhail.*

distributing the geese to old timers in the village, the remainder would fill his freezer nicely. I know of no farmer who welcomes geese for the table.

We did not, however, leave our gratitude at that. We entertained our benefactor and the kindly Mary to dinner at our overnight hotel and it was there, in the local's bar around midnight, that I heard my first rendition of the dog's bottom story.

Under a settle was curled by little Lab Jess, immaculately behaved as ever. But not so the cur accompanying a grizzled shepherd. Her somnolent posture was disturbed by an insistent delving and a good old inspection of her rear end.

'Do ye ken why they do that?' questioned the dog's owner.

'Something to do with sex?'

'That just proves how little ye Sassenachs ken,' replied the hairy old Scot, in tones as rusty as a River Clyde's dredger bucket, and plunged instantly into Matt's hilarious ditty. We were able to grasp enough of the heavy brogue to send us into uncontrollable mirth. The vulgar bit was, for instance, pronounced airsoles. Everything sounds 10 times funnier when you are full of whisky. I requested a written version but this was beyond our raconteur. Since then, as a result, for nigh on 50 years, I have been able only to recount a garbled interpretation until my chance encounter the other day.

I trust you will agree, however, that my version is more suited for my annual Women's Institute discourse on folklore than the unexpurgated.

The book had, as they say in the newspaper world, almost been put to bed when the memory jolt occurred. I only just caught the deadline and I am glad I did.

I have promised myself I will call on Bob's relations again in the near future. I hear the land is still in the same family though our original host has been long departed from this earth.

Perhaps the secret marsh has become an SSSI and is a sanctuary, though on many such designated places shooting is permitted. Those who administer these sites do, thankfully, recognise what superior conservationists many shooting men can make. Bob's uncle was a prime example and this is why I had not pushed his hospitality. I know of some who would not have been able to stay away.

Hopefully it is still unexploited and will serve to show my young son how necessary such wild places are as havens for the wellbeing of our sport.

A BARTER

Still on the doggie theme I was reminded, quite by chance recently, of the remarkable strides that have been made not only in the style of camouflage clothing but in their waterproof qualities also. We had been looking for bedding for a newly arrived pup when my wife remarked, 'We could do with something like that old white jacket of yours.'

It brought so many fond memories back to me. The jacket had, indeed, been slept on by two generations of dogs long after it had ceased to be worn by myself. How it came into my possession is worth the telling.

As already illustrated, an essential part of a goose shooter's winter apparel are his whites, although the call for snow gear is growing less and less with the increase in milder winters.

I have to admit that this favourite white garment of all time was, in fact, merely a woollen donkey jacket. Graham had, over the years, become a good pal after first meeting over my shop counter in Blackpool.

He was one of the local sea defence construction workers and, one day, breezed in wearing a new winter-issue jacket of heavy off-white wool.

'I could do with a jacket like that,' was my knee-jerk reaction to the splendid garb.

'I could do with a tie like that,' was the instant riposte. Graham had long envied my British Field Sports Society black tie with its delicate gold motifs of leaping salmon, stags heads and rocketing pheasants.

Off came jacket and tie with no further words exchanged.

Donkey jacket wearers will be well aware of their superb insulating qualities. Besides being wind and waterproof they offer that cosiness which only the product of a sheep's fleece seems to provide. Unfortunately they are very bulky and make gun mounting a problem. Looking back I reckon I wore my favourite winter gear for something like 30 years! I wore it in downpours, also, and it never leaked.

The event brought back memories of those long slogs over the Solway sand flats to the top of Rockcliffe Marsh, 50 plus years ago, when the heavens poured. Oilskins or waterproof clothing had us all sweating so much that we were as wet inside as we were outside.

The same dilemma was there on the grouse moors too. Especially when one was walking up the wily birds. It is on such places where, today, one can still come across old characters who still refuse to wear our modern gear.

For instance, not too long ago, I was one of eight Guns placed in grouse butts on a Pennine shoot when there came a torrent. We knew we had a lengthy wait in front of us – perhaps half an hour – and while my butt was a traditional cosy stone and turf-built affair, those on either side of me were merely of flimsy board.

I called the respective occupants over to the sanctuary of my den but only one reacted – the younger Gun. The other, an ageing law court judge, stood like a giant oak tree against his scanty shelter unbending and seeming oblivious to the torrent. Perhaps he pulled his trilby a little further onto his balding pate.

'Look at that silly old buffer,' I observed to my companion.

'You mean my Father,' came the reply. 'I am afraid we can never persuade him to wear anything but that old green tweed suit and he never seems to ail a thing.'

Perhaps I am made of the wrong stuff!

Chapter 11

Goodbye Old Times

There is previous mention of intrepid goose chaser BB, Denys Watkins-Pitchford. On many of his sorties went Mac, Douglas McDougall. Both hunted the great grey birds north of the Border before the Second World War but it was not until near the end of this conflict that they joined forces.

The time I found, quite by chance, these same pastures roamed by the indefatigable duo, other goose chasers were still in small numbers and very rarely seen. BB must, surely, be blamed for encouraging the wildfowler to seek the Scottish goose when they read of his exploits in newspaper, magazine and book. Both of these worthies, later in their writings, lament the rush north, which eventually was to reach almost Klondike proportions. Would these goose grounds have been discovered anywhere near as quickly had they not penned their exploits? I doubt it.

While on the subject of goose chasing books, surely the least read has to be the Special Magnum Edition of McDougall's *Goose Fever*? It was by accident that I discovered this publication when I rang David Grayling, the antiquarian book dealer from Shap, in Cumbria, to ask him to find me a copy of the first edition of *Goose Fever.*

'As long as you are not after the Magnum version it will be no problem,' said David.

I had no idea what he was talking about. Surely, if McDougall had produced a second work I would know about it. Not so. It transpired that the Magnum edition was, in the author's own words, printed at the front of his publication, 'For private presentation only,' and, 'Not for sale to the public.' Indeed, the beautifully bound copy now in my possession firmly declares, in gilt letters on its cover, 'Private Edition.' Which is why, I suppose, it took me two years to obtain one after Grayling's first mention.

Nor did my book come from that normally one hundred percent

reliable purveyor of literature. He did hear of one copy during this time but refused to pay the 'extortionate' price demanded. In the end my apparently unopened copy came, would you believe, from far away Denmark! How the deal was done was yet another of those quirks.

On our way north to the goose grounds in October (2004), we had made a detour to one of the world's finest pie makers to stock up on a supply of these scrumptious calorific parcels. Close by was a second-hand bookshop and I asked the proprietor if he had ever heard of the publication. Amazingly, within seconds, his computer had found a copy on the shelves of a Denmark dealer and it would be delivered to my Cumbrian door a week later! The cost, including postage, was still considerably less than the earlier discovered copy.

My contention that the work was unopened comes from the fact that the spine crackled as I turned its pristine pages and the dust cover, bearing the enigmatic painting by BB of McDougall with his 8-bore and a goose, was unblemished.

Now I am able to join Mac once more on his dawn and dusk wanderings.

However, McDougall's accounts of his outings with his old pal from 1976 to 1983 in the new work do not appear to have been as harmonious as when they were younger.

We are told that the ageing BB was driven north by his daughter Angela, and this the man who, in an earlier book, declared that petticoats had no place on goose shooting trips!

Mac's accounts of his exploits with his old pal are, however, just as evocative in this second work.

We hear that, on one venture, all three Guns were in their seventies – as I am now. McDougall is critical of BBs gun placings and even chides him for taking a forward position, thus intercepting the geese before they reached their feeding ground and the other guns. It is all good stuff.

The writer laments, too, the great number of visiting shooters and how he was forced to resort to hiring the services of a goose guide. One feels saddened for an old man who, it would appear, longed for the good old days.

But were those days that good? There was then only a fraction of the number of geese now wintering on these shores and great numbers were slaughtered to be sold legitimately to game dealers. How bad was that? The act, in 1971, which prohibited the sale of wild geese was the best thing to happen to this noble bird in its long history. I am not, of course, suggesting that the pair overshot. This was the doing of others.

McDougall regrets that he could find few places to shoot when he was left entirely to his own initiative. He found he was refused permission on lands where he was once able to roam because the owner felt they were overshot. What joy that, in Scotland, there are so many Lairds of this opinion. I have found this myself and these conservation-minded souls must be applauded. However it is becoming more and more difficult for these folk to refuse the gold proffered by hungry goose guides. On Ponkey's, where I have sole control, no one area is shot more than once a fortnight. Indeed, unless there is an urgent call to move birds from new grass or freshly sown grain, visits are restricted to only twice monthly. Experience has shown that geese can live with this amount of limited disturbance.

We also have our own adjunct to the main inland roost in the form of a pond. This we leave strictly undisturbed if at all possible. If it is shot we strive to do so lightly. I like to see (or hear in the blackness) geese still dropping in as we depart from this water.

BASC seek to control the army of goose guides in Scotland and plead with all to come under their umbrella. If they do one hopes that they will comply with the no over-shooting guide lines.

STUPIDITY

But back to my own chase. Undoubtedly two of the reasons for the geese remaining for so long on their traditional Solway wintering grounds, though admittedly in dwindling numbers as more and more pinks head for the peace of the Norfolk sugar beet fields, is the fact that they fill their bellies relatively undisturbed on Kinmount Estate, due north of the Firth, on Rockcliffe Marsh, to the east, and the Caerlaverock Reserve. Even though the birds now have sanctuary roosts they would still depart if they were over-harried at feed.

Roosting quarters are uppermost in the well-being of the goose. At times, misguidedly, permits have been issued through BASC to shoot inland loch roosts on a limited scale in various parts of Scotland but this, in my opinion, is nothing less than stupidity. During almost 40 years of visiting one Scottish strath I have witnessed such a folly.

Once a year we called at this remote part of eastern Scotland and always found geese feeding on winter stubble, or rough pasture where burns wound circuitously and clumps of heather clung to peat hags.

Then, 20 years ago, the geese vanished. Permits had been issued to shoot the geese on the edge of the nearby loch roost and the birds deserted this wild feeding place.

What great times we had experienced worming our way along those narrow runnels to stalk a party of pinks or greys. Occasionally a cock grouse would explode from under one's nose to clatter away, all alarms sounding, and one would freeze until the feeding buzz emitted once more from perhaps 100 throats. We never harried this place and, in a matter of days after our visits, geese would be back to be left in peace.

This form of goose shooting was as near to red stag stalking as you could get. Sometimes you could pass a rabbit, at feed 20 yards from your ditch, and never halt his chomping.

This was the spot where, one morning, a hen peregrine nigh-on decapitated me. We had espied around 200 pinks feeding each side of a ditch on our arrival on the grounds the afternoon before and were tucked in next morning with the light just starting. I saw the bird arrowing towards me, at great speed, and automatically ducked as it passed inches over my head on flared wings. Whether or not it would have struck, had I not moved, I know not but it was an experience I could never forget.

That morning both grouse and partridge uttered their wake-up calls and blue hares lolloped past before the main party of geese put in an appearance. Earlier, at first light, a small bunch had come in, quietly, from the direction of the coast and pitched on to a patch of grass half a mile away on the side of the valley. They were too far off to have seen our decoys in the dimness and the later arrivals dropped straight in to their feeding cousins.

However, their chosen ley was only a short distance from a little-used track down which we knew farm workers would be journeying shortly. The sun had still not topped the distant Scots pines when this did, indeed, happen and the entire party swung straight for our decoys. During the short time the geese had been at feed we had played them occasional subtle tunes on our calls and it worked.

Richard was directly under the birds and, as they came in on cupped wings, he left it until the last wave was past before he dropped a right and left. My chance was easier for they flared at the sound of the reports. I had time to take a further two, as they fanned against the wind, and then slipped in another cartridge and collapsed a third.

It was interesting to confirm that the early lot had, in fact, roosted at sea. Two of the birds had sand on their legs and feet while the other three bore traces of black peat from the loch.

On the way back to the farm, with two number six game cartridges in the chamber, I tumbled a rabbit for the shepherd's wife whom we knew would receive such bounty with great joy.

In the chapter on goose stalking I have recorded how Simon undertook his first stalk on this same valley bottom many years later. In those in-between-years all the heather disappeared and numerous shelter belts of plantings of spruce had grown up. It is still a wild and peaceful place, untouched by gun save my infrequent presence.

My trips north are, indeed, with advancing years, becoming fewer and fewer. In his later writings McDougall raises a point most pertinent to my own current situation.

He says that, in spite of his age and consequent lack of vigour, he is still content to carry on his goose chasing as long as he is not an encumbrance to others. These days, as a severely disabled Gun, I am very conscious of my condition. I have made those who share my goose lands promise to stand up and speak if they feel I am beginning to get things wrong or I am a liability.

EXPERIENCE

The other day, however, there was an example of how experience can turn what, initially, seemed to be an impossible situation into a favourable one. We arrived at a goose field where around 500 pinks were feeding in the centre of a vast expanse of barley stubble. To my young companion there appeared to be no way we could establish an ambush.

It was mid-morning and the geese, we learned, had found the stubble only the day before. There was plenty of scattered grain and they would be using the same territory for several days. Fortunately not all the bales had been moved off the vast acreage and the attached diagram illustrates how we employed a strategy which resulted in a modest bag – turning what appeared to be a hopeless situation into success.

As soon as we entered the field the geese lifted and we quickly moved the bales to create a triangle of hides with a distance of 45 yards between each. A decoy pattern of 20 shells was laid out and, using matching hide netting, we tucked into the shelter of the bales out of the wind and constant drizzle. For the hiker it would have been a wretched day but for the goose shooter it was ideal. Our third companion arrived as the birds began to return in small lots and we collected seven before departing and

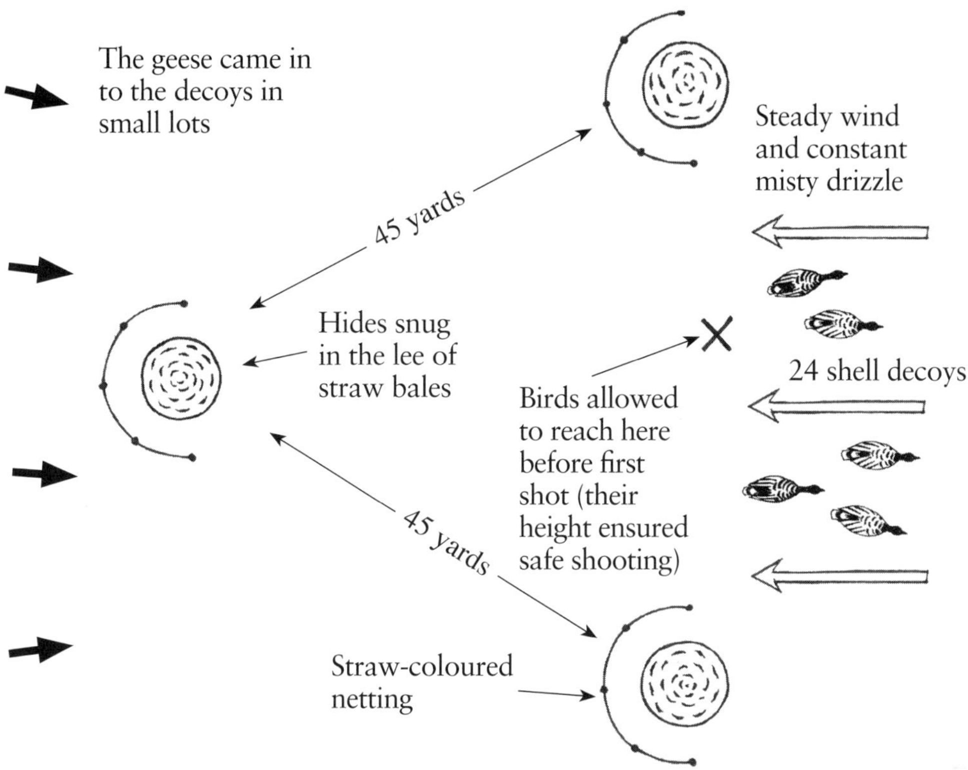

THE AMBUSH LAYOUT – *By employing the above layout all three Guns got their share of shooting. After the first shot the birds went back in the strong wind. After one hour we left the field in peace.*

leaving the remainder to land undisturbed.

The pattern drew birds from all sides and gave us all an equal amount of shooting. They came in low out of the mist and against a stiff wind plus driven drizzle. In the lee of our bale hides we got our positions exactly right.

The fact that there was rain on the plastic decoys destroyed the theory that they will not work when wet. Perhaps this would be so in calm weather. On this occasion conditions were very much in our favour.

What pleasure BB and Mac must also have had in displaying their combined knowledge to their tyros. However, one has to wonder, also, if BB ever regretted introducing his Norfolk friend to his private goose grounds. After the early forays Mac found himself with so many of his own family to accommodate on his trips that there was no room for BB.

BB did not appear to be from prolific stock, while the McDougall clan was the reverse. Fecundity leaps to mind! His sons, nephews, cousins and grandchildren seem endless. All this had to pile much pressure on BB's geese.

But how can one criticise a soul stricken by goose fever for wanting to introduce his offsprings to the overwhelming charisma of goose chasing with all its traditions and secrets? I should be the last to do so, for did I not take up the gun again to do exactly the same when my third-born arrived?

THE OLD WARRIORS

There is a very good reason why a certain day in May 2005 could have been named 'Goose Down Day,' in the Cumbrian village of Hawkshead. It marked the visit of Keith McDougall all the way from lowland Norfolk.

During the compilation of this book many were the communications between myself and Keith, son of Mac. He thought a lunch of Barbary duck in my territory a splendid notion, set off at 5am and was here by noon.

We both agreed our first face-to-face would have been more suited to a pub in Perthshire gooseland but we quickly turned summer into winter as we recalled how we had, unwittingly, shot the same estuaries, lochsides and hedgerows as each other within a very short time in the calendar of events.

Keith had a most welcome surprise for me – photographs of both BB and Mac hitherto unpublished. The captions tell their own stories (see pages 230 and 231).

RETURN TO REDKIRK

The yearning of Douglas McDougall for the old days was very forcibly pressed upon me shortly after the close of the 2004/05 season. March found brother Charles, Ken Watson and myself standing again on Solway's banks where we had first gathered in 1950. Even though a searingly vicious wind tore along the Firth there were numerous longshore addicts abroad that day walking their dogs.

On that first visit there were few motor cars and the lovely carpet-like sea-washed turf was reached mainly by cycle and foot. Then we saw not a soul for a whole week in our cosy lair on Redkirk Point, sheltered

*A RARE SHOT OF **BB***
(Denys Watkins-Pitchford, 1905-1990) – This photograph of BB (circa 1950s), on one of his many trips to Scotland, has never before been published. Its date coincides with my first forays to the Solway and gives a clue to the sort of conditions BB revelled in when he was goose chasing. He is well protected against the elements. The deerstalker flaps are down and muffler tucked inside waterproof coat which reaches long waders. Woollen mitts complete the outfit with briar pipe aiding his central heating system. Under an arm a hammerless side by side double 12 bore magnum. His favourite load was 1½ ounces of BBs. The goose is a greylag and appears to be a very large gander judging by its bulk next to the yellow Labrador.

from the prevailing winds by a deserted farmhouse and its steadings in the crab apple trees. The building housed only the salmon fisher's haaf nets and, in the garage, a double punt, gun and all its paraphernalia. All this was revealed through cracks and chinks in the fabric.

We found a peace and calm on Redkirk the like of which I had experienced on holy Lindisfarne. No doubt a place of worship, built of red sandstone, had stood there in the long ago for kirk is, of course, Scots for church. Was this, too, 'drenched in prayer,' which was how my vicar friend had explained Lindisfarne's aura?

Ken is something of an ecclesiastical historian and, while there are no visible traces of an ancient inhabitation, he points out that the monks of old would have found the Point a perfect location for many reasons. As a priority it would be easily defendable and its uppermost structure would

The Incomparable Mac
(Douglas McDougall, 1902-1993)

The photo of Mac, BB's regular companion for almost 40 years, was taken around the same time. It is the format for the painting BB did to illustrate the cover of the magnum edition of Mac's book 'Goose Fever'. The shooter's powerful physique enabled him to swing a heavy double 8-bore with consummate ease and it was capable of throwing a charge twice as heavy as his friend's weapon. The shot was taken on the reed beds of a northern estuary. The wing tipped greylag under his arm was found by the spaniel and was taken back to his Norfolk home where it joined the established feral flock.

provide the perfect look-out post. Its adjacent fertile plain was ideal for crop growing and animal fodder while the Firth was abundant in marine life. Flight nets, set out on the sandflats, would yield an endless larder of waders, ducks and geese.

On our March day we were rewarded, opposite Stormont Farm, over the Border Esk, by the sight of a large gathering of barnacle geese. They were close enough for us to pick out their stark markings through binoculars and, after a short time, they treated us to a noisy departure towards Caerlaverock.

Another bonus was a purely chance meeting with one of the locals who had become a regular part of our team towards the end of our years on the estuary. George White was out that day with his spaniel. There

RETURN TO REDKIRK – *When three of the fowlers who made the 1950 trip to the Solway met there in 2005 they paused for this shot on Redkirk Point. It was here they parked their caravan for a week. Left to right: Ken Watson, now aged 80, the author 74 and his brother Charles 78. The fourth member of the team, Geoff Holmes, died in 2002 aged 82.*

George 'Whitie' White – *'the truant' (first seen in Chapter 1) 50 years on (2005)*

was recognition on both sides. This was the same Whitie who suffered from goose fever in The Solway Years chapter. And he had a spaniel that day too.

We had last met Whitie at Jim Ritchie's funeral 17 years before. That day was sombre. But this time we were soon recalling the immediate post-war years when Rockcliffe Marsh, opposite where we stood, was a favourite haunt of the pinkfoot.

Whitie confirmed that the barnacle had taken over as the resident goose on the Solway. Since retirement, five years ago, his trips by boat over the Esk to the edge of Rockcliffe have filled his shooting months. In the season there is hardly a day he misses, and there are still enough pinks about to justify his efforts.

'I almost live over there from September to February and am as keen as ever.' In summer he also haaf nets for salmon, hence the weather-beaten features.

There is now a Gretna Wildfowl Association, formed 12 years ago when the locals were threatened with the loss of their age-old flighting territory. The happening was not, however, trauma-free. Raymond Cole is chairman of the club and told of the bombshell that hit himself and the locals.

'We suddenly heard that Carlisle Wildfowlers had secured a lease on Rockcliffe Marsh. They told us they were happy for us to carry on but that we had to join their club.'

The declaration incensed Gretna's fowlers. Heated meetings ensued and the locals were unanimous that they did not want to be dictated by an outside body.

'Eventually it was agreed that the Carlisle club would sub-let the shooting to us. It means both clubs now have rights,' said Ray, who has shot the edge of Rockcliffe for 40 years.

Between the two clubs the rental amounts, currently, to £3,000 per annum.

'It means our members, totalling less than 50, pay £85 a year for their shooting – not excessive by today's standards.'

Ray also contends there are big plus-sides to the situation. A rule permits only full club members to shoot the marsh. Until the lease was secured, up to 20 visiting fowlers were crossing on to the edge of Rockcliffe at the weekends – double the total of the locals using the territory.

'In the end we have benefited,' said Ray. 'The pressure is far less and we are now also allowed 12 yards up the creeks into the marsh.'

Another fowling club granted rights to shoot the edge of Rockcliffe is the South Solway WA based in England. They are allowed to cross the River Eden and proceed over the marsh with guns in slips, where the new grass meets the high merse.

THE GREY LADY

One of my tasks on the day of this last visit was to delve further into the strange case of the Grey Lady, a happening which has been occurring in this part of the Solway for all of 70 plus years.

Charles and I saw her soon after our initial sortie in 1950. We were heading for the salmon stake nets off Dornock Brow, eight miles from Gretna, one pre-dawn when she appeared 20 yards in front of our vehicle. On each side of the single track lane, leading to the estuary, there were no gaps in the dense hawthorn hedge but something had emerged from one side and moved, at walking pace, across our path and through the opposite hedge.

Neither of us spoke until we reached the spot.

'What on earth was that?' gasped Charles.

We were totally baffled. The night was black. There was neither wind nor fog but our headlights had clearly picked out a small bent grey figure. Charles likened it to 'a sheep on its hind legs.'

No geese went into the bag that morning but we did collect three mallard and a greater black backed gull between us. Jim knew of a mallard flightline along this quiet stretch which was visited by himself only occasionally, since it involved a lengthy bike ride. We told Jim's wife Betty about our ghostly sighting and expected nothing more than a quizzical look but she was in no way surprised.

'That would have been the Grey Lady. When we were kids on bicycles we always rode past the Dornock road as fast we could.'

The lane runs past an ancient Church of Scotland graveyard, its lichen-covered tombstones now pitched at crazy angles like tottering drunks. There is nothing spooky about it in daylight but the nearby Annan Library is full of recorded sightings. The Chief Librarian, Rob McLean, was helpful and knowledgeable on the subject.

'There has even been talk of making her a tourist attraction,' he told me. 'How many print-outs would you like?'

Most of the stories, from local newspapers, had a similar theme;

'We were near Dornock when I saw an elderly woman crossing in front of us in what seemed to be a long Victorian dress.'

'She was shrouded in mist, which extended across the road. I was terrified. We appeared to drive straight through her.'

The latter was from Mrs Margaret Ching, from the West Midlands. She was in Gretna Green for her wedding and the headline read, 'New scare adds to 'ghost road' mystery.'

On the way home from this March nostalgic visit we detoured so that I could show my wife Annie where the stackyard had been in Gretna and where our friendly caravan had dwelt many winters. They say you should not go back and the maxim rang true for now there are only stacks of storage pallets and a rusting vehicle.

GOOSE GUIDES

I am firmly of the opinion that a major cause of destroying the 'Old days' on much of Scotland's goose grounds is over-shooting by goose guides. Indeed as I write these pages they are moving into my precious patch to such a degree that I am now distressingly surrounded by goose-let land.

I broached the subject with Alan Myers, big gun specialist from Winmarleigh, near Garstang, Lancashire, himself one of this band of often-abused professionals. It was refreshing that he was completely willing to discuss a sometimes contentious matter.

I have known the 58-year-old Alan since he shot his first goose as a teenager. Was he still as keen?

'I'm afraid the urge started to wear off about five years ago but something has taken its place – punt gunning.'

Next season he will have a 25ft double punt, to be used mostly in Scottish waters. 'I can't get enough of it but should have started years ago. At my age it is rather hard work.'

I suspect, also, that Alan is feeling a tad guilty about the amount of goose harrying that guides are imposing on the Scottish geese. He agreed with my findings that no longer are huge gatherings of pinks and greys remaining on their traditional grounds north of the Border. Alan operates in Perthshire, on territory where I shot 40 years ago. Then the greylags predominated. Now Alan expects mainly pinkfoot.

Where, then, have the greys gone when counting shows that their numbers continue to multiply?

'Many are moving out to the Western Isles where there is also a resident population,' said Alan.

And the pinks?

'Huge numbers are going to their old haunts in Norfolk and South Lincolnshire. There they can feed on the tops of discarded sugar beet and do no harm.'

It is now estimated that almost half of the British Isles pinks winter in that southern North Sea area and Keith McDougall, who lives in Stiffkey, Norfolk confirmed this at first hand. (There was a reported 140,000 birds there at one stage in January 2005.)

Alan was also interested to hear David Wilkins' contention that the pinks and greys are being ousted from the Solway by the ever-swelling numbers of protected barnacle goose. I asked Alan if he felt there was likely to be a restriction put on Scottish goose shooting; 'How can there be? They have to be moved for the sake of the farmers. If the birds were allowed to remain on the crops they would do an impossible amount of damage. Government compensation would have to be huge.'

I have deliberately not lumped all references to goose guides under one heading. They are referred to chronologically throughout the book and, generally, my words are, I hope, favourable.

BARNACLE GEESE *by Rodger McPhail – A big surprise, in October 2003, were large numbers of barnacle geese on Ponkey's. The shoot is close to the flight path for the species from their breeding grounds in Spitsbergen to the Solway. Ornithologists concluded that adverse weather while crossing the North Sea, had forced them to touch down at their first landfall. Numbers were estimated at 3,000. They remained for five days, feasting on stubble turnip green tops, before moving on to the Solway.*

DOUBLE 8-BORE – *The definition of bliss for me was the quietude of The Lakes plus an endless helping of shooting and fishing. Note the double 8-bore: an ideal weapon for the giant Canada geese abundant on lakes like this.*

Chapter 12

Paradise Found

Forty years a goose shooter. Enough cream in any man's lifetime. Four decades chasing the grey battalions would, it seemed, be my lot as I lay, totally immobile, in the Southport Spinal Unit at the age of 57.

Plenty of time to reflect. I was luckier, by far, than most of my room mates. And several Solway friends lay deep inside the earth. In fact Betty, widow of Jim from Gretna, had already driven the 100 miles to see me.

How sweet was it, then, to be sitting on my Scottish goose grounds 10 years later and to be asked by a five-year-old son, 'What is Paradise Dad?'

Questions don't come much easier. From our pigeon hide in an ancient belt of Scots pines, Jago and I were watching a skylark singing his April song high in the heavens. A peregrine had arrowed across our front, possibly attracted by the decoys, minutes earlier and the pinkfoot were still in residence.

'This is Paradise.' And that was enough for a young fellow to take in for the time being.

Four years later, and precisely 50 years to the month after I had shot my first goose, I was again alongside Jago when, on a dark and windy dawn, he swung his gun onto the only goose he had ever aimed at. He brought it tumbling from an astonishing height.

We were tucked behind a magnum straw bale on Ponkey's, in October, when he carried out his feat. There were three hides on the 100-acre field and our arrival, pre-dawn, had not been without its drama.

Paul, now a constant companion on my goose hunting sorties, was behind one bale and Thomas, a clay busting pal from the long ago, manned number two. We had arrived in good time in darkness and set out the 24 shell decoys in the centre of the hides which were in a rough triangle two gun shots apart.

It was the first visit to the territory for Thomas and I carefully instructed him where to leave his motor at the top end of the field on the edge of some pines. He had been gone five minutes – about time enough for him to have parked – when there came a noise like distant thunder and the ground began to shake.

'What's that Dad?' whispered Jago as we both strained our eyes into the blackness towards the rumble. Before I could reply the first of a long column of stampeding cattle swept past 20 yards from where we crouched. Our hiding place felt fragile with the proximity of these charging beasts for our cover was no more than netting round one side of a single bale. Then they were gone.

'Did you see a bull?' I enquired of my sharp-eyed son. Negative.

Soon afterwards, with the sky just beginning to lighten, there came a blood-curdling high-pitched bellow from the direction of Thomas's hide. Barely visible, we could just make out the massive bulk of a one ton bull staring menacingly in our direction. We were up-wind of the animal and he must have picked up our scent.

'Don't move and don't speak,' I whispered while our visitor emitted a constant low threatening grumble. After what was probably only half a minute, but what seemed like an age, the huge shape emitted an ear-splitting roar, stuck its tail skyward, and, with a sudden bound, thundered off in the direction of his long-vanished ladies. Whatever threat we were to his herd he had thankfully concluded they needed his presence more than we did.

We later learned that, when Thomas had reached his parking cover, the cows and bull were already in residence sheltering under the lee of the wood. The herd had spooked and stampeded into the night but the young bull had remained to check him out.

'I picked up a fence post just in case he decided to charge,' said Thomas later. 'Fortunately he just followed me until I reached my hide where he must have winded you.'

THE 'A' TEAM – *the author, Jago aged 9 and Paul on Ponkey's after a dawn flight with Wally the chocolate lab – 'the finest goose retriever I have seen.' On this trip Jago shot his first goose.*

We also later found out that the cattle should not have been in the field. The bull was new, and although he had not shown any signs of aggression to any of the farm hands, the farmer agreed we were wise to be cautious.

For any goose chaser venturing onto new ground it is as well to ask about the presence of bulls, though most farmers will warn you if they do have a touchy one at large.*

Soon after this scary episode came goose talk from the direction of the roost a mile away on the moor top. Our calls brought a bunch of around eight pinks straight towards us no more than 20 feet up.

'Leave them for Thomas,' I instructed my young charge. We were sharing a gun – my shortened Berreta gasser – and the birds gave Thomas a side shot.

Two quick reports and nothing fell. This was not like the Thomas I had known 40 years past. Twice more the same pattern and still nothing in the bag. I learned later that my guest had armed himself, against my advice, with a three inch side-by-side 12-bore bored full and full. Thomas was shooting for the head knowing he would ruin the meat if 1½ ounces of BBs hit the body. When the light improved, and he could take his shots at 40 yards, he was back to his old high standard.

By now there was goose talk everywhere and, suddenly, Jago was flinging up the gun in the opposite direction from where we expected the birds. A single goose, a black dot against the lightening sky, was hurtling down-wind at extreme range.

'Too high,' I whispered but the words were lost in the report and the bird folded instantly. The westerly had reached around a force six and the goose fell a good 100 yards away.

'Mark it by that tall pine. Leave your gun and pick it fast,' I instructed.

I don't know who was the prouder, father or son. I just hope this event stays as fresh in the young fellow's memory as mine has from all that time ago. The momentous event threw up another statistic; the boy was exactly half the age of the man when he shot his first goose!

*Later I asked Rab if the bull could have been a problem.
'No normally, but ye never really ken.'
'Does he have a name?'
'William.'
'Oops, I've been calling him Cyril.'
'Well noo. That could be your problem. What would ye do if someone called ye Cyril?'

A SPECIAL DAY

I have lamented over the difficulty of finding a true wildfowler, whose passion for the goose chase burns throughout his life, but beyond all question the Brothers Wilkins belong there.

The reader has already been introduced to these two country characters and it doesn't take long to realise how totally consumed they are by the lure of the grey battalions. David is 68, John a year older when this is being penned.

A hint of their love and passion for wild geese may be gleaned from the fact that between them they have, for the past 25 years, been the official goose counters for the Wildfowl and Wetlands Trust covering the Fylde area, plus the fertile Morecambe Bay.

It was a great delight for me when Paul, my constant goose companion in recent years, arranged a dawn flight with the brothers. To say then that Saturday, February 5, 2005, was a very special day was certainly no understatement.

'You reckon there aren't many old farts like you still mad on goose chasing. Now you are going to meet two more. And when you hear about their Father it will make you realise that you are only fit to be in the Fifth Division reserve team,' Paul had said over the phone. I knew to whom he alluded.

The weather was foul when we left the Lake District at 5.30am. Continuous rain followed us for 50 miles all the way to the marsh edge. David and John were regular customers in my Preston shop, when I was in the gun trade, but I had never met them together. Both live nearby and they were to tell me they were 'keener than ever' since they had retired from their profession as chartered accountants. They had organised breakfast after flight and we could talk then.

Our venue was Fluke Hall Marsh, owned by Ray Holden of Hy Fly Game Hatcheries near Pilling. It lies at the southern end of Morecambe Bay and is now virtually a wildfowl sanctuary. Leroy, Ray's number two son, arrived with little black Labrador Meg and was keen to drive me onto the marsh and find a suitable gutter, but I declined. Ten hours of constant rain had left the terrain awash and the extreme dampness would almost certainly render my limbs useless. Next time, hopefully.

I knew I would enjoy the dawn. I had a grandstand seat in the cosy 4WD cab and Ray would be joining me as soon as the flight started. I had been driven from my home by tyro Mark. It was his first marsh outing and I was as keen as he was to see him collect his first goose below the tideline.

This trip to this particular marsh was a nostalgic one. I had helped to overshoot the territory when it was a private syndicate 40 years ago. Then there was little chance of putting anything in the bag unless it blew a hooley or snowed.

Since those days the topography had also altered. A new sea wall lies a good quarter mile from the original. Besides the new banking totally preventing the road from monthly inundations by high tide, it has also created a welcome seclusion to the remaining saltings. The outmarsh is now a mere 300 yards to its outer limit, but once over the new bank, you step into a feeling of true remoteness. As dawn breaks there is no longer the intrusion of car headlights behind you as the world awakes. No roar of farm diesels invade the ear as the fowler strains for the sound of geese lifting far out in the Bay.

It is Ray's favourite place. 'I love being there on my own. All the pressures of business leave you. There is just you, your dog and the birds.'

Ray's timing that morning was immaculate. He joined me minutes before the first geese lifted. They were also a good mile to our east and were greeted by the thump of big guns. Ray told me that a lot of fowlers in the Bay were using 8- or 4-bores with the new Hevi Shot manufactured in the USA.

Leroy had given Mark some 1¼ ounce Hevi 3's that morning. He had told me they were deadlier than lead.

'Was this really so?' I asked Raymond.

'Yes, but only if you can shoot as well as Leroy. And I don't think many can. It is heavier than lead and although the actual shot doesn't have the uniformity of lead it seems not to affect its performance.' 12-bore goose loads work out at around £1.50 a shot.

'That really isn't expensive when you consider its extra efficiency and the fact that you don't need many. Who wants to shoot more geese than you can eat? This morning I will be happy if five guns kill two apiece.'

I know Ray enjoyed the flight as much as I did that morning. The big skeins were high but there were plenty of lower bunches well in range. A party of five pinks turned away from the main flight line and headed south.

'Any minute now and we should see one drop,' murmured Ray.

The geese rose sharply upwards. One flailed down, its uncoordinated wings giving the impression it was four times its actual size. Then came the report. We learned later that this was Mark's first goose. He was so spellbound that the second barrel was forgotten.

Return from Flight – Long time friend Ray Holden, MD of Hy Fly Hatcheries, Preesall, owns the marsh at the southern end of Morecambe Bay. When he heard my 12-year-old son was keen on wildfowling there came an open invitation. I am now merely the chauffeur! Pictured are Ray's son Leroy and Paul Moore returning from a successful dawn flight. Paul's artillery this day was a Hammond double eight bore with three ounce loads.

With the flight still under way, Paul and Mark topped the seawall. Paul had dropped two birds and decided it was enough, particularly when Mark had signalled that he had caught his barrels in the mud.

Leroy also downed two pinks and stopped. The Brothers Wilkins had valiantly stationed themselves well behind Paul and Mark and it was their calling that had attracted the low bunches. David uses an old Olt call but John has always relied on his vocal chords.

'He is brilliant,' said Ray. 'His Dad taught him and he says its advantage is two-fold. His throat becomes so dry he reckons he can down two pints while the rest of us are still on our first!'

John has been calling geese vocally long before manufactured aids arrived. He was also an innovator in the decoy field. Fifty years ago he got a friend to fashion a full-bodied pinkfoot in the feeding position out of balsa wood. Armed with his pattern he called on a firm of Preston coach-builders and persuaded them to cast him 12 models in fibreglass.

'They were very reluctant at first but when I told them I didn't care how much it cost they agreed.'

Breakfast was booked in an elegant hotel close to the marsh. An elderly couple were at the next table and were obviously much intrigued by our conversation. It was not of the morning flight: that talk had been disposed of on the marsh. I wanted to know all about the Wilkins family's passion for goose chasing.

Both David and John have kept a record of every outing since they first pulled the trigger as boys. I suppose only someone as meticulous as an accountant would want to do that.

But first their Father. For the last 62 years of his life Dick Wilkins had never missed bagging a goose. Surely a record rarely surpassed, particularly when one realises it included the 1939-46 Second World War years. Maladies, which affect us all in our old age, were shrugged off in his fervour. He died, aged 82, in 1981.

'Dad was remarkably fit and could still do a high kick above his head in his eighties,' said a justly proud David.

My first meeting with the remarkable Dick, who was born in 1899, was soon after I opened the Preston gun shop in 1968. The white-haired lean gent said he was pleased that there was a 'proper fowler' behind the counter. He was fresh back from a dawn goose sortie but you would never have guessed. His garb was that of a country squire.

David and John produced some excellent photographs recording the Wilkins's extraordinary shooting careers but there was one particular event I wanted to ask about. It involved Dick.

Their father was an eminent Preston solicitor and a story had long circulated in Morecambe Bay lore that he had been caught poaching.

'I am afraid it is true,' grinned John. 'It was before the war when Dad said the geese were only ever here in their hundreds. (Today there can be 30,000.) He had been out at dawn on a farm at Cockerham, not far from here, when a bunch dropped into next door's fields.'

It was very much a 'no-go' area. The Lawson brothers, who owned the farm, never let anyone near with a gun but, that morning, one of them must have decided to have a go himself.

'Apparently he was crawling up the ditch when he came across a rucksack, then a hat and finally a pair of gloves. He could see they hadn't been there long and was wondering what to do about it. Was it someone on a suicide mission? Then there was a bang.

'It was Dad. He got his goose and the farmer got the poacher. Dad used to tell us he had to do some very fast talking to persuade the brothers not to prosecute but they never stopped telling everyone about it, even when they were old men.'

And what happened to the goose?

'Dad gave it to him with his apologies.'

Half way through our breakfast the elderly couple, on the next table, made their farewells. 'Thank you for an interesting start to our day,' they had said.

I have made reference, elsewhere, to choosing one's shooting quarters. These two folk had shown no resentment to our tales of goose chasing, otherwise I would have changed the subject. I do have to say, in our favour, that much of the talk had been related to the increase of wildfowl in the Bay, largely due to the influence of sanctuaries and the control of shooting.

I asked the brothers if their long and interesting shooting careers had resulted in any unusual shots and David's reply was to produce a quite extraordinary coincidence.

'For me it would have to be the time I shot at a party of pinks,' he said. 'I dropped two with the first barrel and, as I went to pick them, one was a pink and the other a whitefront. I had never even seen a whitefront before in Morecambe Bay.'

I asked where the incident had occurred, already feeling I knew the answer.

'On a farm near here called Lathwaite.'

This was the same Lathwaite about which I write in the Lancashire Geese chapter and I, too, had carried out exactly the same happening on that same farm. It transpired that David began shooting there in 1964, the year I finished. Over 40 years later he is still the tenant.

I wanted to know if the brothers had a quiet period when shooting took a back seat.

'Not for me,' replied John. 'I got divorced after 23 years so that I could go shooting whenever I wished without spoiling the life of another.'

He shoots clays all year round and can boast one gold and two silver medals in world clay bird shooting competitions.

David sticks to live pigeons in summer. For 14 years, besides his accountancy work, he was the Warden on the Southport Sanctuary Marsh – 'a tremendous experience.'

I was beginning to understand what Paul meant when he said that the Brothers Wilkins eat, drink and sleep goose shooting. They were fanatics in the most complete meaning of the word.

David and John said that, a long time ago, they resolved not to partake in big bag goose kills. Even so, they do admit to shooting more than they need for their own consumption. The sale of wild geese is banned, so what happened to the surplus?

'There never is a surplus, in real terms,' said David. 'Both of us visit many shoots in a season and we know the birds will be readily accepted for the table by both Guns and beaters.'

The Holdens, however, have come up with an even more acceptable way of presenting friends with this most healthy of cholesterol-free commodity. They turn them into sausages and exceedingly delicious they are, too, though I suspect there is a secret ingredient to render them so toothsome.

We parted reluctantly. We were all heading for our respective pigeon woods later that day and I had another old pal to see. Would he also be as keen to talk geese?

A SPECIAL SCHOOL

Peter Taylor was born 55 years ago on Cotewalls Farm, near the mouth of the river Wyre not far from where we had shot that morning. I had heard that the pinkfoot had started to roost in the river alongside his farm. The estuary here is half a mile across and they had been regular visitors for the past five years.

I had not seen Peter for 25 years and I found him hard at work in his barn repairing, of all things, a double punt. He was as keen as ever. It was, he confirmed, quite correct that the pinks were in residence. They had taken root simply because they were left undisturbed.

Peter is Chairman of Fylde Wildfowlers and part of their marshes abutt the roost. There is a strict no disturbance rule on the sands. When the birds flight into Peter's land he largely leaves them alone. They are shot 'extremely lightly' and then only under the November moon. On the opposite shore there is strictly no shooting.

I reflected that this was a situation that would never have existed 50 years ago. The birds would have been harried into the wild beyond. Yet

A Punt is Restored – On one of my fowling trips to the southern end of Morecambe Bay I called on an old customer from my gun trade years. Peter Taylor, of Cotewalls Farm, Preesall, was at work restoring a gun punt. Peter sometimes hosts the BASC Young Shots days on his land where pinkfoot geese feed regularly.

more evidence of the enlightened understanding.

I was then to hear of an extremely unselfish gesture by Peter. The arrival of the birds on his land has given him the chance to show up-and-coming teenage fowlers in the area what goose flighting is all about. Once a year, for two days, Cotewalls is now host to a very special school.

Peter never disturbs the geese at dawn or dusk but allows six youngsters, under careful supervision, to decoy them over two January days. The lads are drawn from the junior membership (under 18) of Morecambe Bay Wildfowlers and Fylde Fowlers and their course begins on a Friday night, in a marsh-side inn, with instructions from a BASC goose guide.

Well before dawn, on the Saturday, they are out on the feeding grounds placing decoys and setting up three hides. There are two boys per hide, plus an experienced adult. Only one gun per two boys is permitted and they take turns to shoot.

'There is always plenty of action but not a great deal of success,' said Peter. 'The lads quickly realise that, although geese appear to be big targets, it takes a long time to overcome goose fever. The excitement that a flight produces is wonderful to behold.'

The course does not end there. During the day Peter lays on a game drive on his farm. Barrels get hot as pheasants, partridge and a great variety of duck pour over the six guns. Most have never experienced anything remotely like it.

Saturday finishes with a duck flight and the team is back at dawn on the Sunday for a last go at the geese before dispersing.

Peter concluded. 'Fewer and fewer youngsters are getting the chance to shoot and so, therefore, cannot be expected to fully understand conservation. Each time we hold one of these events you know you have six committed juniors ready to carry on the good work.'

James Bryan has been treasurer of Fylde Wildfowlers since its inception in 1950. He still shoots, as he nears 80, and was greatly enthusiastic about Peter's input.

'It is thanks to caring country folk like Peter that our sport is able to carry on. It is impossible to thank him enough,' he told me.

James is also Treasurer of the Wyre/Lune Morecambe Bay Goose Roost Sanctuary. He has held this position, also, since its formation in 1963. The sanctuary evolved following discussions between all users of the Bay's sands including the Lancashire Naturalist Trust, fishermen and wildfowlers. It stretches for five miles between the two estuaries and marked the beginning of a steady build up of the pinkfoot in the area.

Before I said my farewells to Peter I told him of an incident in my Blackpool shop a long time ago. His Father, the late Tommy Taylor, was as keen a shooter as his son. He also had another claim to fame – the World Champion Pigeon Plucker, 18 seconds to divest a woodie of its feathers.

The championship used to be organised by WAGBI (now BASC) at the annual Game Fair and one day, on a particularly crowded Saturday morning, Tommy arrived. It so happened that I had a brace of pigeons hanging in the back and asked Tommy if he would give us a demonstration.

At first he was reticent. He protested that he was badly out of practice but when I produced a dustbin and deposited a bird on a newspaper on the counter he took off his jacket and set to work.

By then there must have been 10 customers in the shop and we all gasped in wonder at the lightning gyrations of his hands. The bird whirred through deft fingers before it was deposited, naked, on the newspaper in 21 seconds.

Before we left Peter's farmyard he gave me a pressing invitation.

'When I was a youngster you were always good to me in your shop. I would like to repay that a little bit with a moonlight flight for the geese next November. Please come and bring your lad with you.'

And you want to know why wildfowlers look forward to winter?

THE WORLD'S BIGGEST SHOTGUN

The following Saturday, on the way to another February national pigeon shoot in the Fylde, I called on the aforementioned big bore specialist Alan Myers. His extensive workshops are only minutes from the A6, at Winmarleigh, on the edge of goose feeding grounds used by Morecambe Bay birds. It is interesting to hear that, although he has plenty of goose shooting on his doorstep, including the Ribble estuary birds, Alan, like me prefers to do his chasing in Scotland.

He was hard at work but I had expected to find him preparing for his own pigeon onslaught.

'Far too busy,' he said, as he put the finishing touches to a giant 4-bore barrel on a lathe. He reckoned that if he worked seven days a week for the next two years he would just about complete his orders.

I felt guilty but Alan was willing to talk big guns. He confirmed that, in spite of expensive non-toxic shot, more and more large bores were in use.

Alan began building these heavy guns 17 years ago. They range from 8-bores, to fours, twos and punt guns. His customers are countrywide but many are used by local fowlers who find the extra pattern deadly beyond the standard 12-bore.

Alan is, however, a fan of the innovative Beretta 3½-inch gas operated semi automatic 12-bore. He includes one in his personal armoury and it was on his recommendation that I recently acquired one myself. It was, indeed, a revelation when I first shot a heavy load through the weapon. It had so many anti-recoil systems that its kick was more of a caress.

We returned to talk of the big guns Alan is building.

'Some will have been among the ones you heard on your last morning flight in the Bay,' said Alan. 'They use a slower burning powder that produces more of a boom.'

I had difficulty in tearing my two companions away. Cameraman

Mark, in his first full season as a fowler, was agog at the vast array of machinery and weaponry. And for 12-year-old Jago it well beat an afternoon at a Harry Potter flick!

For me the visit to such a thriving gunsmithing business was nostalgic. In my years in the trade I had employed three full-time smiths and the reek of lathe oil and the scent of fine walnut stock blanks brought it all back.

We were saying our reluctant goodbyes when my eye then caught something rather special. Tucked away in a corner – I rather think 'hidden' would have been a better word – was a giant of a shooting tool. A shoulder gun of such massive proportions that one could only imagine a seven foot giant hefting it skywards.

'What on earth is that?' I asked.

Alan looked almost guilty. I suspect he had not intended anyone seeing this leviathan weapon until it was finished for it will, indeed, need many more hours of work before it is ready.

I was hugely glad I had first asked Alan's permission to wander around his inner sanctum. In the Birmingham gun trade, when I initially visited it in the 1950s, all work would cease when you entered a gunsmith's workshop. Sheets were pointedly placed over functional benches and the men stood back until you were gone.

'That,' said Alan, 'is the world's biggest shoulder gun. It is a 1-bore, proofed to throw one pound of shot, but I know of no man who would be capable of shooting that load.'

We were definitely going to be late for our pigeon shooting!

I refrained, of course, from asking for whom this extraordinary weaponry was being built but I did learn that (a) it had been under construction for two years (b) it weighed a colossal 28lbs (c) stood 6ft 4-inches high and (d) would cost £8,000 – which seemed amazingly undervalued to me.

What sort of enthusiast would want something of such staggering a weight and what physique was capable of taming it?

I learnt that Alan's client already possessed one of his double 4-bores (23lbs and just as tall). He had requested 'something with a bit more range.'

It had taken a while for Alan to agree to produce the gun. He pointed out that, although it was proofed to throw one pound of shot, a viable load must be half of that.

Its estimated killing range will be 120 yards using AAA shot.

Big Gun Specialist – Alan Myers, gunsmith and goose guide, at work in his premises near Garstang, Preston.

No doubt, I reflected, the client had been relieved that he would be able to take his artillery to Scotland where it is still possible to shoot lead at wildfowl away from wetland and SSSI sites. An ideal tool for flighting geese off inland lochs where the shooter could easily avoid the discharge going near water.

Did Alan anticipate any more orders for this bore?

'Even if I were to get any I would refuse. This is the biggest breech loading shoulder gun ever built in the world and I am leaving it at that.'

No doubt the shooting press would be onto the story before my book reached the shelves but, at least I was the first scribe to handle something rather special.

SEPTEMBER GEESE

There were multifarious reasons for my moving to the Lake District and one was the accessibility of sea fishing at Barrow-in-Furness. From my native Lytham there were, nearby, the Ribble and the Wyre estuaries, offering easy routes into Morecambe Bay – but only each side of high tides. Should it suddenly blow a hooley, if there was an alarm or the fishing turned out to be useless, one had to stick it out until the tide made. At Barrow you could come and go throughout the 24 hours.

I was soon to discover a pool of fellow enthusiasts to join me and, one year, booked 42 trips out of the Walney Channel! Not all, of course, turned out to be possible because of high winds but we reckoned to sail on two thirds of the bookings. There were three boats plying out from this channel, which I could reach in little over half an hour from my hillside home.

Being out on the briny, rod in hand, awaiting the thump thump of a telltale winter cod strike or the sudden rush of a silver-sided summer bass was, for me, close to the thrill of goose hunting. And, on September 22, 1983, at precisely 3.10pm there came an added bonus of dramatic proportions.

At first I thought I was hearing things. Was it the bell that old Tommy had clipped to the end of his second rod tinkling in my ear or had I really heard wild geese? The skipper's eyes were keener than mine and he was the first to pick out the thin wavering line bearing down on us from due north. Pinkfoot. On they came all the time dropping ever lower. This first lot passed less than 100 yards off our starboard beam, and at 8-bore height, before finally settling on Pilling sands three miles beyond.

More were to follow, in fact thousands of them, each platoon playing bugles loud. Most carried on due south, no doubt to drop into the Ribble estuary where the Wetlands Trust's Martin Mere awaited them. The remainder swung close to our 40-foot boat, gliding down to settle among the first arrivals at the southern end of Morecambe Bay. This spectacular display was to last for over an hour and even the non-shooters among us were impressed.

The grey army was on schedule. Each year we expected them on either the Solway , off the Lancashire coast or on our east Scottish grounds during the last 10 days of the ninth month. As soon as I reached home (it was in the days before mobiles) I was on the phone to my goose-chasing pals with the exciting news.

ROYAL KEEPER

It is a sad fact of life that, as the older one gets, the more intolerant one gets, particularly when it comes to bad manners. For me, two of these foibles relate to eating. I find it disgustingly rude when folk insist on talking with their mouths full of food. I also find a dog's stare, when one is chomping one's shoot sandwiches, almost as unpardonable.

A while ago, during a break in a goose flight, we had produced our packed lunch when a new companion asked, 'Is there something wrong with your dog?'

'Why?'

'He's turned his back on you.'

I then had to go on to explain how all my dogs were taught these good manners and how it had all begun around 40 years ago, in a keeper's cottage, when I was on a fallow deer stalking expedition.

My gillie on that day was a hugely enthusiastic 18-year-old, name of David Clarke. We had repaired to his quarters, in the middle of the estate, for a brew and, as he placed his sandwiches on the table, his tiny Jack Russell had swivelled abruptly away to face the wall. The move had elicited a similar query on my part.

The young fellow told me that all the Clarke family dogs received the same education and I immediately adopted the trait. It is remarkable how quickly a dog can be taught the habit, particularly if it is caught young enough. I think it should be compulsory in all canines!

Every time this subject crops up I am reminded of the young fellow who passed on this wisdom and what a success story his life has been.

I lost touch with David when he moved from that Lancashire estate to further his career and only came across him again recently by chance. My adoptive Cumbria holds few pigeons (apart from when the abundant oaks have a bumper acorn year) and I had phoned a keeper pal to ask if he had a contact within reasonable travelling distance. When I was put in touch with a keeper in Northumberland his voice immediately sounded familiar. It was the same David of the well-mannered Jack Russell.

Of course I could shoot his pigeons. How soon could I get there? I had to explain that, these days, I need a shooter/driver since my stint behind the wheel lasts little more than the hour. I hoped it would be within the month.

However, it wasn't that long before we were shaking hands. Within a week David arrived on my doorstep, with wife Amanda, and we were soon recalling days of the long ago.

He told me how he loved to visit my Blackpool gun shop, where he was ushered into the gunsmithing quarters. There he saw shot gun chokes being bored, barrels blacked, stocks fashioned from blanks – all fascinating stuff to a teenager.

'The smells were wonderful,' he explained. When you work among gun oil and leather you don't notice it but so often I am told what heady perfume it was to the shooter.

'You always treated me so well I want to pay you back,' was what David said. I was mightily touched. My friend, the local vicar, would have declared, 'For as ye sow, so shall ye reap.' From the Sermon on the Mount.

Yet such Biblical rewards were not to be. A month after David's visit I received an apologetic phone call. He had been appointed the Queen's head keeper at Sandringham!

Who, I pondered, had found their Paradise – the keeper with the world's top job or the father guiding his son to the finest sport of all? I reckon neither of us would swap.

Ray Holden – *When Ray invites you to a goose flight on his stretch of Morecambe Bay marsh you can expect success. Ray, second from left, has carefully controlled the shooting on Fluke Hall Marsh since acquiring the land 10 years ago. Prior to this the territory was under heavy pressure and the chance of bagging a goose was small. Now there are often up to 20,000 pinkfoot in the Bay and a healthy population of greylag.*
The morning I travelled south to meet Ray for the dawn flight we were joined by his son Leroy, Paul Moore and avid goose-chasers David and John Wilkins.
Left to right: Paul, Ray, Leroy, David, John and myself.

CHAPTER 13

The Beginner

In these days of so much opposition to shooting by the anti-blood sports lobbyists how does the youngster or keen older citizen gain a foothold in the world of field sports? Should a boy or girl be born into a shooting family then their path is easy. But what of the erstwhile Shot with no such background?

It has to be said that BASC's wise and thoughtful approach to shooting via its Young Shot Days, when a careful watch is kept for anti-demonstrators, gives the under-16's the better chance. More on this later.

Unfortunately it is the adult prospective Gun who will find they are at a disadvantage. In my gun trade days many were the folk who asked for advice on the subject and then – a quarter of a century and more ago, when shoot saboteurs were unknown – the route was smooth.

The first move was to direct them to a clay bird club or shooting school. Initially they would be taught gun safety and would soon discover if they had an aptitude for the sport. The same advice I would likewise proffer today.

With luck you may also, of course, meet a kindred spirit on your clay days who is already deep into the world of live quarry shooting and here could be your open sesamé. There will be those who specialise in driven birds besides rough shooters and wildfowlers. Many such folk keep their eye in on clays during the close seasons.

There is, however, a huge discrepancy in cost when one deals with the 'real thing.' Top of the scale would be grouse at anything from £200 per gun for a modest walked-up day to £1,000 per gun for a visit to a top driven moor. Many wildfowlers spend only a quarter of that in a year!

Should your pockets be deep, driven pheasant and partridge shooting is the easiest of all to acquire. The shooting press is full of opportunities and roving syndicates now have calendars which may cover the length and breadth of the British Isles.

A determined wildfowler will satisfy his passion for his chosen sport in various ways. If he is lucky enough to live near the coast and his local club has vacancies then entry is simple. This is, however, a lottery. Some clubs cannot even quote a waiting time. Should he live inland, an annual holiday of anything up to 14 days will have to suffice. This procedure is explained in the Foreword.

The passionate rough shooter – the backbone of the shooting world since guns were invented – is the one to suffer the most of all in this modern era. When I became a wage earner all I had to do was knock on a farmer's door and, with the right approach, had permission to control his vermin – rabbits, pigeons and corvids – for nothing. The spin-offs were the occasional pheasant, partridge, woodcock, duck or hare. There would, of course, be much name dropping to your host to make him realise you understood the ways of the countryside and a bottle of scotch was always appreciated. Now, however, each of these farms will be part of an organised shoot and the landowner will, quite justly, be reaping the reward.

I tell, in an earlier chapter, of how Simon had striven unsuccessfully for years to find rough shooting – until he caught me in his arms as I plunged to certain injury aboard an English Channel fishing boat. Such is the hand of fate. He now has more shooting than he can fit into a busy life.

It is encouraging, too, to learn of so many of the fair sex entering the world of animate shooting, even if it is merely that of driven game. I doubt if many womenfolk would make proficient rough shooters when only initiative and expertise fills the bag. But this is not their fault. Evolution dictated that man was the hunter and I am sure the instinct is still latent in the vast majority of males.

The other day I needed to speak to an acquaintance about marauding deer and, when I phoned, I got his wife. She said her husband was out driven pheasant shooting but I could ring after 8pm when he would tell me about 'His day on the hill.'

I could have been rude and explained that the hill was where you stalked deer; the covert was where you shot driven pheasants and, for good measure, the moor was where you found grouse. Instead I left her in her ignorance for I am sure she is a kind and delightful lady deserving of no embarrassment.

What then of the opportunities for the youngster without a rural sports family background? The aforementioned BASC Young Shots Days, part of their programme for the past five years, are becoming ever-

A HEAVY LOAD – *My son Jago at the end of a flight during one of his days on my old shoot.*

more popular. I go into detail, also, in the previous chapter about BASC YS weekends. The most recent near me was hosted, at the end of the 2005/06 season, by the Lytham & District WA and was a huge success. The maximum figure of 12 applicants was quickly reached and the band of under 16-year-olds killed 34 ducks including mallard, pintail, wigeon and teal on the club's Ribble marshes over two flights.

At the YS one day events, held normally in summer, the participants get a chance to shoot clays and handle air rifles under tuition. There may also be demonstrations of dog handling, ferreting, hide building, decoying and even flyfishing. Experts will answer all questions on every aspect of field sports and the participants do not need to be holders of a shotgun certificate since the events are officially registered.

When a YS day was held here in the South Lakes last summer it was a sell-out, with 75 participants. Followers came from far and wide and the event was held on an estate far from the public gaze. Any inquisitive cars were discreetly turned away.

On the subject of shotgun certificates, I found the route to my last son's acquisition of one easy and straightforward. He was granted his when he was nine and, unquestionably, his knowledge of guns and their surrounding spectrum was more profound than that of the examiner's. He did, of course, have the necessary background and began his shooting life at the age of five with an air rifle.

I would, at this stage, make an impassioned plea not to begin your child's lessons with weapons bearing over-long stocks. Reduce then to fit (any qualified gunsmith will advise). Keep the offcut and replace it when he has grown.

The same sort of advice goes for the weight of a gun. Start with a .410. Granted they are difficult to use, because of lack of pattern size, and then move to a light 12-bore with one ounce loads. A 20-bore is an unnecessary expense. Again this has less spread than a 12.

Without doubt the finest way for any young tyro to enter the 'real' shooting world is via a fowling club and it is refreshing that almost all have policies admitting them to supervised shooting. Take any aspiring young Gun onto a marsh at dawn or dusk and it is then, before he has been brainwashed, that you will recognise that inborn instinct to hunt.

Range judging is another vital aspect. Fowling clubs preach it and wood pigeon roost shooting can be an excellent way of learning how far a gun will reach.

I cannot help feeling sorry for the youngster of yesteryear who

OUTRAGEOUS ADVERTS in the 1890s claimed kills for shoulder guns up to 150 yards! They did much damage to the inexperienced shot trying to understand ranges.

appeared to have such a rank bad start to the problem of range judgement when they were bombarded with spurious claims. Take, for instance, the blurb contained in the adjoining advertisement by the famous London gunmakers J & W Tolley, of New Bond Street.

I include extracts from the adverts, from letters written by clients extolling the quite outrageous killing powers of their fowling pieces. Viz.: from J. P. Garnett Esq, Bedford. (10-bore). 'I have shot plover at 120 yards.' The editor of *The Field*, 'Their 8-bores flatten a BB shot to the size and thickness of a sixpence at 100 yards or more.' The Hon. E. Willoughby, York, 'I liked the 8-bore very much. I killed a partridge dead yesterday at 100 yards.' (One wonders what his fellow Guns might think if he turned out today to shoot the dainty partridge with an 8-bore?!) H.R. Shield Esq, Narberth, also an 8-bore addict, 'I killed shore birds the other day at 150 yards.'

Finally, there is an alarming claim this time for the 12-bore. From *The Field*, February 17, 1894: 'I recently bought one of Messrs J. & W. Tolley's 'Altro' 12-bore long chambered guns and find it almost as effective as an 8-bore.' (!!!)

Today such blatant misleading advertising would fall foul of the Trade Descriptions Act.

It has already been explained that BASC will help to provide shooting but what does upset me are the wildfowling clubs where there is no chance of gaining entry merely because selfish older Guns refuse to give up membership 'in case I want a trip out.' For God's sake why, if you do feel the urge, do you not then get yourself a day ticket? For this very reason I left my fowling club when I moved away from the area in my forties.

PRACTISE IS ESSENTIAL

I cannot overstress that, for anyone aspiring to become competent at handling a shotgun, clay bird instruction is a must, be they a youngster or an adult. And if, as a seasoned shot, you are unable to practise the year-round on live quarry then seek out your nearest clay ground. I am lucky to be able to keep my eye in on pigeons out of the game season and happy to travel two hours each way to reach pigeon territory – the lack of cultivated land in the Lake District means we have only a meagre wood pigeon population and this I conserve. What greater joy is there for the countryman than to hear a woodie cooing his sotto voce way through a few bars of his spring and summer love song?

The erstwhile shot who cannot be bothered to practise on clays is merely an ignoramus idiot. It is up to us to ensure we are competent at our sport and to make certain we get clean kills. There is only one way to maintain this standard and that is through practise.

You might say that, as a disabled incompetent, I should not be shooting and you would be right, if I had not readjusted my approach. I gave up shooting when I was severely injured. However, the urge was so great that I tried my hand again with a shortened stock. I pull the trigger only when I feel certain I will kill. In other words, I wait till my animate target is easy and the kills-to-cartridge ratio is above the general average of one bird to three shots.

In maintaining this practice of waiting for the easy targets, my ammunition expenditure has also plunged dramatically. I do appreciate, however, that I am luckier than most in having productive shooting available. Then there are days when I am out with a novice and happy not to handle a gun at all but merely to guide my charge through the joys of the event.

EMERGENCY GUNFITTING

I have touched on the essentials of correct stock measurements. When it comes to stock fitting there are also emergency ways of overcoming discrepancies in length; the reach either too long or too short.

The technique may have to be employed should you, for instance, need to borrow a gun. Let us address the discrepancy more easily cured – that of shortness.

First, mount the gun and reach the aiming hand forward until the stock is forced back to nestle firmly into the shoulder. Then lower the weapon and, without moving the hands, bring the gun back into the firing mode. Remember where to place the hand before each shot and down they should tumble.

You will now have a fit which will not cause excessive recoil and, also, ensure that the mounting is satisfactory. Merely practise the forward hand position a few times with the strange weapon and you should be on song.

The over-long stock is corrected by the reverse positioning of the pointing hand. You may need to bring the hand back initially towards your body to obtain a comfortable positioning even before mounting.

Again, once you have achieved the easy mounting, do practise until you feel proficient.

I repeat, this approach only applies for the use of temporary weapons.

Long ago, in the 1960s, I was privileged to witness a most memorable demonstration of this technique by one of the clay bird world's greatest-ever exponents – Joe Wheater.

Joe was a remarkable character for many reasons. He had left his vocation as a gamekeeper to purchase the highly respected Stanley Duncan gunsmith/dealership business in Anlaby Road, Hull. This was the shop established by the founder of WAGBI early last century.

Joe also created an extensive clay bird layout not far away at Cherry Burton, in the lush Yorkshire countryside, and it was here I saw the performance.

Joe had been explaining the theory side of the technique which I have just outlined, when he went on to demonstrate the practical aspect.

Standing in front of the driven partridge stand, where the bird heads directly over the peg, he organised a queue of shooters with their weapons ready loaded but open at the breech. Taking each gun in turn – they ranged from 12-bore to 20-bore and .410 and in a wide variety of stock lengths – he briefly assessed the weapon before calling for his bird and powdering every one.

Pity the beginner coming under Joe's tutelage. I can only pass on, second-hand, the way he ran his live bird driven days. Many of those were attended by my mentor, Sam Entwistle, from whom I acquired by gun business.

'Step out of line on one of Joe's days and you were sent home instantly,' Sam used to tell me.

As shoot captain his instructions at the commencement of a day's shooting were, I heard, delivered with the sternness of a beadle and, if not taken in to the nth degree, earned severe retribution. Though he was in fox hunting territory Joe did not tolerate the pests on his domain. Shoot on sight was the order.

It led to an eminent Yorkshire Gun having an early bath one day. Reynard broke out in front of the unfortunate fellow's stand and was allowed through. When an incandescent Joe enquired why no shot was fired, he explained he was a Master of Fox Hounds and 'could not possibly.'

Older readers will, no doubt, smile at these reminiscences about a true epitome of the blunt Yorkshireman. Joe had long disputes with the CPSA – the directors of the country's clay pigeon regime. They barred J.

Wheater from all their registered shoots, so he merely changed his name to A. N. Other.

Joe has been long gone and, if there is a shooting heaven, he will be there causing much entertainment for all. His demise left more a chasm than a hole in the shotgun world.

MASTER EYE

There is also a visual discrepancy which can cause big trouble for the tyro – the wrong master eye.

Many are the words written about a shotgunner's master eye by those who strive to explain the difficulties of a dominant optic should it be on the opposite side to your gun shoulder. In simple terms: if you shoot from the right shoulder and your stronger eye is the left, you have big problems.

During my days as a shotgun instructor, the first task was always to establish which was the master eye. For those few who are unfamiliar with the exercise I will explain: With both eyes open point your finger at a distant object. Close one eye to see if the finger moves station. If it does not do so, try the other eye. You are in business if it again remains on target. You have equal vision and must keep both eyes open.

If, however, on completing the exercise, your finger moves to one side you have unequal vision. Should the digit go left then that eye is the stronger and vice versa.

Here, too, another scenario. If you are right handed and your master eye is the right, again keep both eyes open.

What, then, do you do if the stronger vision is on the wrong side? It is a situation applying to myself. I grew up in the days when shotgun coaching was for the wealthy alone. You were given a gun, taught the safety rules in the most stringent way and then pushed off on your adventures. Only trial and error taught me to shoot straight and yet the style I was to evolve I have not yet seen in print – but then I do not profess to have read every word penned on the subject.

The process is simple but does involve some salient points: keep both eyes open even as you bring the gun into the shoulder but, as it meets the body, close your left eye. This ensures that the weapon will be positively on your quarry. Swing through and then, without stopping the movement, squeeze the trigger. By keeping both eyes open you are judging the quarry's distance correctly. Experience will tell you what lead to allow.

For people with this sort of vision there are those who advocate using a cross-over or cross-eyed stock. Do not go there. I have tried it and the punch delivered by one of these monstrosities is like a kick from an enraged bull. A physics don will explain that this is due to ergonomics – an unequal thrust of the recoil on a contorted plain. It really does hurt and will put you off a shotgun for ever!

The ultimate solution is, of course, to do what my brother Charles did. Change shoulders. But then you have to be young and a very, very determined and devoted sort of person.

THE AIR RIFLE

Before I set out to write this book, I was told by publishers that, in order to interest them, it had to be 'instructional.' At first I recoiled.

When I pick up a work which merely sets out to take the reader through the bare facts of a subject, setting out the do's and the don'ts, I find that my interest soon begins to wander. I blank.

So I spent a long time in drawing up a list of what I felt would be of help to the aspiring goose chaser and wove my story around it.

The driving force which thrust me back into my goose hunting was, of course, the arrival of son number three. Jago was born in times of rigorous restrictions but, upon his fifth Christmas, I bought him a Rolls Royce of an air rifle (a Weirhauch model 25 in .177 calibre and shortened the stock from the standard 14-inches to 12.) There is currently a move to restrict even the firing of an air rifle by anyone under 18! May the idea quickly perish. The prevailing winter conditions were easily surmounted by setting up a firing point – a table with cushion for elbow resting and a chair – in the heated conservatory. The side door was opened onto the target with solid backstop at 30 feet. The prime rule here is not to put your charge off by attempting to target shoot in arctic conditions. By the afternoon of Boxing Day the little fellow could outshoot both his Grandma and his Mum!

Step two is to let the protégé accompany you on an outing with the shotgun. A pigeon or duck hide would be preferable when you are solo and when you have plenty of time to talk him, or her, through what, to them, will be an exciting adventure. I was four when I went with my Grandpa pigeon roost shooting and it is probably my earliest memory of anything. It was Grandpa who discovered I needed spectacles. I could not find the bird when it fell but, in fairness, it *was* in head-high ferns.

It will be a while before the tyro is old enough to handle a .410 shotgun for a brief clay bird lesson. Twenty five shots are enough for a start. And, as already stated, you must ensure that the stock is again shortened to fit.

No such care was taken in my young days and I had to be content to struggle with a single adult-sized 12-bore. There was, however, some concession to my diminutive stature in that my Father did load for me a belt full of low-recoil sixes charged with the soft Schultz powder. This was one of the first smokeless powders to follow the belching, reeking, black and we were fortunate to have many pounds of the stuff in the fireside cupboard. This kept us going during the Second World War years when only vermin-slaying War Department cartridges were available.

ROARING ROBBO

One inventive veteran fowler, Ian Cameron, long-time secretary of South Cumberland Wildfowlers Association, solved the problem of excessive recoil by going back in time. He substituted today's cartridges, with their quick-burning propellants, for black powder home loads.

After a lifetime in the painting and decorating trade Ian suffers from an arthritic shoulder. It was a case of giving up shooting (impossible) or finding a solution. A gas-operated semi-auto was suggested and he acquired a state-of-the art Beretta 3½-inch job.

However, he first ventured down the black powder route and found it so satisfactory that his new armoury still reposes in its box.

'I turned out a few loads and found them ideal.' Ian told me. 'I now get a smooth push instead of a painful stab.'

When I got the privilege of handling Ian's ancient fowling piece it was, for me, akin to an introduction to a beautiful woman!

The under-lever 10 bore hammer gun is of Birmingham origin, by P. Robinson, circa 1885. The 30-inch damascus barrels are bored full and full with 3-inch chambers capable of throwing 2 ounce loads but, for comfort's sake, Ian keeps his charge down to 1½ ounces. Weighing a hefty 9lbs the weapon is the sort of tool that, once into its swing, just keeps going – a sure way of producing that generous forward lead for long range shooting.

The gun has the sort of patina only generations of fowler's hands can impart and is in remarkably good condition. It truly was not only a privilege but also a joy to handle. How I wished this work of art could have recounted its journeys to the tide edges from well over 100 years past.

Ian uses the gun for both fowling – on his club's Duddon Estuary marshes – and for pigeon roost shooting. I photographed him knocking down a few carrion with his black powder loads and the reek of the spent charge took me back 50 years to the days when I humped the family Tolley 8-bore over the Solway sands.

When loading bismuth Ian increases his shot to $1^{5}/_{8}$ ounces to compensate for lighter density. With tungsten matrix (slightly denser than bismuth, but still below lead) he goes to $1^{9}/_{16}$ ounces.

Basing his loading procedure on the accepted practice of equal measures of powder and shot he first uses scales to arrive at the precise bulk and then cuts down a cartridge case as a scoop. The end result is ammunition at around half the price of factory loads.

Hevi-shot does not come into the reckoning since this would necessitate boring out Roaring Robbo's full chokes by 50 per cent. Something that would be total desecration to a man of such traditional principles.

READING

The novice starting out on the joyous trail that is goose shooting can also tease his taste buds with a huge selection of reading on the subject. I am often asked to recommend books and where to acquire them.

The easiest, and by far the cheapest route, is to join your local library. They will be able to produce all but the most obscure work and, if you like what you read and wish to have it on your shelves, get on to the internet and track the publication down through a sporting book seller.

My personal collection stretches the length of two four-foot shelves but this does not represent all I have read over a lifetime. Regrettably there are tomes I have loaned out and not received back.

The old timers, starting with Colonel Peter Hawker, Abel Chapman and Millais are a must and are the products from pens of men who can truly be called zealots.

From the last century, there are Peter Scott, Bill Powell, Arthur Cadman and Eric Begbie but by far the king from this period has to be Denys Watkins-Pitchford whose pen name is, of course, BB.

There is simply no-one to touch the style of this great man and we are lucky that 'The BB Society' has been formed not only to perpetuate his memory but also to ensure his writing will always be available. His great pal was Douglas MacDougal and I also put his two books at the

ROARING ROBBO – Ian Cameron, Hon. Sec. of South Cumbria Wildfowlers, damaged a shoulder and suffered from excessive recoil until he changed to black powder. Here he is seen roost shooting with 'Roaring Robbo', his double hammer P. Robinson 10-bore.

forefront of my must-read list. These are referred to in Chapter 11.

Without doubt, however, the most definitive book on goose shooting is a work with exactly that title: *Goose Shooting*, by Alasdair Mitchell, who currently has a weekly feature in the *Shooting Times*, though rarely about goose chasing.

In his book Mitchell sets out to lead the budding goose enthusiast along the path to success and makes little attempt to create a narrative. For this reason it does not totally ignite the coals of goose fever, but what he says is invaluable and all good stuff.

I must also include both Allan Jarret and Hugh Meynell as authors on the subject. Jarret is a prolific, compulsive author who pushes out his books at an amazing rate and they are certainly the most up-to-date works on wildfowling, encompassing both these shores and overseas.

Hugh Meynell's work I class as a real gem. He published it himself and it is only a slender work. It comes across as the jottings of an old man (he and I are the same age) who felt he had to tell his tale. In fact the title is *Saga of a Goose Trail*. His book had arrived at my home while I was on a goose trip north of the Border and I fell asleep with it on my chest when halfway through. When I awoke I finished it before breakfast!

The second half of this work deals solely with his goose shooting on Loch Strathbeg in the far north-east of Scotland and I now regret I passed on the opportunity to shoot this water in the long ago. It was at a time when the late Arthur Cadman was organising three-day trips to the loch and I was heavily involved in both running two hectic gun dealerships and conducting my own goose forays for selective clients. The tales my friends brought back from Strathbeg had my shop floor covered in feathers as the doors were hurled wide by raging nor'easters!

Hugh's book did much to verify these tales and he even sent me an empty 8-bore case that had downed one of his last greylags there. The whiff of the spent powder was erotic perfume indeed to the nose of a longshoreman.

Another absolute must for all goose chasers is Brian P Martin's *Wildfowl of the British Isles and Northwest Europe*. I would even go so far as to say that, for those wanting to hunt down the grey goose haunts in Scotland it is irreplaceable. It is one of only two publications I know which lists each and every recognised roost of these species in Britain. The other is Wildfowl in Great Britain produced by the Nature Conservancy.

In his introduction Martin, a keen follower of field sports, applauds the fact that wildfowlers and the conservationists are united in their efforts these days to improve habitat.

A huge amount of research went into the compilation of this extensive work. Without doubt, had it been available when I was young and fit, I would have used its revelations to work my way round the atlas of Scotland with the challenging task of bagging migratory pinks and greys from every listed locality. What absorbing reading the tales from such adventures would have made!

Finally, for those contemplating a fowling trip, be it for a week or two, I can also do no better than recommend them to the monthly publication *Sporting Shooter*. This most ardent supporter of all aspects of fowling carries a guide, 'Where to find shooting'.

There are more than three pages listing availability in England, Scotland, Wales and Northern Ireland. Out of this multitude, England can offer 48 fowling venues, Scotland 31, Wales eight and Northern Ireland three.

It must be borne in mind, of course, that almost all the foreshore in Scotland has free access and only a very small percentage have restricted shooting reserves. Contact BASC's Scotland office (see Index) and they will give you the finer details.

Most of the recognised coastal goose haunts now have local fowling clubs and it would be advisable to make contact with these organisations' officials before an expedition. With the right approach fowlers are a friendly lot and BASC will provide the contacts. Courtesy at all times must be your guide. It works. I promise.

Soon after I had finished the above lines on fowling literature, a real gem landed in my lap – a catalogue from Marshland books compiled by proprietor Bob Watcham. I had first encountered Bob soon after completing *Golden Dawn*, the book I wrote to celebrate Lytham Wildfowlers' golden jubilee. Bob's praise for the book was most touching. His catalogue did not arrive until recently and I was staggered at the amount of literature available on my favourite subject. Many of the titles I was, of course, familiar with but the potential of the hundreds he had to choose from was akin to prising off a treasure chest lid. Bob refers to himself as, 'The specialist for wildfowling, ashore and afloat'. His contact details are contained in the index.

PLANNING A GOOSE TRIP

When the time comes to head for your goose grounds it is essential to draw up a list of your needs. Richard was always meticulous in the planning of his goose trips. I never knew him to forget anything and a very good reason was his attention to detail.

When his nephew David thoughtfully passed on to me my old pal's familiar red storage box in which he kept various paraphernalia (see Chapter 2) in it was one of his old lists. For the benefit of anyone setting out on a goose safari I can do no better than print it in its entirety:

- Goose gun (cased)
- Game gun (cased)
- Gun cover and sling (there would be a leather sling for the magnum when on a long trek.)
- Goose ammo
- Game ammo (Mostly pigeon loads. Farmers are sometimes glad to give permission to shoot pests.)
- Goose call
- Decoys
- Compass
- Cap, balaclava, face veil, scrim scarf, mitts
- Wellies and over-trousers
- Hip flask, vacuum flask, rum and oxo cubes. (A dash of rum in hot oxo is perfect as a booster on a cold wait but the Scots spit it out!)
- Spare clothes (including thermal long johns and pyjamas for wearing at dawn.)
- Razor etc.
- Alarm clock
- Torch
- Cash/credit cards

Now I would add the mobile phone and two-way radio.

I would have expected to see a necktie included but recall that he would use the one he had travelled in. Richard maintained that a tie was an aid to extra warmth. (It also rounded off his immaculate image.) Gun cleaning kit would have automatically been in a gun case.

In the box also were various ordnance survey maps besides field layouts of the various farms where he had permission to shoot geese. He always made a point, once a farmer had come to know him, of requesting a map. Besides the names of the farmer and his spouse were the names of the rest of the family. A supreme lesson in diplomacy.

In his car also would be another box bearing 'Thank you' gifts. Cosmetics (He was, among other things, a Mary Quant rep) and a cache of whisky. His gratitude never went unrecognised.

There has to be added a footnote to the above. Please do not think that gifts alone will open doors. The gaining of a farmer's trust is not something lightly obtained. There was none better than my old compadre at winning a confidence. He had the supreme approach and most of all, impeccably honoured the trust placed in him. Today I still shoot on farms where he first stepped over the threshold nearly 50 years ago.

In these times of high technology one must not, of course, overlook the internet as a source of information if you are heading for uncharted territory.

It must be remembered that today's aspiring young goose chasers have been schooled in computers these past 10 years, from their earliest days in the classroom. Logging on to the net is as second nature to them as Horlicks at bedtime was to the child of my day.

Computers will plan your route, inform you of just about every form of accommodation along the way, list the gunsmiths in the area (a most useful kernel of knowledge for all sorts of reasons) and give you a list of goose/pigeon/rough shooting guides.

BEWARE ADVERTS

Earlier, I told the story of a ghost and to return to this theme, I have a spooky tale from further west along the Solway and still on the Scottish side. It bears, too, a cautionary note when following up the aforementioned advertised shooting, particularly by hotels desperately seeking to put winter bums in beds.

This particular establishment, a Norman castle-come-hotel, used to offer a first rate deal for both shooting and fishing parties. Their brown trout, sea trout and salmon fishing was often excellent and for those wanting geese and a good mixed rough shoot bag there were few offers better. The proprietor then was a true-born fowler and what he promised, you got. But that was some time ago and the new maitre was young and not very good at communicating with prospective guests.

The conversation went something like this.

'What can I expect from a two-day trip?'

'Well, I neither fish nor shoot but I am a leading authority on both,' was the ignorant response.

Why I decided to try these old haunts (no pun intended) again after that reception I do not know. Perhaps it was sentiment and memories of superb food in wild country. The deal was cheap (that could have been a warning) and it would only be two days out of a week's fowling for it was also on our route north to well-tried goose territory.

My companion was a farmer – a breed I would have thought to be the least likely to believe in ghosts. When we arrived we headed for the village pub, where I knew I would get the rundown on the local goose population. It was bad news but there would be the chance of a wigeon flight at dawn and we were abed before midnight.

Bob (he of the Ross & Cromarty trip) had shivered when we were shown to our rooms earlier and mumbled something about 'spooks.' It hadn't helped when the landlord pronounced that, 'Your dogs will be alright in the dungeon.' That was before we had told him they slept in the vehicle.

I was sound asleep when there came a frantic hammering on my thick, oaken bedroom door. An ashen faced Bob rushed in, slammed and bolted the door, and poured himself a large whisky. Then he began to babble.

'There's something walking about in the room above me and the landlord said no-one else was staying,' he gabbled. We had adjoining rooms and suddenly, sure enough, there were deliberate, if muffled, footsteps on the bare creaking boards overhead. I must have been too whisky-laden to have heard it the first time and I had to admit it truly was spooky.

'Whatever it is it can't harm you in your locked room. Now off to bed and let me get my head down,' I urged.

But Bob was having none of it and climbed into the next bed. There were no more bumps in the night, at least none that I heard, but sleep was fitful thanks to Bob's snoring – which was why I had booked single rooms in the first place!

The locals were right about the wigeon. We had a reasonable flight but there was a pronounced lack of geese and no feeders or game crops on the rough shoot as in the old days. The landlord made no protest when we said we were moving on soon after lunch and the explanation over the ghostly footsteps was also an anticlimax.

It transpired that there truly was no-one in residence above us and the quarters that the landlord shared with his wife and two children were in the opposite wing to ours. He was, however, clearly a considerate soul and was embarrassed to explain that, whenever he took onboard an excess of real ale, (the sort which has a dire effect on one's heavy-duty plumbing system), he shuffled silently along in slippered feet to the distant ablutions which that night took him to the floor above us.

There was, later, a further twist relating to this same establishment. It was their advert which lured Simon to hunt Solway geese many years later. In fact, he then tried another false lead before we met.

How, then, can one guard against falling foul of some such unscrupulous temptation? Again the all-reliable BASC offer the ultimate solution. To the shooter they are our 'mother hen'. Armed with your membership number, phone the association HQ and ask for the section dealing with club membership. They will give you the route to contacting the nearest official of the BASC club in the district where the advertisement is offering shooting. You will find that fellow-BASC members will be only too pleased to give you an honest picture.

A similar service exists in the Association of Sea Anglers and I have used their system on several occasions when exploring fishing venues around our coasts. For the disabled angler it is of paramount value.

I also contacted Steve Woodall, BASC's Northern Regional Officer, and he went even further than merely phoning HQ.

'As with the pursuit of any wild animal, in all honesty nothing can be ever guaranteed. You can, however, make efforts to satisfy yourself that your potential service provider is reputable,' he told me.

'If anyone contacts me for advice about goose shooting I will research the information provided to me on his or her behalf before advising them. I want to ensure that they enjoy the experience they are about to pay for is in the hands of competent, knowledgeable and enthusiastic guides who will go to the best efforts they can to make the trip not only memorable but also provide a degree of education.

'Indeed, many of our members are not there purely for the shooting of geese but to gain an insight into a fascinating pursuit. Hopefully they will take home a few good tips and ideas. I will be happy that they have acted within the best traditions of a sporting spirit and to that end it is essential, therefore, that they are under the care of a genuine professional.'

In other words, Steve will tell you not to bother if he suspects the deal is a bad one.

COMMON SHOOTING INJURIES

Bearing in mind that this chapter is mainly for the benefit of the beginner I refer to minor injuries which can happen in the shooting field. These days all motor cars should carry first-aid kits – an essential part of any shooting trip.

There are, however, some extras which should go into the shooting man's box. Midge cream and antihistamine for wasp stings can be valuable for those pre goose-season pigeon days. I remember only too well the extremely hateful wasp sting carefully planted to the back of my neck only last September when the first of the early Ponkey geese had put in an appearance.

There I was, interfering in no way with a wasp's daily routine when there came a faint buzz and pain exploded like a poisoned dart above my collar. I know not what the wretched creature had been paddling in before its unwelcome visit to what little flesh showed beyond my face net, but there was extreme discomfort until I reached the motor and the tube of antihistamine.

Then there was the ancient Ernie who, unfortunately, chose to site his pigeon chair in a hedgerow slap on top of the entrance to a nest of the yellow devils. The result was several painful stings on his posterior – through lightweight summer breeches. But he got his own back big style. He returned the next day with a sliver of gelignite and vaporised the critters into eternity!

Another item not normally found in your everyday emergency kit is the elastic support – for both knee and ankle. They were always in my gear for the Scottish safaris and more than one affluent magnate was to appreciate their application, particularly during the rigours of deer stalking on the high tops.

And, unless there is always a dog handy, how easy is it to twist the leg joints when sprinting after a winged goose over marshy terrain where small runnels lie hidden in lush vegetation?

A common shooting injury, often seen in my gun-shop days, was the bruised middle finger of the trigger hand. This can be a repetitive problem, particularly when an inexperienced fowler embarks on a goose trip with cartridge loads much heavier than he is used to. It is largely prevalent among the young shots whose hands still have to grow.

On a single trigger weapon the problem does not arise but on a double trigger model the middle digit can be tight against the trigger guard as the forefinger reaches for the frontal position. The extra charge produces a recoil-inflicting, painful bruising. Thereafter the shooter is greatly disadvantaged, flinching as he takes his shot.

In the comfort of a shop the solution is simple. There are two products on hand to provide cushioning between trigger guard and digit. Both are rubberised and take only minutes to fit.

What, though, to do when far from a high street sanctuary?

The cure is, happily, a simple one: cut off a length of crepe bandage from your first-aid box (approximately eight inches to make the handling easier). The item is cheap enough to afford waste. Thread through the gap between the trigger guard strap and the curve, ensuring each end is free. Carry on feeding the ends until the gap is almost filled then, drawing the bandage as tight as possible, knot firmly and push the knot into the last gap.

The emergency job done on my son's non-ejector Sabel, side-by-side on a goose trip at least 12 months ago, is still there. We had then darkened the whiteness of the bandage with the spent powder residue from the insides of my gas-operated auto. Hiding the newness of the latex makes a bodged job much less obvious to those critical eyes.

Perhaps the number one culprit when it comes to minor discomforts is barbed wire. I was taught to use my game bag as a barb protection when straddling. To protect your dog teach it to jump, whenever possible, with your arm on top of the wire.

HYGIENE

As the words of this book were being penned both the daily papers and the shooting press carried stories of the bird flu scare. Shooters were being advised to watch for migratory sick fowl and warned to thoroughly wash their hands after handling ducks and geese.

Apart from these newly arrived precautions it is, of course, as well to pay attention to general hygiene while shooting. Deerstalkers now have their own stringent rules when it comes to gralloching their kills, including the wearing of disposable gloves.

Any cuts, scratches or bites experienced while shooting should be treated with care. The local huntsman in our valley contracted tetanus not so long ago after receiving a cut from the broken leg bone of a road-kill deer he had been given for hound food. He did recover but was perilously ill.

Sometimes injuries come from most unexpected sources. On one occasion, on a pheasant shoot, I was helping to unload grain and discovered a mouse inside one of the sacks. When I picked the rascal up the varmint sunk its needle-like incisors into my thumb and only let go when I thumped it against a post. The amount of blood from such a tiny wound was quite alarming.

The keeper's wife happened to be a nurse and insisted I gave the digit a thorough wash before applying a plaster. By evening it was throbbing incessantly, so I phoned the local doctor.

'Is your tetanus jab up to date?'

'Don't know. It was a long time ago.'

'Come round now and we'll make sure.'

It pays all countryside dwellers and gardeners to keep up-to-date with tetanus immunisation.

Recently there has also been a huge explosion in the numbers of sheep ticks in this county (Cumbria.) Lymes disease can result and we are told to be aware of the symptoms, which can be flu-like. The condition is treatable provided you are not one of those silly people who refuse to see a doctor.

Our very up-to-date village chemist tells me that from 1998 to 2002 there was an immunisation programme in the USA for Lymes disease but it ceased when it was suspected to be the cause of arthritis in those who had undergone the treatment.

My wife happens to be an expert at removing the foul things from both animal and human skin but, if you do not have an Annie handy, there are some very good commercial products on the market designed to do the job without leaving the head in the flesh. Any chemist will advise.

SPECS AND RAIN

This is particularly for those unfortunates who, like me, are forced to wear spectacles. I am sure it is no exaggeration when I claim that 99 per cent of all sportsmen abhor rain in any form. But for the wildfowler a good old downpour, especially accompanied by a stiff blow, can be most advantageous. Rain is misery for the cricketer, footballer, track athlete, even fishermen and the gent on his pheasant peg.

Let me go back a long time, to the middle of the last century, to enlarge on its benefit, however, to the goose shooter. Rain thundered so hard on our Solway caravan roof, that all four of us were prematurely disturbed from our slumbers. Then came an even more insistent and heavier pounding, this time on the door. It swung open and Harry poked a head in. Too dark to see anything, but we all knew he would be grinning his infectious grin.

'We're in luck today boys. Its blowing a hooley and if this lot keeps up they will be walking off!'

Harry said he would wait for us in the barn. His dripping figure would have been about as welcome in our cosy nest as a ferret at a bunny's tea party. The reader might think that, in those far-off days of inadequate clothing, the fowler would be in for a serious drenching in such conditions, but far from it. The Second World War had just ended and every ex-army store in the land was full of cheap 100 per cent waterproof gear. The fowler's favourite was the gas cape. (A lightweight oilskin garment in dun olive which covered the wearer from head to knee. I understand it evolved in the First World War when lethal, skin-searing mustard gas was in use. Combined with a mask it afforded total protection if diligently fitted over exposed flesh.) When not in use the cape could be easily stored in a game bag or tightly rolled and slung over the shoulder with the obligatory spare rope. In fine conditions it ensured a dry hole or a lying pit.

But back to that morning in the 1950s. Within 10 minutes we found Harry, now snuff dry, in the hay barn. He took a swig of the mug of steaming tea we bore to him (few people drank coffee in those days) and we were off down the lane on foot to the boat. It was better that way. The 10-minute walk rather than a Land Rover drive acclimatised us for the stormy river crossing. There would be no chance to cool off by the time we grounded on the far shore.

With five of us aboard, including the man on the oars, our new 12-foot craft rode the mountainous seas like a thoroughbred. That morning we would have only a short walk for we all knew the birds would take the shortest route off along the river edge from their sandbank roost.

There was no argument over positions. We each had our favourite hole and such was the camaraderie that we each knew that the other would not be greedy were he to be in pole position.

As dawn broke, Harry's pronouncement of an hour earlier was borne out. Small parties of pinkfoot beat in low against a fierce crosswind and we had, for those times, an epic flight resulting in 12 birds. In these days of big bags this may not seem a lot among five fowlers but do remember that then the whole population of this goose species in the British Isles numbered a fraction of today's total.

For a teenage longshoreman that morning was an adventure fraught with difficulties. How I must have struggled to keep my vision clear. The prevailing winds on the Solway are westerly, which would mean I had to face the storm. Linen handkerchief would have been in constant use and head would have been kept way down low until the last second. Even then, when the tempest struck, my vision would have reduced the shapes to mere blurs tacking erratically in the crosswind. Three of us were specs wearers and the bag was largely down to the other two. It would have to be a long time before technology came to our aid.

Around 1990 Teflon appeared. An application of this wonder coating meant that, immediately rain hit the lenses, it dispersed so rapidly that vision was virtually unimpaired.

It also had a secondary benefit – the reduction of glare.

Teflon is not something that is applied to all spectacle lenses but, for the shooter, I can promise you it is indispensable. It is not cheap, but worth every penny. Of course the biggest forward stride in ophthalmic improvement came with the introduction of the contact lens but not everyone's eyes are suited to them and I am one of those unfortunates.

The friendly optician then produced another stroke of wisdom – spectacles which fitted high on the bridge of the nose to give me a clearer vision when the gun was mounted – Dennis Taylor type glasses but not anywhere as highly pronounced as the jokey pair worn by that illustrious snooker player.

All these things mean that I can now shoot as well as the next man in rain and at night-time for the first time in my life.

My shooting specs now live in my goose bag – the capacious piece of fishing equipment in which is stowed all I need for both goose and pigeon expeditions. Many has been the time I have been in a February pigeon hide and lost sight of my birds as I mounted the gun. I would still be wearing my everyday specs! Sometimes so stealthy had been my camouflaged movements that I had time to seek out my new visual aids. And should the unfortunate pigeon have settled close enough on a bough, down it would come tumbling to join the bag.

THE VOICE

There is an assumption among inexperienced goose shooters that the spoken word can alert a bird in flight. Under certain conditions this is far from the truth and often a bellowed instruction can result in a considerable addition to the bag.

I will set the scene. Three of you are out at first light on a stubble well hidden in your straw bale hides.

A pinkfoot calls and soon a singleton is spotted winging towards the decoy pattern. Two of the Guns are youngsters and their eyes will be riveted to the oncoming bird. Who will get the first chance, for the old-stager has told them not to shoot if the quarry is nearer your neighbouring Gun? The old-stager does not count in the equation for he will always let the singleton go past him.

Meanwhile, the mentor is not watching the early arrival. His eyes peer beyond, into the ever-lightening sky, and he espies a bunch of eight birds on the same path.

'Leave it!' comes the loud hail and that first pinkfoot will land among the decoys as though it had merely been the cry of a bullock. As the last bird of the bunch passes him, the old-timer swings through and does not interrupt this movement as he squeezes the trigger. By the time his target is plummeting his swing will have taken him to the next bird in line and this, too, crumples.

The rest of the birds have seen nothing and, if it is a gale-riven morning, they may even land unless the tyros are snappy. Usually, however, they will flare and offer easy targets for the remaining four barrels.

There will be times, too, when a single early bird will slip in undetected, probably when you are pouring out that cup of steaming soup.

Do not bother shouting, the bird will believe this to be merely the cry of a mad steer. You must step out of your hide and flap your arms, thus, hopefully, driving it towards your compadre. If he is the right sort of chap, it will be his turn to do the honours the next time.

SOUND

One of the joys of being in the presence of youngsters while abroad in the countryside shooting, fishing or merely observing, is to appreciate the acuteness of their sight and hearing. I never did have the eyesight of Jago (the front desk at primary school was still too far from the blackboard) but I always thought my hearing was exceptional. All my shooting life I have relied on the ears to detect the arrival of ducks on a flight pond but, on a recent fishing trip, I was reminded how much hearing does deteriorate with age.

Three of us were on beautiful Esthwaite Water, a mere mile from my Lake District home, when youngest son enquired, 'What's that racket?'

We were halfway to dark and I had to strain the audio resources to the full to detect the squabble of roosting starlings in a tree on the far bank. Bill, the third member of the party, didn't have a clue what we were speaking about. After a lifetime operating heavy machinery, shooting and dynamite blasting, he was deprived of all but the most strident sounds of the wild.

That evening the fishing was good. Endless September sunshine had reduced the daytime trout catches on the water to nil. Apart from one wily flyfishing local we were the only boat afloat and the trolling method had scored heavily with the onset of dusk. Trolling is actually forbidden on this water but, in deference to my disabled condition, rules are waived. Jago had stowed his fly rod onboard and we would have resorted to the fine art had we blanked with our lures.

(There is another concession for the disabled angler worth mentioning on this water – a wheelie boat which permits a chair to be rolled on and off via the landing-craft-style prow. How we, the severely disabled, are pampered in this enlightened age.)

But our bliss was foreshortened this night by an unusual happening. Bats had just put in an appearance when our young angler clapped hands to ears and almost pleaded for us to head for dock.

'What's up?' I enquired.

'Can't you hear them?' came an anguished response. 'It's excruciating.'

We stuffed tissues into his ears until we had reached our bag limit and headed for land.

I am told that few adults can hear the near-subsonic language of the bat and certainly the pleasure had left me by the time I had reached 70.

TITTLEMOUSE

While on the subject of winged mice, this particular evening reminded me of the time one of their four footed relations came to stay. I was lightly slumbering when the five-year-old came in, aglow with excitement. His chunky hands were tightly cupped together.

'See what I have caught.'

One hand was lifted and inside, oblivious to what might befall it, sat a tiny harvest mouse. It was not much bigger than my thumb nail and could not have been more than a few days old.

'It won't run away. Watch.' And its young captor placed the tiny ball of fur on the top of his head. All day Tittlemouse rode around that way and, at night, he was fashioned a cosy bedroom out of a plastic butter tub.

I suppose Tittlemouse was about six months old when he broke free. One morning there was a hole in one corner of the lid and the search was on. If you have never had a tame mouse running about in your home, don't. We saw him every day sitting, perhaps, on the back of a chair – even on the rug in front of the fire – but try to pick him up and he was gone faster than the blink of an eye.

The havoc he created was way above his weight. At night one could follow his devastating gnawing path – in the desk among the invoices, on the bookshelves, where valuable tomes were decimated in price. Anywhere he should not have been.

Once he visited me in the early morning hours. He awoke me when he dashed over my pillow and soon he was sitting on my chest. A full moon punctured the curtains and he contrasted clearly against the white cover. Tittlemouse finished washing his face and pattered nonchalantly up to my chin where the beard was given a close inspection. Now I had him. All I had to do was move my hands furtively forgetting, of course, that I was a cripple and that they do not work properly. In other words, he melted into the night.

Then, one day, he was gone. We suspected the cat.

THE RIGHT WEATHER

The critical importance of the right weather conditions for goose shooting was clearly demonstrated when artist Rodger McPhail came with me for the first time to Ponkey's. The forecast for a strong southerly had me full of enthusiasm but, by early evening, the wind had died to nothing.

Rodger is, of course, a hardened fowler of many seasons and I use his time with me as an illustration for the tyro. His experiences in the field also gave me a few wrinkles!

For an hour we could only sit and watch as the best part of 3,000 pinks streamed over towards their inland roost four gun shots up. Normally I would have abandoned the plan and hurried down to the lowland duck pond but so dry had been the weather in the area over the grain harvest that there was little more than a puddle where usually there would have been a 50-yard expanse. We had already moved the hides on this flight pond so that our shot fell away from the water in accordance with the new Scottish lead regulations over wetland but we would have to wait for the rains to see how successful the new sitings would prove.

I was not, however, too disconsolate. Most of the geese on the nearby roost had been feeding for over a week on the farm and we were out the next day at dawn on a hillside barley stubble where the straw bales were conveniently still in place – perfect hides with a piece of straw-coloured netting. Rab had reported that around 1,000 birds had been on this particular field on the day prior to our arrival but I blame myself for not having closely inspected the land as soon as we arrived. Nothing came at dawn and, when I checked the stubble, I found it bare. Every grain had been guzzled!

It meant an early breakfast and then a scout to try to locate the new feeding fields. At dawn all the birds had poured out from the roost in a north-westerly direction and I had a good idea where they might be – in a no-go territory.

My predictions were correct but with the advancement of the morning came hope in the guise of an ever-strengthening westerly. So dry was the whole land that I knew the birds would have to return to their roost for a drink and grit erelong.

Meanwhile Rodger had been extremely surprised to see so many hares on our farm during his short stay and told me how much he loved them on the table. It had, apparently, been a long time since one had graced the McPhail larder for, these days, most of his shooting was on driven bird shoots where ground game was banned.

For the uninitiated this strict proviso rules on that type of game shoot simply because, with so many Guns, beaters, pickers-up and dogs in attendance, it can be dangerous to shoot low. The maxim has always to be, 'Make sure there is sky around your target before you pull the trigger.'

On many such shoots woodcock are also off the quarry list for similar reasons. These flitting, jinking birds often maintain a low flight and, in some Guns, imbue an excitement that causes them to take a chancy shot with tragic results. What an enigmatic bird the woodcock is. Most Guns will agree with me when I say that every true field sportsman will remember the day he downed his first.

There has always been an abundance of hares on Ponkey's but, though the farmer would probably like to see their numbers kept at a lower level, we only ever cull if we know a Gun would like to take one home.

An hour later, besides two three-quarter grown *Lepus majors* in the bag plus a couple of pigeons, a mallard, a teal and a brace of pheasants, the wind had reached close on gale-force and we despatched Rodger and another fit Gun to the boundary fence with a supply of heavy shot.

The geese had, indeed, poured back to the roost after a four-hour feed and were desperate for water. They were now beginning to flight back again in small parties to their feeding territory.

There was cover on the fence for only the fittest – it necessitated hunkering down low into clumps of reeds – so Ken and I (the shoot's elder statesmen) elected to sit in our warm cab on the edge of a sheltered wood 500 yards behind the two guns. How gratifying it was for we two old timers to watch our artist friend drop four pinks.

We had a clear view of the flight line as the birds battled over the heather slowly into an ever-strengthening wind. First we were to see the birds suddenly flare and a blob could be seen plummeting earthwards before the bangs reached us.

Those moments are most satisfying for the host who has invited a friend to chase such wild quarry. There is no doubt that Rodger McPhail is the sort of sportsman who fully appreciates that no man can positively guarantee geese in range. It was, therefore, all the more pleasing to see my guest breast the skyline with birds hanging from both fists. I firmly contend that the last time I saw a smile like that was on the face of my mother-in-law when she won a grand on the lottery!

When Rodger returned, the geese were still heading off the moor on the same low path and I asked him if the cold had driven him back to the warmth of the wood. I suppose I should not have been surprised to learn it was because he had achieved what he had travelled north for and felt he had reached his quota. Cold he was not, for one bird had been a runner and had led him a merry chase. And he had also found the small collapsible brolly, I had insisted he took with him, to be a splendid hide. Rodger had spotted the item in my goose bag at evening flight the previous day and enquired what such an incongruous piece of paraphernalia was doing there.

The brolly was of dun hue and a quarter the size of the golf variety. I have been using one of these items for the past 40 years and explained that not only did they provide an adequate hide when used in low cover but also protected one from all the elements. He had been as snug as a grouse in its tussock on the exposed moor top with the open brolly shielding him from the chilling westerly.

My camera captured the occasion as Rodger came down off the hill. The coastal gunner might view inland goose shooting disdainfully but the place where my guest had just lingered will see far fewer human beings in a year than most marshes hunted by the longshoreman in this country.

HARE A LA CELIA

On our journey home I asked Rodger how he preferred his hare cooked. This is where, apparently, the jolly Celia, his wife, comes in. I was relieved to find that the family McPhail are not fond of the jugged hare recipe, which involves using the copious quantity of blood exuding when a hare is paunched. It makes for an extremely rich, pungent dish savoured by only the addicts.

ARTIST AND PHOTOGRAPHER – *Artist Rodger McPhail (left) and photographer Mark Carr. Rodger has shot in many parts of the world but had few chances at pinkfoot. This was taken at Ponkey's in 2005.*

Rodger hangs his hares for a minimal time, only long enough for the enzymes to break down. He reckons the flesh is strong enough without imparting a gamey flavour via the procedure of lengthy hanging. After paunching and skinning, the meat is presented to Celia jointed and she marinates this overnight in beer and onions.

The pieces are then dried, coated in seasoned flour and pan-fried until brown. They are then placed in a casserole dish with the marinade and cooked slowly.

Occasionally one of my guest Guns is an hotelier from my village and he, too, takes back some of these beasties to the delight of his chef. I hear Martin cooks them in a variety of ways including in a pie, a casserole or in a game terrine. In whatever guise, the dish is the most popular on the menu and disappears the quickest. An indication, I suppose, that hare is so rarely seen on menus these days.

There is no doubt that the profusion of hares this year is mainly down to the extremely dry spring, plus the fact that there are so few foxes in the territory – thanks to the efficiency of the keepers in the area. It is worth mentioning that, in all the years I have been on Ponkey's, I have never seen, or indeed, smelled a fox. (Re. the pungency of a fox: if the reader has never experienced Reynard's aroma, when you do, it will be totally unforgettable. It has, to my nasal detector, the reek of rotten diesel and, if the male has been spraying, it will linger for quite some time in a wood).

What entertainment there is on these return journeys from such forays! We discussed the wretched problem of transporting your hare from where it is shot to the game cart or vehicle. I think that, if you were to draw up a list of irksome tasks on a shoot day, near the top would be carrying a hare if you are without a game bag. Holding it by the rear legs necessitates the arm being crooked to prevent the head from trailing on the earth. After more than a few paces it becomes tiresome to the extreme. Rodger reckons he has a simple answer; carry your hare by the front legs. I leave it for the reader to find out if that does, in fact, work.

CAMMO

Rodger had also been impressed by our range of camouflage in the store on Ponkey's. How much easier hide building has become with the introduction of lightweight cammo materials. Twenty feet of the stuff at five feet high makes for superb cover when used in conjunction with four of the handy extending alloy poles. There is also a range of shades, light colours for stubble and reeds and the darker patterns for hedgerow and wood.

Previously we had to hump the cumbersome dark toned ex-army gear which does, however, have one intrinsic advantage – it will not billow so readily in the wind. If your birds are easily spooked, a flapping hide is not a good idea. They will veer off out of range and never bother with your decoy pattern for the rest of the day.

The new material, however, is easy enough to fasten down, but a word of caution about the type of pegs used to do so. Tent pegs are recommended but do make sure they are plastic. The metal jobs can play havoc with farm machinery if one is inadvertently left behind. Farmers have enough to contend with in these hard times without being faced with a wrecked baler. If plastic is not available, wooden pegs can be fashioned easily from tree branches. Make yourself a bundle – I know that on most trips one of my pals will hurry over with the plea, 'Have you any spare pegs?'

Another tip: A 12-inch-wide strip of nylon, trimmed from the end of your hide roll, makes an excellent scarf. You will be surprised at how warm it is and, if you misplace your face veil, it comes in handy to mask a pale visage – the thing for which every goose is constantly searching.

You will find that a 20ft roll will also wrap up easily to go into a standard carrier bag. It will readily fit into your game bag and is invaluable on a field where grain has been harvested but the straw as yet unbaled. Lie down and draw the material over you. But do take care if the straw is wet. It is surprising how quickly cold will strike through your body even though you may be equipped with the latest high-tech clothing.

For times like this I also carry in my vehicle a lying mat manufactured out of a thin layer of foil-backed insulating material. This I have adhered to a lightweight waterproof, subfusc 5ft x 3ft piece of sheeting. This totally stops the cold striking through from the winter chilled earth.

On one occasion I had buried a young chap under a swathe of dry straw – the only way to get under some very wary pinks in Perthshire – confident he would be warm enough. He wore a wax jacket and overtrousers but, over the half hour he was in his covert lair, he was, he told me, reduced to bouts of uncontrollable shivering. Only a spell under the hotel's hot shower expunged the ague from his system. That event prompted the invention of the detailed insulated sheet. The young fellow did, incidentally, say his discomfort was worth it, for he got both a pinkfoot and a greylag. I must add, also, that another species of grey goose came close to being added to the bag that day.

I had warned my guest that a party of five bean geese were in the territory and he admitted he had 'half raised my gun' when a small bunch came to inspect his decoys.

'I just felt there was something odd about their low calls and realised what they were, only because they came so close,' he told me.

FACE VEILS

Still on the subject of camouflage, it is pertinent here to mention face veils. I always carry a supply of this essential commodity, plus mitts. If a companion has not heeded my instructions, he is issued with a set. The biggest giveaway is the flash of pale flesh and, unfortunately, veils are not a cheap commodity. (Mitts are. You can pick them up for as little as £1.50 a pair). And invariably they are not returned.

However, I was able to address this expense after putting out a call in my village for discarded net curtains – every village has net curtains. They are totally essential for covert observation. What else is there to talk about at the weekly WI meetings? Somebody kindly left a useful bundle of them in my newspaper box by the gate within a few days and they were soon in the dye pan.

Unfortunately a lot of this man-made fibre does not take easily to a transformation from white to a donkey brown and shades of dull crayons had to be employed in order to achieve the necessary winter shades. A drop of coloured fencing preservative and coffee were a help also.

Remember, too, that a goose uses its vision in a similar way to the technique employed by a Highland stalker. For example, on Jura off the west coast of Scotland on one of my October red stag forays, I asked my gillie to discuss his method when he was glassing a hill. 'You must look for something different. Something that wasn't there the last time you were out. To the visitor a dormant stag may look like a boulder but to a stalker it will be something out of place and that's when you reach for your scope.'

Binoculars are usually only of 8-10 magnification, whereas a telescope may go up to 60 power.

When geese have been resident in one place for a while they get to know the topography and anything new (like a fresh hide in the open) will cause alarm.

On the marshes pieces of driftwood can be in place for many months and, no matter how small, are capable of concealing a gunner if he lies flat and keeps perfectly still. Even clumps of sea holly or thistle along a foreshore are enough to do the job in prostrate form. A young fit fellow can be up onto his knees and swinging through his bird in two seconds flat. If you let them go slightly past they may not even see you. Having said all that, movement is the number one giveaway.

Before leaving the subject of veils, it must be pointed out that there comes the time in the evening when they are too much of a disadvantage to vision. Then they must be lifted. At times like this, if a bird spots you, it will be too late for its own safety – the quarry will be in range.

CAR CARE

In the early Ponkey days I tell of my acquisition of a 4WD vehicle. At the time there was only the revolutionary Land Rover workhorse, spawned in World War Two and copied from the American Jeep. Then it was not really suited to high speed journeys north, unlike the modern, refined versions.

The Subaru was, I think, the first high comfort price-accessible model to appear and now, today, we have a huge selection. But do beware, should you be one of those husbands delighted to get real farm crud on your wheel arches, if the machine is used by your spouse. She definitely will not like it.

The exterior is not, of course, much of a problem. Something a quick visit to the car wash on the way home can solve, unless you have the misfortune to experience the unusual circumstance which overtook Richard on one trip.

Without knowing it, he had approached a farm in the Scottish Border Uplands, by its rear drive. It was a rough track and appeared to be unusually wet for the prevailing dry spell. Had he known what he was driving into he would most certainly have reversed instantly. Halfway along the extensive route his senses were assailed by something he described as, 'The reek of a thousand bloater trawler khazi doors!'

The ripest of ripe silage had gushed from a silo following the visit of a clumsy farm apprentice who had, unknowingly, punctured its skin during some inept reversing from the cab of a bale loader.

Richard duly took his motor through the car wash on the way home but the pressure jets got nowhere near the underside crevices. Worse still, it was a company car. In the end it became a garage job. The vehicle was taken up on the hydraulic ramp and a hot steam jet applied to the underbelly.

The Americans, I hear, have a similar problem if they are unfortunate enough to run over a skunk. Should the varmint get a chance to deploy its defensive jet mechanism the results are so pungent that the antidote is only the application of liberal solutions of, believe it or not, tomato ketchup! One assumes that this only applies when you live far from a pressure hose.

The interior is, however, where much more caution must be shown. Pay a visit to your nearest builders supplies store and buy the smallest waterproof sheeting you can find. It is easily cut to fit the boot space and gives total protection. Leaky shot game, mud-soaked dogs and grimy boot residue can stay on top of the cover which, when removed, is easily sluiced off by a garden hose. Unless you have done something unlucky enough like leaving a dead snipe wedged between the back seat cover, the darling spouse will hardly ever know the vehicle has left the garage.

BEWARE OLD GUNS

One of the big and unexpected plusses to come my way following the decision to retreat into rural Cumbria was the close liaison I was to have with a registered firearms dealer. I shall name him Oliver, for such people these days prefer, understandably, to remain anonymous to the general public. For those interested in guns they are easily contacted through word of mouth.

Oliver has now had his dealership licence over 20 years and came to see me when he first decided to apply for his qualification. I was amazed at the speed his business flourished. This would, undoubtedly, have been attributed to the fact that he was born and bred in the area and is a member of a much-respected family. Newcomers are inevitably treated with great suspicion. Granted it is the best part of an hour's drive to reach a gun shop from this territory but neither he nor I anticipated the demand his service would engender. In fact, when the Home Office decided, around 10 years ago, to have a purge on the proliferation of dealers who had acquired licences merely because they possessed a large quantity of registered weaponry, Oliver was one of the few without retail premises to retain his. One close scrutiny of his record book instantly confirmed that he was, indeed, an essential part of the county's infrastructure in these parts.

As the son of a farmer he had been familiar with shotguns and rifles since he could hold one but his highly specialist, refined, knowledge was sparse. Which was where I came in. Oliver had done me a lot of good turns since I arrived in his neck of the woods – many more than I would be able to repay – and it was a pleasure to guide him through the minefield that is evaluation.

The bonus side, for me, was the chance to continue to handle some of the finest examples of craftsmanship to come out of the British gun trade.

Courtesy of Oliver, I shot a muzzle-loading .400 calibre Purdey rifle, resplendent with its octagonal barrel and fine rose and scroll engraving on the action. The highly-polished mahogany box, with its brass fittings, still contained reloading tools, oil bottle and turnscrews.

'It drops a lot over 100 yards,' said Oliver as he balanced an end-on log atop a boulder. The backdrop was a substantial drumlin on the valley side.

Holding a good 18-inches over my target I squeezed the so-sweet trigger and the black powder belched out its round ball messenger. The recoil was more of a caress than a thump. The log shuddered slightly and presently Oliver held a stubby forefinger dead centre. It wasn't me. It was the rifle!

Shotguns of equal quality began to filter through and we both desperately awaited the arrival of the micrometer barrel gauge. I had explained to Oliver that this would be his most essential piece of equipment. A barrel enlarged beyond its proof size can burst only too easily.

During my years in the trade I had been horrified at the number of old British shotguns which had landed on my counter out of proof. At first I was baffled why so many were, in fact, oversized in their barrels.

My mentor, the late Sam Entwistle, explained that it was almost certain they had received the attentions of what he used to call back-door gunsmiths – engineers who had the skills to lap out its pitting but not the tools, or know-how, to read the final bore diameter after their operations. Few would, for instance, be able to analyse the original proof marks stamped on the weapons.

(It must be explained that, in the days before non-corrosive ignition caps and powders, the highly polished shotgun bores quickly became pitted if neglected or incorrectly cleaned.)

I pen this as a warning to the goose chaser who, for nostalgic reasons, would want to be the owner of one of the old time fowling pieces be it of 12, 10, 8 or 4-bore calibres. It could be a Tolley, a Bland, or even a Purdey or Holland & Holland. The barrels may look clean but, at no cost must you buy until that all-important micrometer has told its story.

Should you get the chance to obtain one of these weapons privately, do heed the warning and seek the advice of a dealer who is a member of the Gun Trade Association. He will have undergone a strict test before admittance. I know because I was the North West examiner for 10 years!

YET ANOTHER LESSON IN GOOSE STALKING

I have touched several times on goose stalking and I note that, on the final page of his 1976 book *Longshore Gunner*, BB describes deer stalking as one of the finest of all field sports with wildfowling a close second. It would have been interesting, however, to know what the great man meant by his use of the word 'finest'.

There is, also, one other field sport to be included in the same slot for excitement – walked up grouse. I was to first encounter this engrossing pursuit by chance following a futile trip to the Solway while still in my twenties and tell of it in the chapter Greylag Country. For this discipline it helps to be as fit as a mountain guide and to possess the reflexes of an Olympic fencer!

But back to stalking – not of deer but of geese. As a facet of goose chasing this can certainly have its heart-pumping moments. One of the most recent stalks I was involved in was Simon's first – in the last month of the season.

The two of us were in Ponkey territory in mid-January when we found a party of around 100 pinks feeding on sheep-cropped scrub grass in a valley bottom. Here was a wonderful opportunity for Simon to receive his first lesson in the art of goose crawling.

The birds were below us, a good half mile from the road, and, to the uninitiated, a stalk would have looked hopeless. The strategy was to motor 300 yards to the edge of a straggly deciduous wood which ran from the road to join a thick planting of 10-foot sitka spruce where the geese could be a close gunshot from its extreme edge. The binoculars had revealed some birds feeding and some sleeping.

(While on the subject of binoculars – sometime ago I had acquired a pair of the zoom optics which went from 8 to 20 magnification. The higher power was invaluable for goose spotting when the lesser magnification left doubts that the dark smudge on that faraway stubble was either sleeping geese or merely a manure spillage. However, anything over

10 magnification necessitated leaning on something as steady as a car roof, otherwise shakes rendered them impractical.)

From the point where the two woods met, the spruce extended a good 200 yards towards the birds. I had instructed Simon to walk carefully down the far side of the old wood, well out of sight of the flock, but he must have misunderstood. After only a matter of minutes the birds jumped and, when I turned my observations from the flock to Simon's progress, I found he had taken the wrong side of the wood. Even at a distance of half a mile, the wary birds had spotted him.

As the flock disappeared in a thin wavering line towards the coast, we turned the car for home. We would be back in two weeks for the last two days of the season. After telling Simon there was virtually no chance of finding the geese in such an accessible spot again I was to be proved wrong upon our return.

BILLIARD TABLE

The day before we were due to set off on this quest I had received a call from one of my friendly farmers who announced that birds were on a field of new grass in the same locality and could I move them?

We arrived by mid-afternoon to find no birds on the rough land near the wood but around 300 pinks were scattered over the new grass. A scan with the binoculars revealed few places for a hide. This particular farmer was one who did not like the hassle of tending hedges and all his fields were bounded by post and wire. Nor were there any ditches close enough. We really were confronted with the proverbial billiard table.

I was pretty certain from which direction the birds would flight – the field was no more than a mile from one of the roosts – but no winds were forecast and the birds would doubtless come in high and spiral down. Our only hope would be to make a close inspection at dawn. In these days of hi-tech cammo it is surprising how one can conceal oneself but my personal problem was that I can shoot only from a swivel chair and I needed three feet high netting to conceal myself. It may be that I would have to leave it to Simon to lie full-length in the tussocky grass at the foot of one of the fences, as I had so often done in my fitter days.

But first, that evening, we had the prospect of Top Pond awaiting. We had not shot it for a month and Rab reported that the geese had been using it regularly. Hard frosts can put such waters at 1,000 feet above sea level, out of action by the end of January. My pessimism was unfounded, with only half of the pond frozen. Both duck and goose feathers lay thick opposite its windward side.

Because of the extreme wariness of the geese at this time of the year, there was a debate about whether or not to leave Simon's black Lab Zac in the car until flight was over. We opted for him to come with us and it proved to be a costly decision. The rich pickings in the shallow water brought the ducks early and we had downed a mixture of six mallard and teal by the time the geese were imminent. Zac still had a winged teal to gather when the first party of around 10 pinks came in, only to sheer off 100 yards away at the sight of the moving dog. Early in the season they often did not bother.

No one can accuse Zac of not being persistent when he knows there is a bird down and he was to ignore Simon's commands as the only other two lots to come followed the same pattern. It was little consolation when Zac finally collected the duck.

Next morning our close scrutiny of the grass field, half an hour before dawn, paid off in terms of a hide position for my bulk. A heavy steel gate lay at one corner and, when opened, it rested against a fence running at right angles. Goose droppings were scattered as far as the gateway and I was hoping that I was well-concealed with netting forming a cosy triangular hide.

With Zac in the car Simon found himself a dense enough run of tussocks at the fence bottom near the middle of the field boundary and all seemed set – apart from the fact that it was still windless. There was, in our favour, a thin dawn mist but, oh the vagaries of goose chasing! All the birds passed high overhead as if they knew not of the existence of pickings below. The 24 shell decoys did not, as far as they were concerned, exist and nor did they heed our calls.

There had been some clue to this behaviour at first light when we heard distant calling from birds coming in from the coast. As it grew lighter the binoculars revealed party after party dropping in on forbidden land a mile away. This is where our birds also made for.

We left it till 10am before packing up in case the big lot were disturbed, but our luck was out. The thin mist still lay further inland, up the valley, and as Simon swung the decoy bag over his shoulder there came goose talk from this direction. A party must have slept in on one of the lochs. We crouched behind our gate but held little hope. They were, we felt, bound to join the big gathering.

Hidden by the mist the birds, by their calling, seemed to be heading straight for us but, still a good half-mile from our field, the clamour gradually softened and, finally, ceased. They had pitched in and seemed to have done so behind the wood where we had glassed them two weeks earlier. Could this be our big stroke of luck?

With all the haste we could muster we loaded the gear and sped off down the high road. Sure enough, something like 100 pinks were in exactly the same spot. The mist was just thin enough for us to detect the party busy feeding no more than 30 yards from the fir wood edge.

This time Simon made no mistake and I was able to view the whole affair from a box seat. Behind the corner of the deciduous trees I watched him reach the dense cover of the sitkas. Following careful instructions he moved quietly along the edge until, 100 yards from the end, he climbed the fence and sank out of sight on all fours.

A good 10 minutes passed before I saw the birds jump, followed by two bangs. A bird fell and the flock headed away up the valley. Then came a third shot and another was tumbling from above the trees, well behind the main bunch. I was baffled.

Simon climbed over the fence and dashed after a runner which quickly fell to a shot, the report of which came well after I saw it crumple. The bird was collected then, as Simon made his way back to where the bird had jumped, he stooped once, twice, three times. Four birds from his first stalk. This ageing mentor was proud of his pupil.

Ten minutes later I was to learn that the mystery high goose had come from a second flock that had been feeding, unknown to Simon, round the corner of the wood. He had dropped three birds with his first two barrels and had just time to reload one cartridge as the second lot came past.

DESPATCHING GAME

All Simon's geese were dead on this occasion but the problem of despatching game is not one to be passed over lightly. It is something the beginner must be instructed in from the very outset. Unless you are experienced at neck pulling, my advice has always been to carry a small priest, of the type sold in every fishing tackle shop. This is a short piece of metal, or wood, around six inches long and heavily weighted at one end.

The Queen is an expert at administering the coup de grace using her stick when picking up on a game shoot but not everyone is so adept at wielding a long staff. It is something which requires practice, whereas a

A Successful Stalk – Simon's first attempt at goose stalking resulted in four pinkfoot.

priest can be comfortably managed by anyone. The gadget is cheap and easily slips into a pocket.

When using a priest the best method is to hold your bird by the base of the wings where they join the body in one hand and strike sharply, once, on the back of the head by the nape. Hold fur (rabbit and hares) by the back legs and strike in the same place.

A word of warning here concerning cock pheasants. You have not yet received your 'blooding' in the shooting world until you have been wounded by a set of the vicious spurs behind each leg of a longtail. And once you have received your scars you will never forget. To avoid these terrible weapons, if the bird is still alive, make sure you do grip by the wings. Hold him by the neck and he will have you.

DAMN THE MAGNA CARTA

Returning to the theme of this chapter I will now recount tales of marsh outings for three tyros.

Jacob is a school chum of Jago's and is lucky to have a father passionate in his following of rod, rifle and gun. Not only that, his mother is a gamekeeper's daughter. Which is probably why she will have nothing to do with game! This latter parent would, however, explain why he has so much love of wild pursuits in his genes.

The 12-year-old had shot since he could hold a 28-bore but there was a big gap in his field sports education – he had never been on a marsh. His dream was to be a long way out on the saltings when the geese awoke at dawn.

Neither lad needed more than one shake on a bitterly cold January morning and the three of us were soon on an hour's journey to Morecambe Bay. Paul was already at the rendezvous, on top of the sea wall, where I would have a grandstand view as the sky lightened.

Thirty thousand pinks and a smattering of greys were in the Bay and a big tide would have left them close to the grass.

'No ducks and no chatter' was, therefore, the order, for the morning air was as still as a tomb. There would be one first chance and then the birds would be high following the initial salvo.

Minutes after the three figures had been swallowed in the blackness, the wigeon and teal flight began. Wave after wave of wigeon packs swept overhead accompanied by the magic whistle of the cocks and the occasional grunting of the hens. Neither boy had put this species in their game book but that could come another time. The teal were more often heard than seen, the tearing wind through their pinions clearly heard on this stillest of mornings. Mallard were very much on the second shift and the sky was lightening rapidly before the main weight muttered their way out to the sanctuary.

COCKLE PICKERS

By now the geese had begun to talk. At first only a few wake-up calls but these very quickly turned into an incessant clamour. Then as one, they were up. Not to head inland for their feed on the rich fields over the three waiting gunners, but further out into the Bay, disturbed by a phalanx of quad bikes, their riders intent on cockle picking.

I had earlier handed Paul a two-way radio, the better for me to enjoy the events as they unfolded beyond my vision.

'Bloody cocklers!* We might as well pack up. They are working right in from of us.'

I called back, 'They must be in the sanctuary, isn't that illegal?'

'Unfortunately not. Something to do with the Magna Carta.'

Knowing there could still be a chance, albeit slim, of the odd goose moving along the edge of the grass, Paul elected to stay on and gave the all-clear for ducks. As the cloudless sky grew ever lighter, lines of geese could be seen far out over the Bay heading resolutely away from the cocklers. Four- and eight-bores boomed out their messages way to the east and, a while after, came the pop-pop of 12's as the skeins reached their inland feeding grounds. For most of these inland gunners it would be their last outing of the season. February 1 was two days off. Only tidal land would remain open until the 20th.

A family party of eight greylags came off high. Deep, low occasional calls and their slower wing beats made them easily distinguishable from the more garrulous pinkfoot. Tundra whooper swans were still bugling in the middle of the Bay, refusing to be disturbed by the cockle pickers. Some drifted in on the fast-rising tide like giant clods of foam.

Then came a single shot from the direction of the gutter where the two boys and their mentor hid. Binoculars picked out a tiny figure scampering across the grass. He stooped, then turned back at a slower pace, a goose hanging from a tiny hand. It was Jacob.

'The lucky beggar has got his goose,' Paul radioed. 'It came straight at him along the edge of the grass.'

Ten minutes later came two more bangs.

'He's done it again. I've just christened him Golden Balls!'

*Cockling

There is a new phenomenon in the Bay much publicised in the national press – cocklers. On that day none came by way of the southern marshes but, with daylight, binoculars detected line upon line of ant-like figures feverishly harvesting the mollusc glut.

From my Lake District home the nearest point of contact with the Bay is the Grange Wildfowlers' territory. Club committee member and the Countryside Alliance Area Director Tom Fell told me, 'Members have reported that, as they have awaited goose dawn flight, teams of pickers have headed past them out into the Bay, all hopes of a flight ruined.'

There is nothing, I hear, that can be done about it since the environmentalists are happy for the rich harvest to be garnered.

However, it is said to have brought another problem within the hinterland of the Bay – a dearth of apprentices in all sorts of trades. Instead of earning £200 a week they are on a reported £1,000, albeit temporarily.

Jacob's First Flight – Jacob's first dawn flight on a marsh brought him two pinks.

Soon afterwards the sun topped the Trough of Bowland hills and exploded over the marsh like a golden blanket. Three figures rose from their creeks and headed back towards the real world.

Jacob's face told its own story. He is a quiet fellow but I doubt if, for him, Christmas morning just past had been any more joyful.

He told me that the wings of both birds had been iced up when he picked them, certainly a phenomenon few of us have experienced. It proved how viciously cold the dawn had been. Jago said ice had formed on his waders and gun slip.

Both boys had heeded the warning to keep low in their gutters to avoid what slight zephyr there might be. Face veils and mitts had protected tender skins and Paul had chosen hiding places where the easterly would not funnel up their creek.

In spite of the Magna Carta and in spite of 'hopeless' conditions, Sunday 30 January 2006 had proved how utterly unpredictable wildfowling can be. Is that not what makes it so special for those of us lucky to be under its spell? I hoped the fever would last as long for my two young charges as it has for this leathery old crust.

PATRICK'S TURN

The following Sunday it was the turn of Patrick, another marsh apprentice. He also is a school chum of Jago's and has had just as much shooting as Jacob, starting his learning with a 20-bore.

The conditions in the Bay were completely the opposite of a week earlier, apart from the fact that it was, again, windless. Instead of an endless vista, this day was one of a shifting mist, sometimes restricting visibility to 80 yards. We had crept through varying densities of the stuff along the entire journey but still arrived at our rendezvous on schedule.

Paul was minutes behind. 'Don't like the look of this lot. If it doesn't thin there'll be no dawn flight.'

His prediction brought despair to Patrick's face, but Paul was quick to assure him. 'Don't worry. We'll just let it get a bit brighter and then get out there.'

It is most surprising how soon the light gathers on mornings like this. Ten minutes later the three were trudging their way over the close-cropped frozen lea, topped the sea banking and were gone. I motored round to my vantage point a mile south and, out of the vehicle, strained my ears for the sounds of a waking dawn. A cock crowed, a bucket clanked in the farmyard half a mile behind me and then mallard began to mutter on a pond behind a bank of willows close by but nothing flew. Fog disorientates all birds and they hate to move in it.

With full daylight and no wind to move the mist, not even the pipe of a redshank came from out in the Bay. Then the half-tame mallard lifted from their night quarters, did a few turns accompanied by plenty of wake-up calls, and dropped back unsure of their bearings in the blanket.

Almost immediately there came a muffled crump, from the direction of the far off guns quickly followed by Paul's radioed call, 'I don't know why nothing dropped! Bring back lead.'

The geese had decided to come off at last.

Paul's lead words were telling. The day's flight, already unique because of the weather conditions, was to demonstrate the penalty we have to pay for the ban on lead over wetlands. It is a ban which many contend to be senseless.

So far there has been only one efficient alternative to lead and that is the American invention of Hevi-shot previously mentioned in Chapter 12. And what an alternative. Proof of the pudding is, they say, in the eating and this remarkable combination of metals/elements is heavier than lead and, as a consequence, kills further. The manufacturers instruct us to use nothing tighter than half choke. By employing size three shot, therefore, you get not only a wider killing pattern but also one that is more efficient in range. Paul is, however, a traditionalist and refuses to have his full choked English three-inch side-by-side bored out for Hevi-shot and is forced to shoot bismuth or tungsten.

Paul's two shots marked the start of an intriguing flight that was to last all morning. Distant booms reverberated from far over the Bay and soon single skeins hoved into my vision. There was to be no mass exodus.

I was in a sanctuary zone and one party of around 50 pinks topped the sea wall close to my right 40 yards up to pitch into a pasture a bare 100 yards from the road. Inland shooting had ceased five days ago. In a couple of weeks' time, all these fields would hold geese and we would have the privilege of observing these magical creatures from the comfort of our motor vehicles at extremely close quarters. Do not leave your car though. Should you do so, their precious reverie will be disturbed and they will be up and off. They deserve our consideration and respect.

That morning I made a firm decision. Come next season, clan Miller would tread the marshes armed only with Hevi-shot. At £1.50 a shot, it is a small price to pay for what I consider to be, without question, the most intriguing sport in the whole world. Do we not owe it to our quarry to use only the best product available?

For my party, that morning's shooting finished at 9am, in accordance with the marsh owner's ruling. Though all three admitted they had had their chances, their bags were empty. Patrick's face, however, proved it had been a moving experience for him. It prompted me to announce to the two boys a promise that, next season, I would guide them to more coastal goose shooting somehow somewhere. I had a cunning plan – membership of two fowling clubs.

HYPOTHERMIA

I feel it is more than just worthwhile here to emphasise the dire effects extremes of cold can have on both the young and old. Young fit adults, at the peak of their physical endurance, are generally those who undertake wildfowling and it is too easy for them to overlook fellow Guns who are not in this league.

That first morning when Paul took his young charges to the wastes was seriously bitter. He personally wore neoprene belly waders besides the latest in a thermally insulated top. The boys, at an age when growth rate rockets, were clad in whatever could be found to, hopefully, protect what were less resilient physiques.

Most calls on our two-ways that morning were about bag filling efforts but they included, 'I'm just off to check on the lads. I'll bring them in if it gets any colder.'

Paul did, in fact, have both boys doing a couple of circulation-stirring bursts up and down the grass and his suggestions of a return to base were met with indignant rebuffs.

Once, on Ponkey's, when Richard and I were caught in a blizzard on the moor top, my pal fell into deep trouble. We were then far from old men but the January temperature had plummeted with the oncoming of a fierce wind while we crouched in the lee of a gateway. It was one of those extra-wide affairs designed to accommodate modern farm machinery and sheets of corrugated zinc had been attached to the base of the double gates as an emergency sheep shelter.

Snow had threatened all day and now, with the closing of dusk, the clouds belched forth their unfriendly contents. No geese flew. Nor did any bird. Taking to the sky would have been impossible in such a tempest. The grey legion would remain in whatever field they were trapped until the white stuff ceased.

Two over-zealous fowlers knew how they must have felt! It seemed cosy enough in our one-walled igloo for the snow had by then reached the top of the zincs. Unaware of my companion's condition, I was in no discomfort. These were pre-thermal days but I had the great advantage of my sheepskin waistcoat – as effective as anything man has been able, so far, to conjure despite all of his technology. Where today's garments do score is, of course, in their lack of bulk.

Somewhere behind the masses of storm clouds, a waxing moon hid and it was sufficient to produce the faintest illumination to our lonely world, even though blizzard conditions were unabated. All we had to do was to follow the fence downhill until we reached our 4WD and, apart from a bit of bonnet snow-scooping, the rest would be easy. Guns were still in slips and I straightened, with protective hood turned against the tempest.

Richard remained motionless.

'Come on. Time to go time.'

'I can't move,' came the muted response. Richard was curled in the foetal mode, hands thrust inside his jacket. I felt some guilt at not having paid more attention. With both magnums slung over my back I groped for a hand and heaved at the inert bundle. Fortunately, though well over six feet tall, my companion was an extreme lightweight – which probably had something to do with his lack of insulation.

With his body sheltered to leeward, and with an arm tight around his slender frame, we trundled down the gentle incline. Richard did not have the advantage of a hood and I noticed that the curled hair below his cap was frozen solid! At first his feet dragged but soon the circulation began to return and he was in reasonable shape when we reached the vehicle.

What, one might ask, would have happened had Richard been alone that day?

Quite simply, I doubt he would have remained there had he been by himself. He was not one to take chances and would have headed back to the sanctuary of the vehicle at the first hint of such conditions. We had dallied hoping that the snow would be brief and that the geese would fly back under the moon to their roost a mile away.

As it happened the fall was so heavy that it moved both the pinks and greys from our territory and we went north for the remainder of our stay, where the fields were still green.

In those days I had plenty of contacts in Perthshire and we were, I recall, able to enjoy two days among the greylags without seeing another Gun. Now, 35 years on, no geese visit there having been harried away by commercial shooting.

On another occasion, when I was a guest Gun on a pheasant shoot not far from Ponkey's, an elderly gent suffered a lesser form of hypothermia.

He was on the next peg to mine while we waited for the beaters to make a particularly wide sweep. This time snow merely clad the land but it did add its extra chill to a nasty nor'easterly. My fellow guest had turned his collar against the blast and was huddled on a shooting stick. Fearing for his welfare I kept an eye on the old fellow and soon he lifted an arm in a feeble gesture. I hurried over.

'I'm afraid I feel somewhat dizzy. Would you help me to stand?'

I guessed he would be in his seventies and we hobbled over to the shelter of a hedge. The shoot captain happened to be a doctor and, when a flask of hot consommé was produced he by-passed the whisky.

It did the trick and, since this was the last drive of the day, the patient sat in the Land Rover with the heater completing his recovery.

I learned that the disorientation suffered by my fellow Gun that day was an early sign of hypothermia. It is a dangerous myth to claim that a spirit, like whisky, can be of benefit. Alcohol merely enlarges the blood vessels and this would have worsened his condition.

But do not dismiss this spirit as an emergency aid in the field. Its use as an antiseptic, in the story of the wounded Jura stalker in Chapter 6, well illustrates this aspect.

CHAPTER 14

Goose Dogs

There are so many myths and fallacies surrounding gun dogs that I decided to make a short journey to talk with John and Sandra Halstead, breeders of what few will dispute is one of the world's most renowned line of working Labradors. This is, of course, the Drakeshead strain derived from John's early days of fowling retrievers.

Wildfowling was John's passion as a young man and the kennel name is an amalgam of mallard DRAKES and HalstEAD.

'It gives you an idea of how committed I was to wildfowling. It was a long trail by motorcycle from my Burnley home to the Dee Estuary but I was there whenever I had half a day to spare,' said the 66-year-old John.

This truest of outdoor men and I met briefly many years ago in my gun shop days on a grouse moor but this was our first face-to-face encounter. There was an instant empathy and it was no surprise to discover we had the same birthday!

The husband and wife team run their thriving operation from Brinscall, near Chorley, tucked away in a haven of woods, trout lakes and rough pasture. Rabbits scuttle and there is a profusion of waterfowl. Some flaunt on open water while others skulk in the reed beds. A dog-training Utopia. There is a feeling of peace and quiet belying the fact that industrial Lancashire is only mere minutes away. There would, I mused, be an epic dawn chorus and I congratulated John on his lack of grey squirrels.

After dog training, shooting is still John's number one passion and, on the day I went to see him – shortly after the close of 2005/6 fowling season – he had just returned from a clay session. He likes to keep his eye in but, with advancing years, has had to change to a lighter gun. He now uses a 20-bore and finds it much more compatible on his rough shooting forays.

'I have swapped the marsh for walked-up game. It is challenging and helps to keep me in trim.'

The Drakeshead trophy count is impressive, boasting an astounding 28 field trail champions – close to one for every year the couple have been in the business of breeding and training their pedigree line.

I began by asking John, forthright and emphatic in his views, to settle the age-old contention that a fowler's dog should go on the drop i.e. when a bird has fallen to shot.

'No way. Imagine it is the start of a morning goose flight and you have Guns to the left of you and to the right. You have downed a bird well out and there are more coming. If your dog runs in to retrieve, you have spoilt it for everyone.'

John does not pull punches. 'I would like to bet that those who say retrievers should go on the drop quite simply do not have control. I watch my dog, particularly at dusk, and can tell instantly if it knows a bird is down. Then, if it will not spoil the other people's sport, I give the command to go.'

John has an adage all his own: 'Learn to read your dog.'

We discussed the sometimes-freezing conditions dogs have to work in and queried if it was true that yellow Labs have a thicker coat than blacks.

'Another myth. All Labs should be thick coated – an outer and inner layer. This insulates them against extreme cold. If there is only one layer then that animal has a fault.'

He is very opposed, too, to a relatively recent trend in protective man-made dog body warmers and classed them as 'totally unnecessary.'

While still on the comfort theme I asked about background heating in kennels.

'Again an unnecessary expense. Many of our dogs prefer to be under nothing more than overhead sheets even when it is snowing.'

John advocates gentle towelling for a soaking dog before it goes into a vehicle or kennel. The under coat will still be dry.

What of gun dogs living in houses where there is a family?

'Quite acceptable, if you insist, but a dog living in a kennel will always have a better coat.'

And there was, he said, another vital dimension when a dog shares family life. 'If there are children involved, a dog can soon learn bad habits. You just have to balance the situation. If your dog is both a pet and a workhorse, what standard do you require? Certainly if you are wanting something of field trial level then living closely with youngsters is out.'

When we reached the subject of feeding, John's theories were interesting. He is a fan of all-in-one mixed diet products.

'When they first came on the market they were inefficient simply because they were uncooked. A dog would push the meal through its system and leave a lot undigested. Now that it is pre-cooked (and therefore easily absorbed) it is excellent.'

At Drakeshead Kennels all the dogs are fed at varying times, 'So that they don't become too anxious if their meal does not arrive right on schedule.' And if they are to be subjected to a hard, full day's work, picking up or rough shooting, John is a believer in giving them a light meal two hours before shooting begins.

The feeding of Mars bars was also placed firmly in the box of old wives tales.

'This very probably began when a dog was found to have a deficiency and required a quick energy boost. Any dog in normal health should not need feeding until the end of the day.'

John is not, however, against the proffering of the odd titbit but chocolate for human consumption is poison to a dog.

My next poser was what I maintain to be one of the most contentious among dog owners – the neutering of both sexes if they are not to be used for breeding. The question came close, I felt, to inducing a frown over John's friendly countenance. His answer was dismissive.

'If, on a shoot, a dog shows any urge to look for a bitch, then it is poorly trained. As far as bitches are concerned, we have them injected to repress their coming on heat if that's what we want.'

John maintains that one of the few acceptable reasons for castrating a dog is if it has aggressive tendencies.

(From my experiences among dogs I can confirm that this drastic measure, performed on a mature animal, can work efficiently.)

Besides his individual successes, John has also captained the England gun dog team seven times.

I found my afternoon with this remarkable duo both intriguing and revealing.

'Sum up the Labrador for me as a fowling dog,' was my final request. The answer came straight off the cuff.

'The Labrador is the best. Through selection over many generations it has become internationally accepted as the finest retriever breed in the world. And, without question, the British Isles had the highest standard of trials dogs anywhere.'

John's advice over choosing a shooting companion is simple. Pick your pup carefully from proven breeding and you have close on 100 per cent chance of getting it right. Shoot straight and the dog will take care of the rest.

DOG THEFT

We addressed, finally, what John described as a 'huge worry' – dog theft. Every month there are adverts in the shooting press appealing for sightings of stolen dogs.

'It is something which appears to be happening more and more,' said John. 'The thieves can't possibly be getting what these dogs are worth. We just seem to be living in an age where the unscrupulous will steal anything.

'Only the other day a friend near here had all his terriers stolen. The thieves were seen by neighbours who thought they must have been friends since they acted so openly.'

All kennels like John's have the highest security systems. Nor are the dogs ever left unattended day or night.

A keeper pal not far from me, in a quiet part of Cumbria, runs cocker spaniels. Until recently he was happy to go on holiday and leave his dogs in their familiar kennels. A friend went twice a day to exercise and feed, but not any more. He disperses his dogs among relations and friends. It is a lot of trouble but would appear, these days, to be the only option.

Personally I am a fan of the feisty Jack Russell as a minder for my soft retrievers. Should a stranger even try to pat Bobbie he would get a growl and an eye-roll thus causing an instant back off.

So far he has only bitten once and meant it. Soon after we moved back to the Lakes – about six years ago – a friend, whom our Jack Russell had never met, rapped hard on the front door and strode in with a loud haloo.

You could almost see Bobbie's mind working. 'This is what I'm here for,' and something like 28 pounds of solid muscle and teeth flew through the air and attached itself firmly to a naked forearm! How he leaped so high I know not.

The arm was wounded but Dave, an avid dog man and lurcher keeper, suffered no long-term ill effects. In fact he was most impressed and entirely blamed himself.

There is another Jack Russell story which illustrates their worth as defenders of their territory. This fellow was owned by a pal living on the southern side of the Ribble (to be close to his goose shooting).

Barry had a smallholding and, like all farmers, left the keys in his vehicles. He was unaware that his Land Rover had gone until he received a call from the police. A patrol car had come up behind a Land Rover on the motorway with the driver's door open and a small dog hanging onto a foot!

The driver was trying frantically to beat the unwanted appendage free of his boot with a stick while steering erratically and ever slower.

Rather fittingly the little fellow was already named Grip and was undamaged. The thief got a hefty custodial sentence with all sorts of charges thrown at him. I would like to have been in court at the time, for it must surely have been a mirthful affair. Fortunately it was not necessary for the dog to attend!

What place, you might ask, has a terrier in a book about goose hunting? Plenty. Goose chasing and rough shooting are synonymous and terriers make excellent flushing animals once they have been taught the rudiments of behaviour. In other words, they must return to their beater/handler immediately on the whistle and not worry fallen game.

Terriers can have as good noses as most dogs and, even if they may not retrieve your goose, can readily locate one that has fallen into thick cover. And what a security measure with guns in vehicle or hotel bedroom!

John Halstead does give some sound security advice: have your dog micro-chipped. The chip comes in the form of a small electronic pill about the size of a grain of rice inserted under the loose skin round a dog's scruff. It is virtually painless in its application and, at around £20 to £40 a dog, it is little enough to pay for some peace of mind. If ownership is challenged, the chip, easily read electronically by a vet, gives proof positive via a database.

My local retired vet friend Jane told me another horror story, which illustrates what tortuous lengths dog thieves will go to.

A dog owner was exercising his pet in a 'dog friendly' park when another canine and its handler joined in. After the two animals had frolicked for a while they disappeared behind a small coppice never to return. A car park abutted the wood and it can be only assumed that the thief had bundled both dogs into a vehicle.

Another breeder, Barrie Gannaway-Jones, of Richmond Kennels, near Southport, also a gun dog trainer, micro-chips all his puppies at eight weeks but regrets that the devices do not have the sophistication of the type of chip employed to track wildlife and detectable by satellite.

'I well appreciate that going down this route would, at present, be financially prohibitive but, with the lightning advance in technology, I can see it arriving in the not-too-distant future,' said Barrie.

Proof of how deadly such a system would be was instanced not long ago here in Cumbria. The incident was related to me by a retired police officer who could vouch for its authenticity.

A director of a large chemicals processing firm was disturbed one evening by a call from a police officer and a water bailiff. When they asked if he was in possession of a fresh salmon he replied in the affirmative. It was in the deep freeze.

He had innocently bought it from one of his employees but with the aid of the microchip under the skin of the fish, the officers were able to prove it had been poached by net out of season. Satellite tracking had pointed to the unfortunate fellow's larder. Charges were not pressed but the poacher was not so lucky and received a sizeable fine.

Retired vet Jane is not over-enthusiastic about the current chipping system and gives other advice. 'Be aware, constantly, that there are ruthless people about and protect your dog at all times.' Sound reasoning but, for we rustics, unused and unseasoned to the 'real world,' not easy to take on board.

A SOLWAY DOG

In the early Solway years, gundogs were a rarity. Jim Ritchie was the first of the locals to buy one. Rock was a chocolate dog Labrador from show strain and turned into a fine heavy chested fellow ideally suited to the strong Solway tides. He had a thick double coat but, sadly, suffered at a relatively early age from the then little heard-of hip dysplasia.*

Jim was diligent over Rock's training and, come September 1, in the mid-1950s, he was ready for real action. Early mallard saw him retrieving well but then came a blip with the arrival of the pheasant season.

Longtails were occasionally to be found in the gorse clumps on the Scottish stretch of the estuary. Four of us were working the shore one afternoon, before flight, when a Gun, out of sight of Rock, dropped a bird

*Today it is accepted to test all Labradors as early as possible for both hip dysplasia and eye defects. The tests are both straightforward and relatively inexpensive when the alternative is contemplated. Unfortunately there is no cure for either and a responsible professional will have the dog's life terminated rather than see it suffer. It is imperative that dogs like this do not breed – the only way to eradicate the faults.

into thick cover. Jim was called over and duly sent his young and eager dog into the drop zone. To say that the cover was dense would not be an understatement and, after a long spell exhorted on by his handler, Rock returned birdless.

'Are you sure we are in the right area?' enquired Jim. After being assured that the bird was stone dead, and that the line we were seeking was exact, Jim sent his dog again. This time there was violent activity in the heart of the cover. Branches snapped and the bushes shook until, eventually, Rock emerged – with a stick!

In fairness to the dog this was an area used by Jim during training sessions and the stick was almost certainly one he had thrown earlier that year.

The problem was solved, soon afterwards, when one of the locals turned up in a long wax-proof coat which stretched well down over his waders and he was able to force his way into the jungle to where the dog had previously concentrated his interests. The bird was, indeed, stone dead and firmly wedged in the topmost tangle of a gorse bush.

Experienced dogs will often point dead game stranded above ground and it pays the beginner to heed this.

Probably the saddest declaration I ever heard relating to gundogs came one day when an old fowler's bitch died. He was 70 and his wife pronounced, 'You are not to get another, the dog will outlive you!'

After a year, and observing his loneliness, she relented. That was five years ago and man and dog are doing fine.

HOTEL BEHAVIOUR

A simple ruling on whether or not to take dogs into bedrooms is, 'No.' Particularly gundogs.

There is another tale, indirectly related to myself, which more than makes it clear why it is a no-no. In fact, there is a second hair-raising incident from the same goose-chasing trip which also goes to illustrate how one must, again, be careful about the selection of one's shooting companions also.

My connection with the two stories came merely through the fact that I had introduced a pal – Syd of the Ross & Cromarty chapter – to the territory and he had phoned asking if I minded if he took two pals to what was free and very worthwhile shooting. I was impressed by his courtesy, but when I heard of the tales I am glad I was not there!

First, the doggy one.

We shall call this guest Phil, proud owner of a two-year-old black Lab bitch name of Tillie. Besides being a very biddable gundog, Tillie was also a spoilt family pet used to sleeping indoors.

When Phil arrived he asked the hotel proprietor if he could take Tillie into his bedroom and the reply was positive, 'Provided she doesn't jump onto the bed.'

Now Tillie must have been one of those remarkable canines (and I have known the occasional one) who easily understood the human voice for, while Phil was at dinner that evening, she did not jump onto the bed but, instead, craftily pulled the thick, feathered duvet onto the floor. She must have decided it was much more comfortable than her blanket.

Other owners will know that all canines paw frantically at their bedding in order to make a cosier nest as their ancestors did when they all slept outdoors. Unfortunately Tillie's pawing was over-vigorous and the luxurious duvet burst its contents. To add to the mayhem, Phil had thoughtfully opened the window wide to lower the temperature to the level he though his treasured companion would better appreciate. What he had not anticipated, however, was the arrival of a gale-force wind while he partook of his leisurely wining and dining.

When Phil finally retired to his abode, towards midnight, he was greeted by a whirling snow-like storm of down as the open door funnelled the violent wind.

For an accountant, for that was his profession, he was a fast thinker. Back in the bar, he found George who was still dispensing alcohol to an indulgent clientele. Taking him to one side, he thrust a fist-full of banknotes under George's nose and asked if he knew who might be the chambermaid attending to his room the next morning.

After George heard the tale he said he could do better than a chambermaid. His wife was the housekeeper and, yes, the bundle of notes would certainly ensure all traces of the seriously-abused duvet, and its contents, would be gone over breakfast and a fresh cover put in place.

Tillie slept in the car for the rest of the week and the proprietor never missed the duvet.

Syd didn't think things could get any worse but, frighteningly, they did.

Two mornings later his second guest, a solicitor, nom de plume Jeremy, behaved in a very unlawyer-like manner.

It was the morning all three had agreed to go out for dawn flight and they would muster on the car park at 6am when it was still dark.

On his way out Jeremy tapped on Syd's door – or at least, what he thought was Syd's door. On getting no answer he turned the knob to find a darkened room. The light switch revealed a somnolent figure underneath the bed covers, so Jeremy thought he would give the laggardly Syd a shock and pulled down his new covert veil to completely mask his face. He was also clad in an all-in-one SAS-style suit.

Shaking the still-slumbering form, he remained silent and awaited the response which he felt, no doubt, would contain a torrent of abuse. Instead, there came an ear-splitting scream as the elderly female occupant took in the scene.

Jeremy's reaction was to flee from the bed-chamber as fast as his trembling legs would allow and, upon reaching the car park, fling himself into the waiting 4WD.

'Go. Go. Quickly. Drive,' he cried.

'What's wrong?' asked Syd as he obeyed with great alacrity.

Though clearly badly shaken, Jeremy refused to say more and changed the subject as only a courtroom lawyer could. The bag that morning is irrelevant for, unfortunately for the lead character in the play, the affair did not go away with the end of flight.

Syd set the final scene.

'As we turned into the hotel drive there was a police car outside the entrance and the proprietor was talking to two officers. Jeremy jumped straight out and apparently asked if the four of them could talk in private.'

That was when the shroud of mystery was pulled over the affair.

'Jeremy told us what had happened in the bedroom but wouldn't say how he smoothed it over,' Syd said.

It is generally supposed that a large sum of money was offered to the hapless lady and both the police and the hotel proprietor were satisfied when she accepted.

Unfortunately, Jeremy has now gone where all goose shooters and geese eventually go, so it must be assumed that the old adage, 'Money solves everything' (or words similar) had prevailed.

DOG TRAINING

Having shared the shooting field over more than half a century with just about every species of hunting dog, I readily agree with the Halsteads that the Labrador is the prime choice for the wildfowler. It is also a most versatile all-rounder.

For rough shooting (walked-up game) and flushing on driven shoots there is, of course, nothing to touch the spaniels. In my early days of dog handling my mentor was Donald Kippax, a Panel A field trial judge who was a regular customer in my Blackpool shop. When I contended that the spaniel was the better flusher he shook his head.

'The spaniel will go through cover whether there is anything there or not. A Lab will only go in (unless ordered) if there is something there.' He also contended that the main difference between the two species was that a spaniel had to be trained to retrieve (natural in a Labrador) and a Lab had to be trained to hunt (natural in all spaniels.)

The number one basic is, of course, to instil total obedience: sit, stay, heel and stop to the whistle.

Training any dog is so rewarding – and fun. By diligent use of the whistle you will find that your dog is always watching you for directions. A retriever that sets off on its own, head down and heedless, is worse than useless. Its wayward careering will inevitably disturb quarry out of shot.

There are a great many books available on basic dog training and it does no harm to stack them on one's shelves. Not many, however, stress one all-important facet which almost all of us are guilty of – the fact that you must never lose your temper while schooling any animal.

One of the first books I acquired as a novice was a delightful tome by Countess Lorna Howe entitled, The Popular Labrador Retriever, first published in 1957. In the passage on training she says that while misdemeanours have to be punished the method applied needs to be regulated according to your pupil's temperament. Some are so sensitive that a mere scolding is sufficient. Others may need corporal punishment but only of the mildest kind. The Countess favours a light switch in these instances but is careful to cause no physical damage. Should you feel you are in danger of losing your temper she stresses that, at such times, the handler must put the dog away until you have calmed down!

We hear more and more these days of the Newfoundland as a fowling dog – something I have never witnessed in marsh conditions but Countess Howe explains that, originally, there were two classes of this species which originated, of course, in Canada. The largest strain was used as a draught animal while the smaller was employed by wildfowlers to retrieve birds and also to bring back fish 'which might otherwise have escaped.'

We also learn from the Countess that when Europeans first discovered North America, around 1,000 years ago, there were no dogs on this continent. It is generally assumed that it was the Europeans who took various varieties over there. Around 1800 Colonel Peter Hawker, in an attempt to classify the strain, referred to the larger as the Newfoundland and the smaller as the Lesser Newfoundland or the Labrador or St. John's dog. Thus the name Labrador stuck.

An interesting statistic from the Countess was that, in 1957, the Kennel Club registered 4,672 Labradors which was second only in popularity, including all breeds, to the cocker spaniel. In 2005 a staggering 45,779 Labs were registered and the cocker had gone into second place at 17,468.

When I contacted the organisation, the helpful KC spokesperson was not, of course, able to indicate what proportion of that figure were working dogs. An intelligent guess would, I reckon, put this percentage at around 10%. Over the months of July and August 2006 I conducted my own research in the tourist-trap Lakes village where I live. It is remarkable how so many of us dog-loving Brits take their canines on holiday.

'Does he (or she) work?' I would ask of the dog's owner. The positive came out at about 1 in 10 although, surprisingly, many declared, 'I wish he/she did!'

The third most popular these days in the KC records is the springer spaniel at 15,180.

One variety of spaniel I have to include in this chapter is the fascinating Brittany. I have already mentioned that I was only ever tempted to join a driven pheasant shoot because of its extensive wild quarry and it was here that I had the great privilege to shoot over this species. I deliberately use the term 'shoot over.' This is applied to dogs with the pointing or 'setting' characteristic. In other words, when they wind a quarry then remain motionless until commanded to move in to the flush.

Our keeper then was Frank Blackburn, an artist and countryman of the old school. As one who was used only to the explosive mannerisms of the springer and cocker I was in total wonderment when Frank's delightful little bitch froze for the first time on one of our rough shooting days. And, when ordered, she was no slouch at stylish retrievals.

So impressed was I at this dog's technique that I resolved to try my hand at running one of her next brood of pups but my dramatic neck injury ruined that dream. The Brittany are, characteristically, longer legged than the average springer and, like all spaniels, excellent in water. She would have had no trouble in coping with the largest grey goose.

MIGHTY MAX

Another dog I have had the pleasure of working with is the German short haired pointer. As the name implies its coat lacks the density essential for extreme cold weather fowling and had the insulated neoprene dog's waistcoat been available then, our courageous four-legged companion would definitely have sported one.

Though the breed's style is more suited to the grouse moor or rough shoot (the main reason for which the dog had been acquired) than the marsh, they do make extremely powerful retrievers.

Max was already owned by the aforementioned Roy Hardcastle when we met. The handler was keen to see how his dog performed in water and he really came into his own on inland ponds under icy conditions. Frozen waters can be treacherous when the covering is neither thick nor thin. A lightweight dog may head out onto a seemingly solid surface only to crash through a less frozen spot where fowl have kept the water relatively open. We always keep a stout rope to hand should we need to plunge in for a rescue.

Max, however, had his own method or, one might claim, canine reasoning. Generally his great strength enabled him to smash his way from the bank to retrieve like some armour-clad ice breaker. Should he not be able to employ this method and, over several years, I saw him fail only once – he refused to walk over the ice. We were then able to retrieve the bag ourselves by simply employing a clothes line to sweep the birds in.

To witness Max displaying his immense power – thundering his way through the arctic conditions – really was awesome. Ignoring his thin coat, he never baulked. Perhaps his extreme endeavour kept his circulation racing sufficiently to guarantee ample insulation. He certainly never suffered from rheumatics and died at a ripe old age. I do hasten to point out that Max was kennelled outside and was thus more equipped to cope with extreme cold.

As a footnote to iced pond conditions I must stress the need to take great care. The winters were harsher when I was young and we even purchased a lightweight fibre glass dinghy, when they first appeared, to use in emergencies. The plan was to smash our way through, such was the enthusiasm of youth. We often amassed considerable bags but did cease shooting altogether before the birds began to suffer from a shortage of food.

POWERHOUSE DOG – *Max, a German short-haired pointer was an outstanding fowling dog who used his immense strength to smash through ice-covered ponds. To Max a goose retrieve was akin to a cocker spaniel picking a snipe!*

CLARISSA – *When I wrote to Clarissa Dickson-Wright for her favourite pinkfoot goose recipe she replied instantly. Here she is at a book signing with her co-author, Sir Johnnie Scott.*

Clarissa's Christmas Goose

What would those of us forced into a sedentary life do without Radio 4 (start with *Farming Today* at 5.45am) and *The Times* crossword? The BBC produced another jewel for me pre-Christmas 2004. That absorbing country lady, Clarissa Dickson-Wright, was a guest on a food programme when she was asked to name her choice of Christmas dinner.

'I have asked Johnny (Sir Johnnie Scott, her countryside sidekick) to shoot me a pinkfoot,' she told us.

These days, with the sale of wild geese banned, there are few who would know what Clarissa was talking about. Those of us who do gave her a generous round of applause.

What wonderful viewing Clarissa and the late and much-lamented Jennifer Paterson, treated us to with their sumptuous banquets in the *Two Fat Ladies* slot on TV. We might be saturated with cookery programmes on the box these days but I would lay long odds at that intriguing duo coming top of the pile in the popularity stakes. And did you notice their form of conveyance? Nothing less than the previously much-lauded Triumph Speed Twin motorcycle! (see *The Solway Years* chapter) How about that for a chance eventuality?

But would the so, so busy barrister/chef/public orator/celebrity find time to give me her recipe for her favourite Christmas dinner if I asked her – or even be bothered to reply?

Shame on me that I should ever have doubted when a fowler contacts a fowler. (Did we not see Clarissa out with her gun at dawn, on TV, among Norfolk's teeming pinkfoot?) Her answer came almost by return and it is with much gratitude that I print the talented lady's detailed procedure for addressing an already tasteful meat. Her full recipe follows, overleaf.

Clarissa's Wild Goose Recipe

1 x Pinkfoot
Castor sugar
1 tablespoon olive oil
1 onion, chopped
3 sharp apples – not Bramley's
1 sliced red cabbage
2 tablespoons black treacle
1 wine glass of sharp cider
Salt and pepper

Pre-heat oven to 180°C/360°F
Rub goose with salt, pepper and sugar.
In a heavy casserole heat oil and fry onion till golden.
Cover and roughly slice apples, shred cabbage and add both to onion.
Add treacle and cider, stir well and cook for 10 mins.
Place goose on top. Cover and cook in oven for 45 mins.
Remove lid and cook in oven for another 25 mins. or until goose is cooked.

It must be added that Johnny would have made sure his friend received a young bird. For old geese I would humbly suggest the Solway Caravan Method. I intend to subject one of these veterans to Clarissa's recipe. If it does not tenderise after a reasonable time I shall return it to the closed lid system until ready. I strongly suspect a culinary orgasm. Hey-Ho!

The Vicar's Poem

Though I rarely attend any of our village churches I enjoy, immensely, the time spent in discourse with Canon Stephen Pye, of Hawkshead. He is a true country vicar, aware of how lucky he is to be in a rural parish.

One of the perks is the accessibility of fresh trout and game. He is particularly fond of pinkfoot and looks forward to giving Clarissa's recipe a try.

Stephen listened, with interest, to how I had felt when I feared my hunting trips to Scotland were over when I was confined to a wheelchair. I likened my feelings to those of the Scot forced to leave his beloved land when the crofters were moved two centuries ago. It inspired him to write the following poem (*overleaf*).

THE POETIC VICAR – *Hawkshead's Vicar, Canon Stephen Pye, loves wild game. Here he starts on a pinkfoot.*

Where Wild Geese Fly

The days would pass by him now
bowing their heads with the prow that
dipped, incessantly, towards the
horizon, where beyond he imagined
the wild moors beckoning.

Calling him now through the salt spray
towards the estuary and the narrows
where the salmon leaps upwards,
willing itself inland to the place,
that still pool, he longs for.

At the dawn of one day he had
awakened to their calling and rushed
to deck, swaying, eyes heavenward;
A skein heading from their arctic land
to his place of the deer in high hills.

The place where he had stood, motionless,
awaiting nature's bounty in his homeland.
Now he stands, gazing upward, longing Icharus-like
to journey with them to the land
of spring water, burn and purple heather.

Their song, now, is in his heart aching
as the rigging creaks, and the ocean
beneath anchors his thoughts to the
relentless tasks of his voyage,
while the geese fly on.

A.S. Pye

MOUNTAIN GEESE *by Rodger McPhail*

Epilogue

Richard died before my book was concluded. At his funeral the eulogy was read by his constant fishing companion, Graham Holmes. Together they had flogged waters from Wales to the far north of Scotland in their hunt for salmon over the last 30 years of his life.

Graham had asked me for 'an amusing story' from our goose chasing times to lighten the ceremony.

'It would have to be The Night of the Indian Princess,' I had replied.

Graham's account was tailored to fit the ceremony, when there was standing room only in the chapel. The following is the unexpurgated version:

Richard, Ken Hargreaves and myself had arrived at our Scottish HQ late one wild January night. Our familiar cosy quarters were on the ground floor of the landlord's solid granite house adjoining his inn. It was built to withstand all weathers, and it had stood for many winters in the middle of an empty landscape. The stunted, wind-bent sycamores thrashed their bare branches bordering the field across the road where we had carried out many successful dawn ambushes a few minutes walk from our beds. Tomorrow, our reconnaissance told us, we would have a three-mile drive to our goose fields. Tightly drawn bar-room curtains and raucous laughter indicated that the revelry was in full flow next door. There would be only light imbibing for us. We had an early pre-dawn rising and we had been caught before when we were young.

Landlord George had said, on the phone, that our usual rooms would be ready and he would leave the house door open. We went about our routines. Richard headed for the kitchen, where a pot of his favourite Indian Prince tea would soon be brewed strong and sweet. Ken hurried to his abode, (we had a room apiece for we all held gold medals at snoring) to crack a bottle of best doctored peat water into three tumblers and I fed my dog.

The kettle had sung, the dog was satisfied and I was just reaching for my glass of refined barley when Richard burst into the room, collapsed onto a chair and called for 'A whisky – quickly!'

His hand shook as he downed it in one.

'What the hell's wrong with you?'

'Give me another. There's a woman in my bed. Young. Naked.

Beautiful!' he croaked.

The silent disbelief that fell on the room was broken by a light tap and the door opened slowly. There was, indeed, a beautiful woman in the house. By now she was clad in gossamer white; and long, glossy, black hair tumbled about her shoulders. Richard told us later that she had been sitting in 'his' bed when he walked in, combing the luxuriant tresses which only partially hid her ample womanhood.

'I'm sorry for the surprise,' announced the vision. She did, we all later agreed, resemble an Indian Princess. 'I'm George's niece and should have flown out of Edinburgh Airport this morning. My flight was delayed and I leave in two hours.'

Richard shared my twin-bedded room that night (or I think he did). None of us heard any snoring. An empty bottle saw to that.

Next morning, an hour before dawn, there was an untouched pot of Indian Prince when we went to brew up. On our way out, into the pre-dawn icy blast, the 'Princess's' bedroom door stood open, revealing an empty double bed.

Richard died, aged 71, on Jan 11, 2005.

At the end of the service, when the throngs were making their way to their motors, a young fellow approached with a heavy container. It was Richard's nephew David.

'My Uncle wanted you to have this – its in his will. He said you would like his goose shooting gear.'

The so-familiar old plastic storage box was placed carefully in the boot. So often it had sped north with us on our long journeys to Scotland. I knew what would be inside but this was neither the time nor the place to delve into a man's private effects. At home the box was left in the hall. My 12-year-old son should be home from school soon and would soften the moment for me. I had not seen such a glow of sheer anticipation on a boy's face since dawn on Christmas morning as he lifted the pile of scrim scarf that hid the contents.

How many times had Richard lain in the rushes on the moor top of his goose shoot with that same scrim around his neck? 'Warmest scarf ever invented,' he would say. When geese approached it was drawn over his face and he melted into the landscape.

The two pairs of mitts would not go over my ponderous paws. Richard knew Jago would be wearing them. Black balaclava, for flighting among the peat hags, and a green midge face net for the pigeon hide were there.

We had talked of a spring pigeon trip and one cartridge belt was already filled with 1oz 7's. The other belt was half empty – the left-overs from our last goose chase.

There was the odd, unopened and scuffed, box of No. 1's – Richard's favourite goose load. A box of 10 buckshot cartridges announced that there were only 27 pieces of lead in each round. One cartridge was missing and I had witnessed him bowl over a fox with it at 50 yards many years ago.

Yellowing maps, of the considerable lands over which farmers had trustingly permitted him to roam for the geese, lay neatly folded at the bottom of the box. And, in one corner, was tucked what I had been hoping for – Richard's American Olt goose call he had bought from my old gun shop when they were first imported nearly 40 years ago. He had thoughtfully given it a brand new cord. Mine had long since lost its tone and I knew this one had not. But had it always sounded so melodious courtesy of its handler?

A blast brought the young spaniel out of her reverie and someone shouted from the kitchen, 'Stop that, you know it upsets the parrot!'

I went outside into the night and played on it something that I hoped sounded like The Last Post.

Instructional Index

N

O

P

Q

R

S

T

Acknowledgements

Annan and District Library Services, Mark Carr, David Grayling, John and Sandra Halstead, Ken Hargreaves, Ray Holden, Peter J. Lawson, Keith McDougall, Rodger McPhail, Hugh Meynell, Keith Miller, Alan Myers, Stephen J. Pye, Betty Ritchie, David Ritchie, Ken Watson, George White, John and David Wilkins, Karen Wilson, Clarissa Dickson-Wright.

Recommended reading from Merlin Unwin Books

To order: www.merlinunwin.co.uk
Tel: 01584 877456

Vintage Guns for the Modern Shot

Diggory Hadoke

At the back of many a gun cabinet lurks a neglected old shotgun. This book will encourage its owner to bring it back into use. It also provides practical advice on buying the right gun for restoration. It describes the steps and potential pitfalls on the path to renovation so the gun can be used and enjoyed.

The author's passion is for old guns and for their continued use in the field. He argues that the quality of craftsmanship in many old guns, as well as the sheer pleasure of handling them, makes them superior to the machine-made over/unders of the modern shooting field.

Hadoke covers all aspects of collecting and restoring shotguns for use – on an affordable budget. He writes for the shooter rather than the engineer or historian, and his fascinating book is presented in an easy-to-read style.

£30

Private Thoughts from a Small Shoot

Laurence Catlow
Illustrated by Ashley Boon

Catlow's shooting diary records his year as pheasant rearer, gamekeeper, forester, dog-handler and all-round shooting enthusiast. He has robust views on: the right to roam, the nanny state, game cookery, friendship, disobedient dogs and beloved hats. This is Catlow at the top of his form.

£17.99

Confessions of a Shooting Fishing Man

Laurence Catlow

Highly topical, thought-provoking diary. Catlow's best-seller.

'If you are looking for a present for a friend who shoots or fishes, then you need look no further than this book.' – Roger Scruton, The Times

£14.99

Rough Shooting in Ireland

Douglas Butler

For all who rough shoot, the sporting options are endless:

- snipe in the marshes and wet pasturelands
- woodcock in the forests and scrubland
- pheasants and wood pigeon generally
- grouse in the heather uplands
- mallard, wigeon, teal and many species of duck on lakes and ponds

Douglas Butler has extensive first-hand experience and his wisdom is applicable to all European rough shooters.

'The first book of its kind in more than 60 years' – Irish Times

£20

The Shootingman's Bedside Book

Compiled by 'BB'

These pages are packed with evocative and stirring passages for sportsmen to enjoy after a day out with the gun.

'It will fan into flames the hunter's instinct which smoulders in many an urban heart' – The Independent

£18.95

The Practical Guide to Man-Powered Bullets

Richard Middleton

This book explores in practical detail many of the ways, old and new, in which people can shoot bullets by their own force without the aid of explosives. Middleton's narrative is lively, humorous and full of exciting information and experimentation. In this quirky and clever book, he invites you to share the thrills of his garden shed experiments with him.

'*A dangerous man to live next-door to...*' – Shooting Times

£20

What a Chap Really Wants in Bed: A Shooting & Fishing Book

Giles Catchpole & Roderick Amery

A hugely entertaining collection of 125 short stories about shooting and fishing, each accompanied by a witty cartoon by Olly Copplestone.

'*Achingly funny writing – and brilliant cartoons*' – Sporting Shooter

£20